Ecstasy, Catastrophe

SUNY series in Contemporary Continental Philosophy

Dennis J. Schmidt, editor

Ecstasy, Catastrophe

Heidegger from *Being and Time*
to the *Black Notebooks*

David Farrell Krell

Published by State University of New York Press, Albany

© 2015 State University of New York

For information, contact State University of New York Press, Albany, NY
www.sunypress.edu

Production, Emily Keneston
Marketing, Anne Valentine

Library of Congress Cataloging-in-Publication Data

Krell, David Farrell.
    Ecstasy, catastrophe : Heidegger from Being and Time to the Black Notebooks /
David Farrell Krell.
        pages cm. — (SUNY series in contemporary Continental philosophy)
    Includes bibliographical references and index.
    ISBN 978-1-4384-5825-0 (hc : alk. paper)—978-1-4384-5826-7 (pb : alk. paper)
    ISBN 978-1-4384-5827-4 (e-book)
    1. Heidegger, Martin, 1889–1976. Sein und Zeit.   2. Ontology.   3. Space and
time.   4. Heidegger, Martin, 1889–1976. Schwarze Hefte.   5. Heidegger, Martin,
1889–1976—Notebooks, sketchbooks, etc.   I. Title.

B3279.H49K7393 2015
193—dc23   2014045612

10 9 8 7 6 5 4 3 2 1

To our *Being and Time* seminar leader, Salomé Maria Krell,
and to my fellow students, Kevin Miles, Harold Brogan,
and Walter Brogan

Das faktische Dasein existiert gebürtig . . .

Factical Dasein exists natally . . .

—Heidegger, *Sein und Zeit,* 374

Contents

Preface

In late winter of 2013–14, I received an invitation from Professor Gerhard Richter to deliver the Brauer Lectures in German Studies at Brown University, as well as the further invitation to deliver some of these lectures at Rutgers University. Since 2012 I have been happily associated with Brown's German Studies Department, thanks to the initiatives and support of Gerhard Richter and his colleagues. It was Professor Michael Levine of the Department of Germanic, Russian, and Eastern European Languages and Literatures at Rutgers who extended the further invitation. My thanks to them both and to their colleagues, and also to the wonderful students at both Brown and Rutgers.

The invitations came with the freedom to choose any topic, and to my surprise I reverted to one of my earliest interests, namely, Heidegger's "ecstatic interpretation of temporality." I had already written about that interpretation in the opening chapters of *Intimations of Mortality*, published in 1986, but the topic persisted. The moment I began work on the Brauer Lectures in March 2014, however, the first three volumes of Heidegger's *Schwarze Hefte* appeared in print. The early reviews were so damning and so polemical that I decided to take a break from my work on *Sein und Zeit* in order to read them. The three volumes, over a thousand pages of text, presented an extraordinarily different Heidegger than the one I had been working with; even though there is precious little in the *Black Notebooks* on the theme of ecstatic temporality, I followed the impulse—and the importunities of friends—to read them and then to write about them.

As a result, the present book has two parts and is the result of either a bicameral brain, the Janus-headed nature of all life, or my own galloping schizophrenia. For, whereas I take *Sein und Zeit* to be one of the greatest books of contemporary philosophy, the first three of the eventual nine *Schwarze Hefte* are surely not. Whereas one never finishes reading *Being and*

Time, in the sense that its analyses provoke ongoing thought as strongly in our own time as they did back in the 1920s, one completes a reading of Heidegger's *Notebooks* from the years 1931 to 1941 with a strong desire never to return to them. If the temporal ecstases of Heidegger's *Being and Time* represent the best of thinking, the *Notebooks* represent something else—something akin to tragic collapse. Perhaps this Janus-head, or bicameral brain, or galloping schizophrenia is the situation in which Heidegger leaves his readers today.

My thanks to Alexander Bilda of Freiburg University for his unstinting help throughout the writing of these lectures, and to Daniela Vallega-Neu and Walter Brogan for their discerning criticism and suggestions. Thanks also to Dennis Schmidt and to Andrew Kenyon, Emily Keneston, Laura Glenn, Trudi Gershinov, and the entire staff at SUNY Press.

Finally, I beg the reader's indulgence for the fact that I have not altered the lecture style, so that a certain informality marks—but I hope does not *mar*—the book as a whole.

D.F.K.
Strobelhütte, St. Ulrich, and
Providence, Rhode Island

Key to Works Cited

Works by Heidegger

BW   *Basic Writings.* 2nd ed. San Francisco: HarperCollins, 1993.

EGT   *Early Greek Thinking.* 2nd ed. San Francisco: HarperCollins, 1984.

EM   *Einführung in die Metaphysik.* Tübingen: M. Niemeyer, 1953.

FS   *Frühe Schriften.* Frankfurt am Main: V. Klostermann, 1972.

G   *Gelassenheit.* Pfullingen: G. Neske, 1959.

H   *Holzwege.* Frankfurt am Main: V. Klostermann, 1950.

HA   Hannah Arendt und Martin Heidegger, *Briefe 1925–1975 und andere Zeugnisse.* 3rd, expanded ed. Edited by Ursula Ludz. Frankfurt am Main: V. Klostermann, 2002.

KPM   *Kant und das Problem der Metaphysik.* 4th, expanded ed. Frankfurt am Main: V. Klostermann, 1973.

N I–II   *Nietzsche,* two vols. Pfullingen: G. Neske, 1961.

Ni 1–4   *Nietzsche,* four vols. 2nd ed. San Francisco: HarperCollins, 1991.

SB   *Die Selbstbehauptung der deutschen Universität; Das Rektorat 1933/34: Tatsachen und Gedanken.* Edited by Hermann Heidegger. Frankfurt am Main: V. Klostermann, 1983.

SCH   *Schellings Abhandlung über das Wesen der menschlichen Freiheit
          (1809).* Edited by Hildegard Feick. Tübingen: M. Niemeyer,
          1971.

SZ   *Sein und Zeit.* 12th ed. Tübingen: M. Niemeyer, 1972.

US   *Unterwegs zur Sprache.* Pfullingen: G. Neske, 1959.

VA   *Vorträge und Aufsätze.* Pfullingen: G. Neske, 1954.

W   *Wegmarken.* Frankfurt am Main: V. Klostermann, 1967.

WhD?   *Was heißt Denken?* Tübingen: M. Niemeyer, 1954.

ZS   *Zollikoner Seminare.* Edited by Medard Boss. Frankfurt am Main:
          V. Klostermann, 1987.

20   *Prolegomena zur Geschichte des Zeitbegriffs. Gesamtausgabe,* vol. 20.
          Marburg lecture course, Summer Semester, 1925. Frankfurt am
          Main: V. Klostermann, 1979.

24   *Die Grundprobleme der Phänomenologie. Gesamtausgabe,* vol. 24.
          Marburg lecture course, Summer Semester, 1927. Frankfurt am
          Main: V. Klostermann, 1975.

26   *Metaphysische Anfangsgründe der Logik im Ausgang von Leibniz.
          Gesamtausgabe,* vol. 26. Marburg lecture course, Summer Semes-
          ter, 1928. Frankfurt am Main: V. Klostermann, 1978.

27   *Einleitung in die Philosophie. Gesamtausgabe,* vol. 27. Freiburg lec-
          ture course, Winter Semester, 1928–29. Frankfurt am Main: V.
          Kostermann, 2001.

29/30   *Die Grundbegriffe der Metaphysik: Welt—Endlichkeit—Einsamkeit.
          Gesamtausgabe,* vol. 29/30. Freiburg lecture course, Winter Semes-
          ter, 1929–30. Frankfurt am Main: V. Klostermann, 1983.

39   *Hölderlins Hymnen "Germanien" und "Der Rhein." Gesamtaus-
          gabe,* vol. 39. Freiburg lecture course, Winter Semester, 1934–35.
          Frankfurt am Main: V. Klostermann, 1980.

52   *Hölderlins Hymne "Andenken."* *Gesamtausgabe,* vol. 52. Freiburg
        lecture course, Winter Semester, 1941–42. Frankfurt am Main:
        V. Klostermann, 1982.

53   *Hölderlins Hymne "Der Ister."* *Gesamtausgabe,* vol. 53. Freiburg
        lecture course, Summer Semester, 1942. Frankfurt am Main: V.
        Klostermann, 1984.

54   *Parmenides. Gesamtausgabe,* vol. 54. Freiburg lecture course, Win-
        ter Semester, 1942–1943. Frankfurt am Main: V. Klostermann,
        1982.

61   *Phänomenologische Interpretationen zu Aristoteles: Einführung in
        die phänomenologische Forschung. Gesamtausgabe,* vol. 61. Early
        Freiburg lecture course, Winter Semester, 1921–22. Frankfurt
        am Main: V. Klostermann, 1985.

63   *Ontologie (Hermeneutik der Faktizität). Gesamtausgabe,* vol. 63.
        Early Freiburg lecture course, Summer Semester, 1923. Frankfurt
        am Main: V. Klostermann, 1988.

65   *Beiträge zur Philosophie (Vom Ereignis). Gesamtausgabe,* vol. 65.
        1936–38. Frankfurt am Main: V. Klostermann, 1989.

94   *Überlegungen II–VI (Schwarze Hefte 1931/38). Gesamtausgabe,* vol.
        94. Frankfurt am Main: V. Klostermann, 2014.

95   *Überlegungen VII–XI (Schwarze Hefte 1938/39). Gesamtausgabe,*
        vol. 95. Frankfurt am Main: V. Klostermann, 2014.

96   *Überlegungen XII–XV (Schwarze Hefte 1939–1941). Gesamtaus-
        gabe,* vol. 96. Frankfurt am Main: V. Klostermann, 2014.

Works by Jacques Derrida

DE   *De l'esprit: Heidegger et la question.* Paris: Galilée, 1987. Trans-
        lated by Geoffrey Bennington and Rachel Bowlby as *Of Spirit:
        Heidegger and the Question.* Chicago: University of Chicago Press,
        1989.

DG   *De la grammatologie.* Paris: Minuit, 1967. Translated by Gayatri Chakravorty Spivak as *Of Grammatology.* Baltimore: Johns Hopkins University Press, 1976.

É   *Éperons: Les styles de Nietzsche.* Paris: Flammarion, 1978.

G 1–4   The four "Geschlecht" papers: (1) and (2) are published in *Psyché*, while (4) is in *Politiques de l'amitié*, with English translations as follows: (1) by Ruben Berezdivin in *Research in Phenomenology* XIII, 1983, 65–83; by Ruben Berezdivin and Elizabeth Rottenberg in *Psyche 2: Inventions of the Other*, ed. Peggy Kamuf and Elizabeth Rottenberg. Stanford, California: Stanford University Press, 2008, 7–26; (2) translated by John P. Leavey Jr., in *Deconstruction and Philosophy: The Texts of Jacques Derrida.* Edited by John Sallis. Chicago: University of Chicago Press, 1987, 161–196; by John P. Leavey and Elizabeth Rottenberg in *Psyche 2,* cited above. The third "Geschlecht" is not yet published. The fourth, "L'oreille de Heidegger: Philopolémologie (*Geschlecht* IV)" appears in *Politiques de l'amitié.* An English translation by John P. Leavey Jr. appears in *Commemorations: Reading Heidegger.* Edited by John Sallis. Chicago: University of Chicago Press, 1993.

Gl   *Glas.* Paris: Galilée, 1974. Translated by John P. Leavey Jr. and Richard Rand. Lincoln: University of Nebraska Press, 1986.

HQ   *Heidegger: la question de l'Être et l'Histoire.* Edited by Thomas Dutoit and Marguerite Derrida. Paris: Galilée, 2013. In process of translation by Geoffrey Bennington.

M   *Marges de la philosophie.* Paris: Éditions de Minuit, 1972. Translated by Alan Bass. University of Chicago Press, 1985.

Works by F. W. J. Schelling

7, 8   F. W. J. Schelling, *Abhandlung über das Wesen der menschlichen Freiheit und die damit zusammenhängenden Gegenstände*, in vol. 7 of *Sämtliche Werke.* Stuttgart et Augsburg: J. G. Cotta, 1860. The third (1815) version of *Die Weltalter (Die Vergangenheit)* is published in vol. 8 of the same edition; an English translation by Jason Wirth for SUNY Press is available.

DW   *Die Weltalter Fragmente in den Urfassungen von 1811 und 1813.*
        Edited by Manfred Schröter. München: Biederstein und Leibniz
        Verlag, 1946.

IP   *Initia philosophiae universae: Erlanger Vorlesung WS 1820/21.* Edit-
        ed by Horst Fuhrmanns. Bonn: Bouvier, 1969.

WF   *Weltalter-Fragmente.* Edited by Klaus Grotsch. Stuttgart-Bad
        Cannstatt: Frommann-Holzboog, 2002.

Works by the Author

AO   *Derrida and Our Animal Others: Derrida's Final Seminar, "The
        Beast and the Sovereign."* Bloomington and London: Indiana Uni-
        versity Press, 2013.

DL   *Daimon Life: Heidegger and Life-Philosophy.* Bloomington and
        London: Indiana University Press, 1992.

IM   *Intimations of Mortality: Time, Truth, and Finitude in Heidegger's
        Thinking of Being.* 2nd ed. University Park: Penn State Press, 1991.

LV   *Lunar Voices: Of Tragedy, Poetry, Fiction, and Thought.* Chicago:
        University of Chicago Press, 1995.

OM   *Of Memory, Reminiscence, and Writing: On the Verge.* Bloomington
        and London: Indiana University Press, 1990.

PH   *Phantoms of the Other: The Four Generations of Derrida's* Geschlecht.
        Albany: State University of New York Press, 2015.

TA   *The Tragic Absolute: German Idealism and the Languishing of God.*
        Bloomington and London: Indiana University Press, 2005.

Works by Other Authors

AC   Augustine, *Confessions.* Two vols. Translated by William Watts.
        Loeb Classical Library. Cambridge: Harvard University Press,
        1977.

AP   Aristotle, *Physics*. Two vols. Translated by P. H. Wicksteen and F.
          M. Cornford. Loeb Classical Library. Cambridge, MA: Harvard
          University Press, 1934, 1957.

CHV   Works by Hölderlin are most often cited from Friedrich Hölder-
1–3   lin, *Sämtliche Werke und Briefe*. Three vols. Edited by Michael
          Knaupp. Munich: Carl Hanser Verlag, 1992. See also the refer-
          ence to DKV, below.

DK   Hermann Diels and Walther Kranz, *Die Fragmente der Vorsokrater*.
          Three vols. 6th ed. Zürich: Weidmann, 1951. Cited by fragment
          number.

DKV   On occasion I cite Hölderlin in this edition: *Sämtliche Werke und
          Briefe*. Three vols. Edited by Jochen Schmidt. Frankfurt am Main:
          Deutscher Klassiker Verlag, 1992.

És   Jacques Lacan, *Écrits*. Paris: Éditions du Seuil, 1966.

HC   Hannah Arendt, *The Human Condition*. Garden City, NY: Dou-
          bleday Anchor, 1959. In German: *Vita Activa: Vom tätigen Leben*.
          Stuttgart: Kohlhammer, 1960.

HP   Hermann Paul, *Deutsches Wörterbuch*. 6th ed. by Werner Betz.
          Tübingen: Max Niemeyer Verlag, 1966.

HW   G. W. F. Hegel, *Werke in zwanzig Bänden—Theorie Werkausgabe*.
          Edited by Eva Moldenhauer and Karl Markus Michel. Frankfurt
          am Main: Suhrkamp, 1971. (See, however, PG, below.)

KrV   Immanuel Kant, *Kritik der reinen Vernunft*. Edited by Raymund
          Schmidt. "Philosophische Bibliothek." Hamburg: Felix Meiner
          Verlag, 1956.

KSA   Works by Nietzsche are cited from Friedrich Nietzsche, *Kritische
          Studienausgabe*. Fifteen vols. Edited by Giorgio Colli and Mazzino
          Montinari. Berlin and Munich: Walter de Gruyter and Deutscher
          Taschenbuch Verlag, 1980.

PG   G. W. F. Hegel, *Phänomenologie des Geistes*, 6th ed. Edited by
          Johannes Hoffmeister. Hamburg: F. Meiner, 1952.

PP   Maurice Merleau-Ponty, *Phénoménologie de la perception*. Paris: Gallimard, 1945.

SA 1–10 Works by Sigmund Freud are cited from the *Studienausgabe*. Ten vols., with an *Ergänzungsband*. Edited by Alexander Mitscherlich, Angela Richards, and James Strachey. Frankfurt am Main: Fischer Verlag, 1982.

VI   Maurice Merleau-Ponty, *Le visible et l'invisible*. Edited by Claude Lefort. Paris: Gallimard, 1964.

Note: When repeated references are made to the same text in any given chapter, so that the source is clear, I do not always cite the code.

Introduction

Sections 65–68 of Heidegger's *Being and Time* elaborate what he calls the "ecstatic interpretation of temporality." He calls it that, not because he is beside himself with joy while developing the idea, although who can tell, but because he finds that the "temporalizing" of human temporality, in all three of its dimensions—future, past, and present—can best be described as "ecstatic." The minute description of these *Ekstasen der Zeitlichkeit* is surely one of the principal contributions of the second division of *Sein und Zeit*. If the first division of the three planned divisions of "Part One" of *Sein und Zeit* presents the "Preparatory Fundamental Analysis of Dasein," the second division, "Dasein and Temporality," is to repeat the preparatory analysis, showing why and how *time* constitutes the horizon of human existence. However, even though in later years Heidegger takes pains to defend *Sein und Zeit* as his breakthrough work, it remains true that when he turns from the temporality of Dasein or human existence to the time of being (*Sein*) "as such" and "in general," he lets these analyses and descriptions of the ecstases go. When one examines his work from the 1930s until 1961, the year of "Time and Being," one finds very few references to the ecstases of time. Heidegger no doubt has his reasons for dropping these ecstatic descriptions of "original" or "primordial" temporality. Yet the conviction that undergirds these lectures of mine is that the ecstatic interpretation of temporality remains one of Heidegger's greatest achievements.

Part One of the present book is titled, "Ecstatic Temporality in Heidegger's *Being and Time* (1927)." A brief synopsis of the four Brauer Lectures on ecstatic temporality might be useful here. Chapter One, "The Ecstases of Time," introduces the theme of the ecstatic interpretation of temporality. At the center of the analyses of sections 65 and 68 of *Being and Time* is the word *Ekstase(n)*. On the periphery of these analyses is the even odder word *Entrückungen*, the "sudden seizures," "rapid removals," or "raptures" of

1

time. I try not to succumb entirely to the temptation of searching for those moments in the history of philosophy that might have given Heidegger his notion of ecstasy and of the *Ekstasen* of time, or his image, captured in the word *Entrückung*, of the "suddenness" of the ecstases. Yet it is difficult to ignore certain echoes in Heidegger's descriptions, echoes of Schelling's *Ages of the World* and Erlangen lectures (ca. 1811–1821), and also of Augustine's *Confessions*, but especially of Aristotle's account of ἐξαίφνης in his treatise on time in *Physics* (4:10–14), that word itself meaning "all of a sudden." Plato, in his Seventh Letter, if indeed he wrote it, uses the word to describe the hard-won yet always surprising and always sudden arrival of insight into the ideas. Plotinus, and after him a long and rich tradition of mystical literature, find this notion of sudden seizure apt. The text of Augustine's *Confessions* is filled with instances of suddenness and seizure, that is, of "rapture" (*raptus, rapere, raptim*), and one is not surprised to find this idea in the later literatures of Pietism and Romanticism. There it might be expressed as *Augenblicklichlichkeit*, the instantaneity or suddenness of momentous occurrences or feelings or insights—events that in the blink of an eye transport one outside oneself. A moment of little death, perhaps. Indeed, the notion of suddenness in Aristotle is joined by other words, all marked by the ἐξ- of *ecstasy*, that have to do with displacement, departure, passing, and loss, the ἐξ- of *exitus*, as it were. Aristotle himself cites the otherwise unknown Pythagorean philosopher Paron, who says that because time causes all things to pass away into decay it is something "altogether stupid," ἀμαθέστατον τὸ χρόνον (*Physics*, 4:13; Diels-Kranz 1:217). Aristotle objects that one might also say, with equal justice, that in time all things come to be, but after thinking it over for an instant he agrees with Paron: it is more fitting to say that in ecstatic time all things depart and decay, so that time is an ignoramus—or an ogre, the original ogre, K(h)ronos devouring his children. Perhaps that is why the mystical tradition wants to think of ecstasy as a way of escaping time, exiting from it for a spell; ecstasy would be a way of letting oneself be seized by rapturous eternity. For his part, Heidegger insists that the ecstas(i)es themselves are *of time*, which, however incorrigible and harsh it may be, is inescapable. Chapter 1, the first Brauer Lecture, closes with some old stories about time and suddenness, stories from Plato's *Gorgias*, the myth of Prometheus as dramatized in *Prometheus Bound*, and the epic of Gilgamesh.

Chapter 2, "Raptures and Ruptures of Time," begins with a reference to Hölderlin. That great poet, when reading and translating Sophocles, comes to see that the high velocity or "ex-centric" suddenness (*Rapidität*) of the sequence of a tragic play's scenes pertains to the very essence of tragedy.

Such speed alone produces "tragic transport," which is important for what Aristotle calls *catharsis*. The imposition of caesurae or dramatic pauses in *Oedipus the Tyrant* and *Antigone*, produced in both cases by the detailed and dire predictions of Tiresias, slows the action of the tragedy just long enough for us who are watching and listening to sense the *acceleration* with which what is coming in the dramatic presentation (*Darstellung*) *will* come, and to know that what is coming is catastrophic.

Our reading of section 68 of *Sein und Zeit* confronts two major difficulties in the ecstatic analysis of rapture. The difficulties have to do with (1) the *closure* of the future ecstasis and (2) the *oblivion* that is powerful in the ecstasis of having-been. The first difficulty arises from the suspicion that our resolute *openedness* to the future, *die Entschlossenheit*, is threatened if the future itself is *closed*. The second difficulty has to do with the temporalization of anxiety, or of our "readiness" for anxiety, as analyzed in section 68b. How does *readiness* temporalize? Or, for that matter, how does the resolute openedness that runs ahead, *die vorlaufende Entschlossenheit*, temporalize?

The second lecture ends by looking ahead to Heidegger's later use of the word *rapture*, *Entrückung*, primarily in his *Contributions to Philosophy: Of Ereignis*. Here we note another aspect of "suddenness," namely, the sudden change in Heidegger's rhetoric in the 1930s, that sudden change constituting something like a rupture rather than a rapture. Along with that change, we note that "ecstatic temporality" no longer plays the role it did in *Being and Time*. This might suggest the failure of Heidegger's ecstatic enterprise, which perhaps should indeed be dropped. Or it might suggest, more powerfully than any successful demonstration could, that ecstatic time is utterly finite. The only sure sign of progress in philosophy, Heidegger says repeatedly in *Being and Time*, is shipwreck: *Scheitern*.

Chapter 3, "Ecstasy at the 'Other End' of Dasein," begins by elaborating briefly on the "hard and heavy" rhetoric of Heidegger in the 1930s, a rhetoric that includes the word *Entrückung*, or "rapture." Such rhetoric is one of the central themes of the second part of the present volume. However, Heidegger's Nietzsche lectures of 1936–37, which also refer to *rapture*, eschew the "hard and heavy" rhetoric. For in these lectures Heidegger offers a reading of *rapture* in the context of Plato's *Phaedrus*, a reading that is quite remarkable and not at all polemical.

The chapter then follows a suggestion Heidegger himself makes in section 72 of *Being and Time*, a suggestion that Hannah Arendt took up and developed in her *Vita activa*, or *The Human Condition*. What would happen if, in a repetition of fundamental ontology, we took the "other end" of Dasein, not *death* but *birth*, as the principal theme? "*Das faktische Dasein existiert gebürtig*," writes Heidegger; the human being exists throughout the stretch of its existence *between* birth and death, from end to end, by way of *birth*. Dasein is a "native" of birth, so to speak; existence is not only mortal and fatal but also *natal*. What would change in fundamental ontology if we were to take birth as the privileged "end" of our "being toward the end"? The chapter undertakes some descriptions of infancy and early childhood, guided by two figures heretofore unknown in philosophy, as far as I am aware, namely, Bébé Dasein and Childe Heidegger. Among these descriptions are the grownup Heidegger's brief yet telling remarks in his 1928–29 *Introduction to Philosophy*.

Finally, something of Merleau-Ponty's project of a phenomenology of the living human body may help us here. It may be that the unity of the ecstases of time is a *corporeal* unity based on the body schema, not an intellectual, cogitative, or apperceptive one. And this rootedness of time in the body, with all its *épaisseur* or "thickness," might be the best evidence for one of Heidegger's most deep-seated but least demonstrated convictions, namely, that human temporality and time itself are finite, *endlich*. It would be ironic if birth, and not death, were the most telling revelation of human finitude.

Chapter 4, the final Brauer Lecture, alludes to the familiar title "Through the Looking-Glass," although in the present instance Alice becomes Dasein. Among the most powerful and influential accounts of infancy and childhood is Jacques Lacan's "mirror stage" in the formation of the ego, which he says occurs in children (or infants) aged six to eighteen months. Surprisingly, Lacan's own text appeals to what he calls "the ecstatic limit" that every patient—and arguably every analyst—must confront. Because that ecstatic limit has to do with "the patient's destiny as a mortal," Lacan's text invites a reading in terms of Heidegger's fundamental ontology.

A second account of the importance of birth as "the other end" of Dasein, admittedly a very different account, is to be found in Derrida's first seminar on Heidegger at the École Normale Supérieure during the years 1964–65. True, Derrida's seminar focuses on sections 72–76 of *Sein und Zeit*, on the theme of "historicity," and does not comment explicitly on the ecstases of time in sections 65 and 68. Yet his analyses raise a number of important issues for our understanding of the temporal ecstases. Derrida notes that in the final "breathless" sections of Heidegger's never-completed book, the temporal ecstasis of *the past* or *having-been* seems to overtake the ecstasis of the *future*, which earlier on in *Being and Time* is privileged for the existential analysis. Dasein is always cast ahead of itself, says Heidegger, so that existence means futurity above all. Yet as Heidegger's magnum opus draws to a close, history and the past do take on increasing importance—

precisely in the context of our *natality*. In Derrida's view, the "other end" of Dasein, its birth, prefigures nothing less than the end of the metaphysics of presence, inasmuch as *my* birth as well as *my* death, like all origins and ends, cannot be thought in terms of *presence*. The ecstatic, for Derrida, is a *sortie hors de soi* that disrupts all proximity to self-presence and all "philosophical invulnerability." To be sure, Heidegger's insistence on "resolve" or "resolute-ness" (*Entschlossenheit*) asserts a privilege that can no longer be maintained. Derrida concludes that to live in ecstatic time is to move or to be moved within a present that is nothing more than "the past of future," so that the enigmas of future and past—and of time itself—retain their mystery.

Part Two of the present volume, "On the *Black Notebooks*," consists of two chapters preceded by an interlude titled "Some Indefensible Ideas About Polemic and Criticism." The interlude is, if I may say so, a lighthearted introduction to a dismal theme. In the 1951–52 lecture course, *What Is Called Thinking?* Heidegger makes the strong claim that polemic never achieves the level of thinking. Only what magnifies the greatness of past efforts in the arts and sciences, as well as in philosophy, attains to that level. Because so much academic criticism and scholarship is carping and mean-spirited, however, this poses a problem. How does one magnify greatness? And can polemic ever be entirely overcome? Are these ideas, "magnification of greatness" and "suspension of polemic," utterly indefensible? I develop here the simple or simpleminded thesis that the German word *Hingebung* gives us some help. *Hingebung* or *Hingabe* is "devotion" or "devotedness," literally a "giving-over" to the matter under consideration. The problem, of course, is that "giving-over" should not be mindless; critical intelligence must accompany magnification. How do the "critical distance" we prize and an intense devotion to the texts or works of art we most admire coexist? Does not "giving-over" close the distance? Can criticism survive such a closing of the distance? Must devotion therefore be mindless? I present my ideas on these questions and offer the most helpful examples of creative criticism I can think of, but I do not even try to defend my ideas. Perhaps there is something about our creative and scholarly practices *at their very best* that defy defense?

Lightheartedness ends with chapter 5, "Does Rescue Also Grow?" "Where the danger is," sings the great Hölderlin, "the rescuing also grows." Who am I to doubt one of my heroes? Yet after reading the first three of the nine *Black Notebooks* that are scheduled for publication, I do doubt rescue.

These three volumes of Heidegger's private notes from 1931 to 1941 met with universal condemnation when they were published in March 2014, principally because of a number of anti-Semitic remarks that Heidegger makes in them. The bulk of these remarks on *Judentum*, most of them from the years 1938 to 1941, are mindless and vulgar, and one is shocked to read them. Yet some of those remarks are more difficult to comprehend, inasmuch as Heidegger is often mocking or berating the National Socialist regime precisely for its racism and biologism. Whereas it is never a question of "exonerating" Heidegger for these defamations, it *is* a matter of showing how complicated a reading of the *Notebooks* turns out to be. For the remarks on "*Weltjudentum*," or the "international Jewish order," is only one part of a wide-ranging—indeed almost universal—polemic that takes all of modernity to task. Heidegger takes the "gigantism" and "machination" of the contemporary world, whether in Germany, Russia, or the United States, to be an expression of the "oblivion of being." The root of the problem goes back beyond Descartes to Plato, at the very outset of the history of metaphysics. Whatever the "root" of "oblivion" may be, however, Heidegger's polemic castigates virtually every political and ecclesiastical institution, every cultural politics, every aspect of the university, every science, and every form of contemporary philosophy. The most succinct of all the entries in the *Black Notebooks* reads, "You dolts!"

Is there then no hope of rescue? There is, says Heidegger. But the sole hope, in his view, is that some sort of "decision" alter the very tendency not only of the times but also of the entire epoch of metaphysics, exchanging calculative thinking for meditative thinking, *Besinnung*, and surrendering our preoccupation with beings for a meditation on beyng, *Seyn*, as he begins to spell it in the 1930s. At this point Heidegger's polemic shifts to a different kind of rhetoric, one marked by lugubrious piety. Fealty to beyng and preparation for the coming of what he calls "the last god" constitute the sole possible rescue. Yet when piety and polemic collide in Heidegger's *Notebooks*, the result, it seems to this reader at least, is that the piety is crushed. One is left with a very bleak picture not only of Heidegger's Germany in the 1930s, but our own world in the twenty-first century.

Chapter 6, "The Tragedy of the *Black Notebooks*," takes its cue from two of Heidegger's notes on tragedy and the tragic. "*Das Seyn selbst ist 'tragisch*,'" writes Heidegger. "Beyng itself is 'tragic.'" What is as horrifying as the anti-Semitic (and anti-Catholic and anti-everything) remarks is the apocalyptic tone of the *Schwarze Hefte*. I try to analyze this tone not from the outside but from within Heidegger's text and on its own terms. I develop a thesis, first presented in the book *Daimon Life*, on what I call Heidegger's *paranoetic thinking*. I argue that Heidegger's situation is worse than paranoia. The paranoid sufferer can blame this or that being (*Seiendes*) for menacing his or her life and making them miserable. For Heidegger, by contrast, no one and no thing is to blame, but only beyng. That is to say, when one surrenders the preoccupation with beings (again, *Seiendes*), and when one turns to beyng (*Seyn*) instead, one discovers that the sole menace derives from beyng itself. It is not we human beings who have abandoned or forgotten beyng, but beyng that has abandoned and forgotten us. But, to repeat, because beyng is not some identifiable being or person out there in the world, *no one* is threatening Heidegger. Hence his Polyphemic rage. *Nothing* is plaguing him. Except that precisely the nothing *is* plaguing him.

The paranoetic tendency of Heidegger's thinking in the *Black Notebooks* is therefore ultimately tragic, even catastrophic. When Heidegger blames "the international Jewish conspiracy," as it were, for what is wrong with his times, or when he blames the Catholics or the Bolsheviks or even the pragmatic Americans for their "machinations," it may be a sign that he has regressed even farther, slipping from paranoetic thinking to a paranoid nonthinking, pure and simple. His vituperative polemics make no sense. They make no sense especially on Heidegger's own terms and in the light of what his own thinking has achieved. Neither the piety nor the self-stylizations of Heidegger's rhetoric can therefore rescue him from the dire history of beyng, that is, the history in which beyng comes to nothing. The piety and the self-inflation, along with the strident polemics, are mere lapses—they are collapses of thinking. It is therefore not a question of whether Heidegger is to be condemned or forgiven: these texts of the 1930s are *unforgiving*.

Does this mean that Heidegger's books—all of them—are to be burned? There is precedent for that, but perhaps it is a precedent we should not follow. Are Heidegger's books then to be banned, or ignored? No, not even his books and essays of the 1930s, some of which are the most thought-provoking things he ever wrote. What, then? The situation, as always, calls for *critical* reading, and what that necessitates is the hard work of *reading* in the first place.

Part One

Ecstatic Temporality in
Heidegger's *Being and Time* (1927)

1

The Ecstases of Time

"Ecstatic temporality," or the "ecstatic interpretation" of "original," "primordial" temporality, is one of the major achievements of the second division of Heidegger's 1927 *Sein und Zeit, Being and Time*. When does Heidegger first come up with the idea of the "ecstatic"? What does he mean by it? Do we know where in the history of philosophy Heidegger may have found this idea? And was that idea ever applied to *time* in the way he applies it? If the ecstatic analysis of temporality is as remarkable as I believe it is, and if it alters in a fundamental way our idea of human existence in time, why does Heidegger soon drop it after the publication of *Being and Time*? And even if *he* drops it, does that mean *we* have to? These will be my questions not only today but throughout the series of the four Brauer Lectures.

Let me begin with section 65, and not with section 64. Section 64, on "Care and Selfhood," seems to me highly problematic: its appeal to a self, an αὐτός or *ipse*, and especially to the independence and autonomy of that self, even to some sort of *permanence* of the self—all of these suggested by his emphatic and repeated use of the hyphenated word *Selbt-ständigkeit*—seems to me to be as problematic as all the other terms he urges his readers to avoid, namely, *spirit, soul, body, person, personality*, and *subject*. Indeed, the problematic notion of a standing self, problematic if only because it does not seem to be submitted to that *Destruktion* or "dismantling" of ontological notions on which Heidegger otherwise insists, accompanies Heidegger after *Being and Time* as well. In the 1930s, for example, he counts on such selfhood for the grandiose "decision" toward which he feels his times are compelling him.

No, let me begin with section 65, "Temporality as the Ontological Meaning of Care." Three preliminary questions obtrude, however, before we begin to read section 65, which is where Heidegger first introduces his interpretation of "ecstatic" temporality. We have already heard these questions. First, when does Heidegger first come up with this idea of ecstatic temporality? Second, do we know where in the history of philosophy Heidegger may have found this idea of ecstasy, which he was able to apply to time? Third, if the ecstatic analysis, along with the analysis of being toward death, or toward "the end" of our mortal existence, is the great achievement of Division Two of *Sein und Zeit*, why does Heidegger soon drop it?

When does he first come up with the idea? Apparently, quite late in the writing of *Sein und Zeit*. During the summer semester of 1925 Heidegger teaches a lecture course titled *Prolegomena to the History of the Concept of Time*, now published as volume 20 of the Heidegger *Gesamtausgabe*. Surprisingly, the words and the idea of ecstatic temporality do not appear there. Time itself is understood to be "the guideline" of his inquiry "into the being of beings" (20:8), and yet, remarkably, there is not a hint of the ecstases. It is not as though the theme of time were new to Heidegger, either in 1925 or 1927. Indeed, his *venia legendi* lecture in July 1915 is on "The Concept of Time in the Discipline of History." Heidegger, we remember, serving as Husserl's assistant, had as his special assignment the phenomenology of the historical sciences. We could hardly expect the word *Ekstase* to appear in the *venia legendi* lecture, but what does appear there, presumably for the first time, is the notion of time *proper,* "authentic" time, as it were, *die eigentliche Zeit*. In his preliminary discussion of time as the measure of motion and acceleration in modern physics from Galileo through relativity theory, Heidegger comments on what it means to declare a particular instant of time the starting point of a measurement: "We make an incision into the timescale, so to speak, thereby destroying time proper [*die eigentliche Zeit*] in its flow, and we cause it to cease. The flux freezes, becomes a plane surface [*Fläche*], and only as a plane surface is it measurable. Time becomes a homogeneous place-order, a scale, a parameter" (FS 366). Time for an historian, by contrast, is a matter of *qualitative* determinations, as Dilthey and Bergson have already insisted, qualitative in terms of (1) our assessing the authenticity of the historian's sources, (2) elaborating the context of the period under discussion, and (3) estimating in some nonarithmetic way the distance of our own world from the world under discussion. Periods and distances in the historical sciences do not succumb to measurement. Heidegger is particularly attuned to the problem of the historian's selection of themes for discussion and even his or her decisions about what counts as evidence; for these matters are shaped by his or her own history, indeed in ways that are seldom evident. By 1915 Heidegger is sensitive to issues of hermeneutics, although that word too does not yet appear.

Heidegger's focus on questions of time and history is clearly visible in every course he teaches and in every text he writes between 1915 and 1927.

It is to *Being and Time* that we must now turn, and yet I find it impossible to finish discussing the *venia legendi* lecture before mentioning the final example Heidegger offers to show how the historian reckons with, but does not measure, time and time periods. Heidegger cites the twelve weeks that it took the Prussian general August von Mackensen to reach the Russian-Polish *Festungsviereck*, a recent event in World War I. Those twelve weeks assume their proper importance, Heidegger says, only insofar as they reflect "the vast and powerful thrust of our allied troops [*die ungeheure Stoßkraft unserer verbündeten Truppen*]," the assuredness with which the "operational target" was chosen, and the "resistance" of the Russian army (FS 374). Such military examples will not be missing from Heidegger's lectures on Nietzsche two decades later, to say nothing yet of other texts from the late 1930s and early 1940s. They show how difficult it is for a philosopher as well as a historian to avoid those intrusions by contemporary events into one's selection of themes and examples. Indeed, in *Being and Time* Heidegger will take pains to show how existential-ontological analysis, in the pursuit of its aims, has to purge itself of the news of the day, as of "everydayness" or "dailiness" altogether. These military examples also show how impossible it is for Heidegger to purge himself of his *deutsch-nationales Denken* and the militancy that clings to it. The very "principle" of historical conceptuality, Heidegger concedes at the end of his *venia legendi* lecture, lies in the "value relation," *Wertbeziehung*, that permeates historical institutions such as the Church and the historians themselves. To repeat, these "value-relations," are seldom visible to the historian—or philosopher—him- or herself.

I realize that I may be getting sidetracked by this, but I cannot drop the matter before mentioning that, at least according to some reports I have seen, Walter Benjamin hated Heidegger's *venia legendi* lecture, which he may have heard—the two of them were students of Heinrich Rickert's in Freiburg during the years 1912 to 1913—and which in any case Benjamin would surely have read. Nevertheless, it would be worthwhile to compare in detail Heidegger's views in that lecture with Benjamin's *Kunstkritik* essay and the "critical-epistemological preface" to his *Trauerspiel* book, both of which appear to conform with Heidegger's main theses; it would be most instructive to compare that lecture with the late "On the Concept of History," which, with its stringent critique of historicism, opens a gap between Benjamin's mature conception and Heidegger's early conception of historical time. Yet even here, for instance, in Benjamin's criticism of our belief in progress and the "homogeneous" notion of time that underlies such a belief, we hear echoes of Heidegger's most strongly held views. In the *Schwarze Hefte* (96:183) we hear Heidegger say, "Expelled to the farthest remove

from the truth of the historic are the historians," and Benjamin would be
hard put to disagree, even though his sense of the "historic" would differ
sharply from Heidegger's. But enough.[1]

Our second question was: Where in the history of philosophy might
Heidegger have found, if only quite late in his writing of *Sein und Zeit*,
the idea of ecstatic temporality? Not in Husserl, surely. And even though
Heidegger does find Bergson's *Données immédiates de la conscience* compelling reading, which does not mean to say that he always interprets it well or
fairly, "ecstasy" is not there, even if something of Bergsonian *élan* is already
present, and *élan*, as *Schwingung* and *Schwung*, will be important for Heidegger's later thinking of time. Could it have been in Kierkegaard, then, or
in the literature of mysticism? Perhaps. But there ecstasy would have to do
with some sort of intervention of "eternity" into time, or at least with the
temporary suspension of the temporal. Franz von Baader (1765–1841), in
"On the Concept of Ekstasis as Metastasis," defines ecstasy as the temporary
suspension of the interlacing of body, soul, and spirit, in anticipation of their
complete separation in death.[2] Whereas von Baader is an important source
for Schelling, however, he is not such for Heidegger. Could it have been
Schelling himself who gives Heidegger the word and the idea of ecstasis,
inasmuch as Schelling uses the word ἔκστασις during his years in Erlangen?
Let me take a moment to examine this possibility in detail.

Heidegger mentions "ecstatic temporality" briefly in the notes for his
lecture course on Schelling during the Summer Semester of 1936. Among
the three principal terms at the outset of Schelling's 1809 treatise on human
freedom—*Wesen, Grund, Existenz*—the last means not the being on hand of

---

1. One more word on the question as to *when* ecstatic temporality becomes a theme for
Heidegger. Even if ecstatic *temporality* is not discovered until quite late, it is important
to note that both the "Dasein" of 1927 and the "factical life" of the early 1920s are
"ecstatic" in many senses of that word. Dasein, as being in the world, is "out there";
and even when "factical life" bolts the door on its existence, preferring to live in dispersion and distraction (*Streuung, Zerstreuung*), something of its transcendence survives.
Heidegger stresses that factical life is essentially "away from itself" and even "outside
itself" (*Von-sich-weg, Aus-sich-hinaus*). It will therefore be a matter of remembering such
ecstasies—as "everyday" and as "ruinous" as they may seem—when it comes to *time* and
temporality. See my discussion of this at PO 40–41.

2. Franz von Baader, "Über den Begriff von Ekstasis als Metastasis," in *Schriften*, ed.
Max Pulver (Leipzig: Insel Verlag, 1921), 232–42. My thanks to Alexander Bilda for
the reference.

a thing, or a thing's *existentia* as opposed to its *essentia*, but precisely what Heidegger calls *Ex-sistenz*, "that which steps out of itself," *das aus sich Heraustretende* (SA 129). What undergoes this stepping out? Heidegger replies, *das im Heraus-treten sich Offenbarende*, everything that "in stepping out reveals itself," or "enters into the open" (ibid.), and that of course means beings as a whole, not merely Dasein. By 1936, both "existence" and "ecstasis" have less to do with the unfolding of human temporality than with "the truth of beyng" as such and in general.

Yet temporality is also discussed in terms of Schelling's discussion of God's "becoming" (SA 135–36). Such divine coming to be cannot be measured in terms of Kantian "succession," *das Nacheinander*, inasmuch as a certain "simultaneity," or *Gleich-Zeitigkeit*, prevails in the divine. Heidegger adds, "The original temporal simultaneity [*Gleich-Zeitigkeit*: 'at or in the same time'] consists in this, that having-been and being-futural, and equally originally [*gleichursprünglich*] being-present, assert themselves as the plenitude of essence [*Wesensfülle*], coining themselves within one another" (SA 136). This odd phrase, "coining themselves within one another" tries to translate *selbst ineinander schlagen*. This last word means to strike or to imprint, hence, "to coin." It is a word Heidegger will use decades later in his interpretation of *Geschlecht* in the poetry of Georg Trakl. If I am right, it is not a word Heidegger uses in his account of ecstatic temporality in *Sein und Zeit*. Here in the Schelling course the stroke, imprint, or coinage (*der Schlag*) has to do with "appropriate temporality," or "temporality proper," which Heidegger identifies with the *Augenblick*. Thus, according to Heidegger, Schelling does not think of eternity as the *nunc stans*, "the standing now." Rather, he thinks of it in terms of a living, moving, processual eternity in which each temporal ecstasy is "struck" or "coined" in all the others. Heidegger later in the course identifies "the moment" in which future, having-been, and present collide, or mutually imprint one another (*zusammenschlagen*), as the moment of decision, *Entscheidung*. In it the human being achieves its freedom, indeed as a form of "resolute openedness," *Entschlossenheit* (SA 186–87).

In a later seminar on Schelling's treatise, taught during the summer semester of 1941, Heidegger takes some distance on Schelling's claim that the divine, in its ostensibly full and perfect freedom, "overcomes" time. Beyng, argues Heidegger, can never be independent of time: "Being is 'dependent' on ecstatic time; this is an essential characteristic of the 'truth' of being; but this 'truth' belongs to the essential unfolding [*Wesung*] of beyng itself" (SA 208). It is somewhat surprising to see the term *ecstatic temporality* still being used, yet an entire section of Heidegger's notes in 1941 bears the title, "Temporality as Ecstatic Temporalizing" (SA 228–29). Here Heidegger calls time "a preliminary name for the region in which the truth of being is projected"; he adds, " 'time' is the ecstatic between (time-space), not the in-which of beings, but the clearing of being itself" (SA 229).

When one turns from Heidegger's own notes to Schelling's texts, one notes initially that the word *Ekstase* is absent from the *Treatise on Human Freedom*. Nor does the word appear in the 1811, 1813, and 1815 versions of *The Ages of the World*, as edited by Heidegger's colleague Manfred Schröter. Yet Schelling does use the word in an important way during his Erlangen lectures of 1820–21, and we will take a moment a bit later in the chapter to examine that use. But could Heidegger have found the term *ecstasis* anywhere in Schelling during the period in which he is writing *Being and Time*? That seems highly unlikely. He knew of Schelling's 1809 treatise, and he may already have read *Die Weltalter*, to which he refers, albeit rarely, in the 1936 lecture course. Yet the Erlangen lectures were edited only much later (1969, 2002, and 2012–14 are important years for the new and more complete editions of the *Weltalter-Fragmente* and the Erlangen lectures), so that, to repeat, it is highly unlikely that Heidegger would have seen these materials.

Surely, we may say, indeed we *must* say, that Heidegger gets the idea of ecstasy from Aristotle's treatise on time (chapters 10–14 of *Physics* Δ). Not only "ecstasy" but also the very word and thing called "existence" must have Aristotle as their origin. In the thirteenth chapter of Book IV of the *Physics*, Aristotle is discussing μεταβολή, "alteration" or "change" in the most general sense. He takes up the theme of "sudden" change, ἐξαίφνης, translated by Schleiermacher (in Plato's *Parmenides* at 156d) as *der Augenblick* and *das Augenblickliche*, "the moment," "the instantaneous." The "sudden" seems to occur somewhere between motion and rest, and seems to be outside of the time series as such; it occurs too quickly for us to be able to count it, or to count on it. Rapid change seems to involve dispersion and scattering rather than languid alteration or augmentation through growth. Recall the words of the chorus of crazed Maenads in Euripides's *Bacchae*, who want to see Pentheus dead. "But first," they cry, "drive him out of his mind!" (l. 850: πρῶτα δ᾿ἔκστησον φρενῶν). In his essay on memory, Aristotle designates those who confuse their fantasies with actual memories as ἐξισταμένα (451a 10). In his essay on the soul (406b 13) he uses the word ἔκστασις to mean "departure" or "displacement": "All movement is displacement of that which is moved." In his discussion of sudden or instantaneous change in *Physics*, Aristotle employs words related to ἐξίστημι and ἔκστασις three times in only a few lines, lines that must have struck Heidegger, who in his early days was above all else a reader of Aristotle. Starting at *Physics* 222b 15, we read this:

> The term ἐξαίφνης ["all of a sudden," "instantaneously"] refers to what has departed from its former state in an imperceptible time [τὸ ἐν ἀναισθήτῳ χρόνῳ διὰ μικρότητα ἐκστάν]. . . . Yet all change is by nature a departing [or dispersing—and here for the first time the word ἐκστατικόν appears]. In time, all things come into being and pass away, for which reason some called it the wisest, whereas the Pythagorean Πάρων called it the most stupid, since in it we also forget; and his was the truer view. It is clear, then, that in itself time must be . . . the cause of corruption [φθορά] rather than of generation. For change in itself is a departure, whereas it is only accidentally the cause of becoming and of being.

I repeat, this *must* be the source of Heidegger's notion of "ecstatic temporality." Not only does Aristotle establish the relation of the ecstatic to existence in general, but he also sees that ecstasy entails departure and loss: the tragic tone of both his and Heidegger's thinking would here be set in stone or, better, branded on the flesh of each.

And yet when Heidegger himself analyzes in detail Aristotle's treatment of time he does not mention this passage: in *The Basic Problems of Phenomenology*, from the summer semester of 1927, he would have had at least to mention it at either of two places (26:334–35 and 358–59). True, at 334 he discusses the "sudden" or "instantaneous," but he pays no heed at all to either ecstasy or existence, no heed at all to time as radical departure and corruption. Fifteen years later, in a lecture course on Parmenides (54:223), Heidegger again discusses the meaning of ἐξαίφνης, and in the context of time, but he says nothing about the ecstatic analysis of temporality or the *Augenblick*, either as Schleiermacher's translation or as "the moment of insight" in his own magnum opus; here, in the Parmenides lectures, it is a question of "incipient upsurgence," *das Anfängliche*, in the history of being, or of beyng.

Now, I know what you are thinking: you are thinking of those moments, not in your own treatment of a given text, but in treatments by colleagues who succumb to the temptation to suppress a reference in order to claim an insight as their own. Yet Heidegger is more likely to savor any and every connection with the Greek, proclaiming these connections rather than concealing them. Heidegger's silence is therefore mysterious. And, as

if that were not enough, and as though to demonstrate the perhaps cryptic
nature of what Aristotle is discussing here, Jacques Derrida, in his remarkably thorough essay "Ousia and Grammè," an essay that often succeeds in
showing what Heidegger seems to have neglected in Aristotle's and in Hegel's
accounts of time, disregards this crucial passage altogether. It is as though
Aristotle, writing for everyone in the history of philosophy to come, is here
writing for no one. It is as though Paron were right, and time is incorrigible.

The third preliminary question was: If ecstatic temporality is a genuine
achievement, why does Heidegger soon drop it? Why, after the end of the
1920s, is there scarcely a reference to it? Heidegger's remarks in his "Letter
on Humanism" and in his letter to Father Richardson do not satisfy me,
although I will not take the time to review them once again here.[3] The 1930s
are years dedicated to the thought of ἀλήθεια, "truth" as unconcealment.
The theme of time withdraws in the face of Heidegger's questioning of the
history of metaphysics, better, the history of the truth of beyng. The meaning of being as presence, whether as παρουσία, Anwesenheit, or Gegenwart,
seems from hence to be taken for granted, so much so that it could seem
to Derrida that Heidegger had merely taken his place in the epoch of metaphysics as a history of presence. "Clearing" and "letting-come-to-presence,"
Lichtung und Anwesenlassen, are the words that in Heidegger's final years
come to replace the notions of being and time, "clearing" and "coming to
presence," along with the vocabulary of Ereignis, "the granting" or "reaching" of time-space. The "interplay," Zuspiel, of time-space "dimensions,"
rather than "ecstases," occupies his final reflections (IM 52–53). Yet why
not Ekstasen, inasmuch as this word is so much richer than the shopworn
word dimensions? We do not know. The truth is that neither Derrida nor
I nor anyone else I know has genuine insight into the question as to why
Heidegger abandons the ecstatic analysis. Yet, if I may repeat my adolescent
remark, does Heidegger's dropping it necessarily compel us?

Let me put these preliminaries aside so that we may begin to read
section 65. We may well feel unequal to the task. Heidegger calls us there
to "unbroken discipline." For what we must get into our view, indeed,
into our "undistracted existentially understanding view," im unzerstreuten,
existenzial verstehenden Blick, are (1) precisely that problematic autonomy
and permanence of self mentioned a few moments ago, Selbst-ständigkeit,
and (2) the totality of human existence, die Ganzheit des Daseins. Now, the
notion of totality, for its part, has been problematized from the moment

---

3. See IM, chapters 2 and 3, where I rehearse these "self-interpretations" of Heidegger.

it is introduced. If human existence, as possibility-being, is fundamentally futural, thrown toward the future that is coming toward it as its *Zu-kunft*, then there seems to be always something "still outstanding" about Dasein, some possibility that is not yet actualized, some debt that is not yet acquitted, some deed that is not yet done. If existence "stands out" as always ahead of itself, *sich vorweg*, it will be difficult indeed to understand it as a totality, and just as difficult to understand it as "standing" in its selfhood. How to think totality and permanence without turning Dasein into something present at hand? The moralizing undertone of the call to unbroken discipline—that cool, grave tone that Nietzsche so mercilessly exposes as the tone of the ascetic ideal in the scholar or scientist—lets us know that what is at stake here is the entire analysis of existence proper, *die Eigentlichkeit*, as of that recalcitrant notion of a *vorlaufende Entschlossenheit*, an open resolve that runs ahead, revealing to Dasein its being toward the end. Yet the stakes are even higher: Heidegger stresses that the *ontological* meaning of the temporality of Dasein will shed light on the temporality—and the finitude—of beings in general, hence on the very meaning of being as such: something like a horizon, a backdrop, ground, or upon-which (*Woraufhin*) onto which we project beings of all kinds, handy items in our everyday world or even scientifically investigated entities, discloses to us the being of beings (*das Sein des Seienden*). If the ontological meaning of care and concern lies in temporality, then the upon-which of all projection may well be time as such, and we will have arrived at the crux of the book called *Being* and *Time*.

Now, Heidegger has claimed that the fundamental projection of existence proper, that is, Dasein in its most proper mode, is the open resolve that runs ahead. The problem of such a claim, and Heidegger sees the problem (which he develops in section 62), is that all this talk of resoluteness and resolve, *Entschlossenheit*, seems to reflect an inherited ethics of some kind, a "factical ideal" that imposes itself on the analysis and that therefore needs to be dismantled and tested. It may help if we inquire into this odd *Vorlaufen*, "running ahead," that is said to accompany resolve. (Note that when we translate *Vorlaufen* as "anticipation," and *vorlaufende Entschlossenheit* as "anticipatory resolve," we muddle Heidegger's sense entirely: nothing about our ownmost possibility, our death, which is nonrelational, unsurpassable, certain and yet as certain indeterminate as to its "when," can be "anticipated." It may be that Heidegger takes the verbal form *Vorlaufen* from the current and readily understood modifier *vorläufig*, "preliminary," as though resoluteness itself is proleptic, provisional, preliminal, even "preliminary." Derrida will translate it, literally and brilliantly, as "precursory.") Whither does running-ahead run? Presumably, into its own future, the future that is coming toward it. The future of Dasein, as ability to be, as possibility-being, comes toward it, *auf sich zu*. That is the meaning of *Zu-kunft*. Yet as long as Dasein *is*, it has been undergoing this; its future *has been* coming toward it out there in the world all along. Dasein exists the way it always already has existed, and thus in moving toward its future it is in some sense thrown back on its factical having-been. Heidegger says that Dasein *existiert wie es je schon war*, "exists as it always in each case already was," a phrase that seems to capture the Aristotelian notion of "essence," τὸ τί ἦν εἶναι. It is important to note that the temporal ecstasy of the past, and it alone, receives a new designation from Heidegger. Not the past, *Vergangenheit*, is his theme, but the present-perfect *Gewesenheit*. This word, which contains the root *Wesen*, or *essence*, designates the ecstasy in which we come *back* to ourselves. Perhaps this is a part of the problem of the "self," namely, that it has its primacy not only in the future of possibility-being but also in its factical having-been. Nietzsche might wonder whether there is something "monumental," if not "antiquarian," about the self, especially if it regards itself as "standing."

Thrown into the future that is coming toward it, cast back on its having-been—where is the ecstasy of the present? We are always, replies Heidegger, while projected futurally and cast back on our having-been, "alongside" handy items in our everyday world, simply "with" them. These handy items dominate our present for the most part, we with our toothbrush, fountain pen, or iPhone in hand. What is surprising in this first exposition of the ecstases is that the present to which Heidegger refers here is not the "moment of insight" into our mortality, not *der Augenblick*, which would surely be the ecstasis of a resolve that runs ahead toward its most proper mortal possibility; rather, our present ecstasis opens onto the handy items of our everyday world, the world that ensnares us and to which we fall prey. Yet why does he mention the *Augenblick* at all? We do not need the "moment of insight" for our access to handy items in our everyday world. Indeed, Heidegger consistently associates the future with our *appropriate* existentiality, having-been with our *appropriate* facticity, but the present with *Verfallen*, our falling prey to or being ensnared in our everydayness. Whereas the future and past are projections of our proper self, the present seems to be the projection of our *inappropriate*, "inauthentic" mode of being. The problem then would be: When and how do the ecstases of future and past, in their ecstatic interaction and interpenetration, yield the all-important *Augenblick*? When does the present that is absorbed in its everyday concerns yield to the present of insight—sudden insight—into our mortal condition?

In general, what we most need to know is how inappropriate and appropriate ecstases interact, and especially how the inappropriate ecstases open onto, call up, invite, enable, allow in some passive way, yield or yield *to* the *appropriate* ecstases. For these too must unfold in and as temporality.

But we are going too fast, and things are already too confusing. In *Intimations of Mortality*, I began my discussion of section 65 by listing the four theses that Heidegger offers at the end of the section by way of summary, and it may be useful to list these four theses again. Section 65 argues for the following four points:

1. "Time is originally the temporalization of temporality [*die Zeitigung der Zeitlichkeit*], which makes possible the constitution of the structure of care."

2. "Temporality is essentially ecstatic."

3. "Temporality temporalizes originally out of the future."

4. "Original time is finite."

A few remarks, in all brevity, about each of these simply stated but infinitely complex theses.

1. Discovery of the care structure is the result of the entire first division of *Being and Time*. The word *Sorge* embraces every aspect of human existence, all its deeds and omissions. Formally defined, care is "being ahead of itself already in (a world) as being alongside (beings encountered in the world)" (SZ 327). In the words *ahead, already,* and *alongside* we hear the structures of existentiality, facticity, and ensnarement or falling prey. We also hear intimations of a temporality at work, with our being ahead (our existentiality) indicating the future, our being always already in a world (our facticity) indicating our having-been, and our being alongside or with handy items in the world (ensnarement) indicating the present. The structure of care implies a temporal unfolding, *Zeitigung*. Temporality is no sort of being at all, says Heidegger. It *is* not; rather, "it *temporalizes* itself" (SZ 328; 20:442). Temporality *is* not; it *ensues*, in Joyce's sense. Recall those remarkable lines from *Finnegans Wake* (I, 18), lines I entered into my copy of *Being and Time* decades ago: "In the ignorance that implies impression that knits knowledge that finds the nameform that whets the wits that convey contacts that sweeten sensation that drives desire that adheres to attachment that dogs death that bitches birth that entails the ensuance of existentiality." In case you were wondering, that is the structure of "care."

2. Heidegger now, at SZ 328–29, uses the word *Ekstasen* to designate what we otherwise would lamely call the "dimensions" of human
temporality:

> Future, having-been, and present display the phenomenal char-
> acteristics of the "coming-toward," "the back upon," and the
> "enabling to be confronted *by*" ["Auf-sich-zu," "Zurück auf,"
> "Begegnenlassen *von*"]. The phenomena of the toward, onto,
> and with [or alongside: *bei*] reveal temporality as the ἐκστατικόν
> without qualification. *Temporality is the original "outside itself"*
> *in and for itself.* We therefore call the designated phenomena
> of future, having-been, and present the *ecstases* of temporality.
> Temporality is not prior to that a being that only later emerges
> out of *itself*; rather, its essence is temporalization in the unity
> of the *ecstases*.

Note the Hegelian tease: in-and-for-itself, that is, at the supreme
moment of what Hegel would take to be dialectical insight, the moment
of conscious interiority, intelligence, reason, and spirit as such, temporality
is "the original 'outside-itself,'" and it is outside itself, not at some early or
intermediate stage, and not as a preliminary exteriority that will soon be
swallowed by an all-consuming interiority, but as the very essence of temporality. We have to wonder whether an outside-itself can have an essence, or
a self, or whether it can be named at all in terms of earlier metaphysical or
logical systems. Not for nothing was the word ἔκστασις associated with the
mysteries, with Demeter and Dionysos, and not with logic and metaphysics. For the young Nietzsche at Basel, ἔκστασις was the Dionysian actor's
stepping outside of his everyday self, speaking as the outside and sustaining
the outside. For Schelling, to whose Erlangen lectures we ought to return if
only for a moment, ἔκστασις is the radical displacement we call *astonishment*.

In his Erlangen lecture course of 1820–21, Schelling uses the word
Ekstasis to designate the "stepping out of itself," *sich heraustreten*, of what he
calls "the absolute subject," which we may understand as the subjectivity or
personhood attributed to the God of Christian ontotheology.[4] The most rad-

---

4. F. W. J. Schelling, *Initia philosophiae universae: Erlanger Vorlesung WS 1820/21*, ed.
Horst Fuhrmans (Bonn: Bouvier Verlag, 1969), 35. Hereinafter IP in the body of my
text. For this and all references to Schelling, I am indebted to Alexander Bilda of
Freiburg University, who is coediting with Philip Schwab the Erlangen lectures for the
historical-critical Schelling edition.

ical departure in Schelling's interpretation is that this egression or emergence of absolute subjectivity, which he had earlier understood as "intellectual intuition," is *not* a kind of knowing, *Wissen*. It is not subjectivity projecting itself to the outside in order to "know" itself. Rather, it is "*E k s t a s e*, a 'being posited outside itself,'" *ein "Außer sich selbst gesetzt werden* (IP 39). Or, if "posited" is too Fichtean a notion, let us translate Schelling's *gesetzt* as a being placed or even *propelled* outside itself. Schelling equates such ecstasis with Plato's θαυμάζειν, philosophical "wonder" or "astonishment," viewing it as a complete "surrender" of self, *Selbstaufgegebenheit* (ibid.; cf. 47). Such ecstasis is a "two-faced expression," a *vox anceps*, inasmuch as it may mean either an expulsion from what is properly one's own place or an emergence into that proper place (IP 41). Schelling is well aware of the Aristotelian sense of ἔκστασις as "displacement" and "departure," so that it is a question (as we say in English) of whether ecstasis is "a point of departure for" or a "departure from" what is proper to the absolute. For Schelling, and equally for the later Heidegger, the positive sense of ecstasis would be that which leads a human being "to the beginning of meditation," that is, to *Besinnung*, which is Schelling's own word for thinking (ibid.). Again, what is remarkable is Schelling's insistence that such meditation is not an interiorization, as it is with Hegel, but a removal to the outside, "*das außer sich.*"

The "fragments" of notes surrounding Schelling's *Ages of the World* say precisely the same things about ecstasis.[5] A note in *Konvolut NL 94* describes the "free knowing" that one might identify with absolute subjectivity as a knowing that experiences everywhere a kind of defeat in the face of the power of beyng (*vielmehr erliegt es überall d[er] Macht d[es] Seyns*); the thinker of the absolute is thrown from the midpoint of his or her meditation and experiences beyng as central (*heraus geworfen aus dem Mittelp[unkt] u[nd] dagegen d[as] Seyn central*) (WF 297). Here too Schelling stresses the fact that "knowing" departs from (*hinweggeht*) its earlier position of mastery, such departure being precisely the sense of the Greek ἔκστασις (WF 301). Later in the same *Konvolut* Schelling describes ἔκστασις as related to intellectual intuition, precisely as the doubling of subject and object within consciousness; yet he now describes the ostensible interiority of such "intuition" as precisely a being thrown outside of oneself, "something," he adds, "that does not please the egoist" (WF 309). One is tempted to identify Schelling's notes on birth, especially the "birth that occurs in lightning,"

---

5. F. W. J. Schelling, *Weltalter-Fragmente*, ed. Klaus Grotsch (Stuttgart: Bad Cannstatt: Fromann-Holzboog Verlag, 2002), hereinafter cited as WF in my text.

which is to say, the birth of Dionysos of a Semele blasted by Zeus, with the ecstasis in question. Yet that is where the darker side of the *vox anceps* of ecstasy manifests itself: ecstasy may well be the movement (the *thrown* movement, Heidegger would say) of consciousness from freedom to necessity, from a superior form of being to nonbeing. "Here," writes Schelling, in *Konvolut NL 81*, "the full concept of ecstasis—the great doctrine—illness [*Hier voller Begriff d. Ekstasis—grosse Lehre.—d. Krankheit*]" (WF 260–61). This would be the ever-living fire of Heraclitus interpreted as *Sucht*, that is, as both that for which one is searching or longing and that which eats away at one's health. Once again we meet here the Schelling of *contagion*, the Schelling who meditates also on the dire forces of nature.[6]

Schelling's language and thinking in the *Weltalter-Fragmente* and in the Erlangen lectures—with the sole exception of his reflection on illness—are so close to the later Heidegger's understanding of the truth of being that one cannot doubt the force of Schelling's "influence" on Heidegger. Yet, to repeat, such "influence," when it comes to the theme of ecstatic temporality, cannot realistically be said to have begun by 1926 or 1927, the period during which *Being and Time* was written. And, in any case, Schelling is not applying the notion of ecstasis specifically to temporality. Let us return, then, to the second thesis of section 65, "Temporality is essentially ecstatic," and ecstatic "in the unity of the *ecstases*."

In the *unity* of the ecstases, says Heidegger. This leads to one of his most daring claims, one that seems to militate against his thesis that the future is primary for existence. He insists that the ecstases of time are "equally original," *gleichursprünglich*. He has used this word before, to suggest the equal originality of *Welt* and *Wer*, that is, of Dasein as being-in-the-world and as answering to the personal pronoun, *who*. Likewise, the principal forms of *Erschlossenheit*, or disclosedness, are equally original: how one finds oneself to be, that is, caught up in this or that mood or attunement to the world (*Befindlichkeit*), understanding as a projection upon possibilities (*Verstehen*), and discourse (*Rede*). None of these can be derived from the others; all are interwoven *ab ovo* in our existence. At some point, all genetic or genealogical accounts must cease, says Heidegger:

> The nonderivability of something original does not exclude a multiplicity of ontological characteristics that are constitutive of the original in question. If such a multiplicity shows itself, then

---

6. See Krell, *Contagion*, Part II.

the characteristics are existentially equally original. The phenomenon of the *Gleichursprünglichkeit* of constitutive moments has
often been overlooked in ontology on account of an unbridled
tendency in the methodology to seek the birth certificate of each
and every thing on the basis of one simple "primal ground"
[*"Urgrund"*]. (SZ 131)

Yet even if we should overcome our lust for an *Urgrund* with regard
to the temporal ecstases, we will still want to know more about their unity
and their interweaving. Does not unity require some sort of enclosure? How
enclose traits that in and for themselves are outside themselves? We will
want to know more about this essential exteriority, which Schelling calls a
birth by fire. For this would be the key to the animation of Dasein, the
fact that it is not self-moving but is *set* in motion. Not "animation" but
Bewegtheit, the past participle of *Bewegen*, is Heidegger's word in *Sein und
Zeit*. This important word designates the way in which Dasein is *moved*,
presumably by the ecstases of time. Such "movedness" would give us the
essential connection between "existence" and "ecstasy."

Heidegger uses an equally strange word to suggest the kind of "movedness" (please excuse the odd English locution, especially if you have always
thought of yourself as a self-mover) in which existence is caught up: in
sections 68 and 69 (SZ 338–39, 350) he calls the ecstases of temporality *Entrückungen*, "raptures." In section 69 he writes: "The ecstatic unity
of temporality, that is, the unity of the 'outside-itself' in the raptures of
future, having-been, and present, is the condition of the possibility of there
being a being that can exist as its 'there'" (SZ 350). When you finally get
there, there isn't any there there, but there there do unfold the raptures
of temporality. Ironically, Heidegger's raptures or ecstases are not there to
propel us outside of time by way of some mystical experience that would
bring time to a standstill. They temporalize as *finite* time itself. About which
more in a moment.

3. Concerning the primacy of the future, that is, the priority of existentiality for Dasein, let me say only this. The primacy, priority, and perhaps
even "apriority" of the ecstasis of the future, the *Zu-kunft*, is implied in my
being able to confront my ownmost possibility; my existence is characterized chiefly by the *Umwillen*, the "for my own sake," such that my being is
always an issue for me. I am "involved" in it, even if I understand nothing
of its whence and whither. The futural essence of "existence" Heidegger calls
"existentiality"; the pleonasm or tautology is meant to be instructive. Yet it
is important to note that this priority of the future becomes increasingly

dubious to Heidegger in the lecture courses immediately following the publication of *Being and Time*, and perhaps even in the final chapters of that
book itself. It is of course difficult to see how the "equal originality," *die
Gleichursprünglichkeit*, of the temporal ecstases will allow the thesis on the
priority of the future to stand. Yet Heidegger makes the primacy of the
future even more problematic when he italicizes the following sentences (at
SZ 350): *"Temporality temporalizes completely in each ecstasis. That is to say,
the totality of the structural whole of existence, facticity, and ensnarement, that
is, the unity of the structure of care, is grounded in the ecstatic unity of any
given complete temporalizing of temporality."* What could the "completeness"
of "any given temporalizing" mean? And how can temporality temporalize
"completely" in each of the three ecstases? Why are there three, if any one
of the three includes all three? Did I say *includes*? Is there, must there not
be, only one "outside-itself"? "In-and-for-itself"?!

4. The finitude of original time is perhaps the most difficult of the
four theses for us to affirm, inasmuch as Heidegger says so little about
it, fails to *demonstrate* it in his otherwise remarkably systematic work. Yet
how could one demonstrate such a thing? And what does *finitude* even
mean? Heidegger is not theorizing about cosmic time, the time-space of
astrophysics. From the outset he takes such theorizing to be derivative with
respect to a suppressed or repressed "original" time, the time that does not
submit to measurement (as Bergson would agree), but that we get a sense
of when we say that someone's time is "up." The time that runs out, that
is exhausted or perhaps truncated quite suddenly, the time that Paron felt
was really stupid is what Heidegger means by "original" time. Again, it is
difficult to say why such time is "original," "more original" than the time
that can be measured by clock and calendar. Finitude of time? There can
be no doubt about the seriousness with which Heidegger argues for it, no
matter how recalcitrant the notion and how resistant to demonstration. For,
in all modesty, even without high-flying references to astrophysics, we all
will admit that time is bigger than we are, and that when our time is up
"infinite" time will go marching on as it always has—recall that sea, after
the *Pequod* has gone down, rolling on as it rolled five thousand years ago,
and think of those stars that will still be enjoying their parallax a million
years from now; think even of humankind bungling its way along without
you or me to some unseen destiny and probable if unpredictable catastrophe. Such "infinite" time seems to be the "original," with you and me as
mere epigones. This is precisely what Heidegger denies. One of the most
stringent statements of his book is the following: "The problem cannot be:
how does 'derived,' infinite time, 'in which' what is at hand comes to be

and passes away, become original, finite temporality; rather, the problem is: how does *in*appropriate temporality spring from finite temporality proper, and how does inappropriate temporality *as* inappropriate temporalize a *non-finite* time from finite time?" (SZ 330–31). Original time is—we *know* not how—finite.

The word *endlich* has appeared earlier in the book. Section 53, "Existential Projection of an Appropriate Being Toward Death," while elaborating the third characteristic of the existential conception of death, which is ownmost, nonrelational, *unsurpassable*, certain, and as certain indeterminate as to its *when*, takes the *Unüberholbarkeit* of death to be an essential marker for the finitude of *time* as well. The end of Dasein that we call *death* cannot be overtaken on the highway of life. That is why we never get a good look at it. Similarly, time as futural cannot be overtaken: *my* time is forever on the hither-side of the finite time that advances toward me. By running ahead in resolute openness, Dasein heeds Zarathustra's remonstrance (KSA 4:94) not to grow too old for its truths and its victories. Heidegger adds that by running ahead (*Vorlaufen*) Dasein becomes free "for the ownmost possibilities that are determined on the basis of the *end*, and that means possibilities understood as *finite* . . ." (SZ 264). *Endlich* here could be translated as *final* and even *end-like*. Yet the "end" is not simply the place where Dasein ceases to be. Indeed, Heidegger will later say that existence has "another" end: the "other end" of Dasein is *birth*. This birth-end will later, in chapters 3 and 4, occupy us at some length. However, even the death-end is not some point that is still outstanding. Rather, *Dasein existiert endlich*, "exists finitely" (SZ 329). True, time marches on even when any given Dasein, you or I, is no longer "there." Yet this is no objection, Heidegger says, "to the finitude of original temporality" (SZ 330). He adds, driving his analysis to the twin peaks of paradox and oxymoron:

> The question is not what all can transpire "in a time that goes on," nor what we might encounter in letting something come toward us "beyond this time"; the question is how this coming toward us *itself and as such* is originally determined. Its finitude does not suggest primarily a cessation, but is rather a characteristic of temporalizing itself. The original and appropriate future is coming toward itself, toward *itself*, existing as the unsurpassable possibility of nullity [*Nichtigkeit*]. The ecstatic character of the original future lies precisely in the fact that it closes [*schließt*] our ability to be, which means that the future itself is closed [*geschlossen*] and that as such the future makes possible the

resolutely unclosed [*entschlossene*] existentiell understanding of nullity. (Ibid.)

How the *closed* future *opens* us to the insight that we ourselves are the ground of a nullity (SZ 283–85) is perhaps the ultimate question of the second division of *Being and Time*. For this too is the very meaning of *Zukunft*: the *zu* of *Zu-kunft* means the advent of what is *closed*. In German, one closes the door, *zu-machen*. What is closed in the present case? Our ability to be anything other than a nullity.

The burden placed on the temporal analysis here seems to be strained to the breaking point. What would happen if Heidegger himself were to come to doubt the relation between our future, as the primary ecstasis, and our finitude? For this is indeed what seems to happen as soon as the book is published. In a lecture course of 1928–29, Heidegger is still keen to demonstrate the finitude of human existence, but he dwells less on time and its "closed" future than on the uncanny finitude of philosophy: "Because philosophy is essentially a human possibility, that is, a finite possibility, there is a sophist hiding in every philosopher" (27:24).[7]

In *Being and Time* itself the thesis concerning the finitude of time is still closely tied to that of the primacy of the future. Heidegger writes, "The future proper, which temporality primarily temporalizes insofar as it makes out the meaning of the resolve that runs ahead, thus reveals itself *to be finite*" (SZ 329–30). As I am thrown toward my future precisely as my future comes toward me, I come to myself as possibility-being (*Seinkönnen*); yet my ownmost possibility "is the insurmountable possibility of nullity" (ibid.). If the fourth thesis (on the finitude of time) is closely tied to the third (on the primacy of the future for existential analysis), and if this third thesis becomes less and less tenable to Heidegger himself, how is the finitude of temporality—indeed, the finitude of original time as such—to be reconfigured? If the priority of the future ecstasis cannot be maintained, what can possibly conjoin ecstatic temporality and the finitude of time? It may occur to us that our being bound to a factical past is also strong testimony on behalf of the finitude of time, and the way my present enables me to fritter away my time with things that are infinitely pointless may also testify to such finitude. You may recall Emerson's rueful confession that

---

7. That is, Martin Heidegger, *Einleitung in die Philosophie*, Winter Semester 1928–1929, 2nd ed., *Gesamtausgabe*, vol. 27, ed. Otto Saame and Ina Saame-Speidel (Frankfurt-am-Main: V. Klostermann, 2001 (1996), 24.

the only demonstration of finitude we need comes when we correct our page proofs. Yet let us search for other testimonies, other witnesses. A key witness might be the very notion of ecstasy. Or perhaps that other word, used four times in *Being and Time* to describe the motion or the movedness of ecstasy, namely, *Entrückung*.

Let us examine the four appearances of the latter word, *Entrückung*, but not before asking again one of our preliminary questions: Whence the notion of *Entrückung*, sudden seizure or "rapture"? Could it be Augustine? Here again Heidegger does not reveal the source of his *Entrückungen*, either in terms of the verb *rapere*, "to seize," or the adverb *raptim*, "rapidly, suddenly," even though at one point he himself "translates" the German *Entrückung* with the Latin word *raptus*. When Heidegger refers to Augustine's *Confessions* in his 1924 lecture, *The Concept of Time*, he cites the passage from chapter 27 of Book XI, in which Augustine speaks of "the times that I measure in my mind," but he says nothing of *rapere*, *raptus*, and *raptim* in their many appearances throughout the *Confessions*. We know that in Heidegger's own education Augustine plays a key role: in a 1925 lecture course he explains that seven years earlier, that is, in 1918, he "stumbled across" the notion of *Sorge*, "care" or "concern," in Augustine, namely, as *cura* (20:418). As far as I know, however, there is no such attribution on Heidegger's part, no such "stumbling across," in the case of *rapere*, *raptus*, or the adverb *raptim*. In the Marburg lecture courses on "the phenomenology of religion," published as volume 60 in the *Gesamtausgabe*, in which Augustine plays a major role, there is talk of "sudden temptation," "sudden fall," and the equally sudden *kairotic* moment of grace; yet here too there is no explicit reference to *raptus*. This is surprising in the light of Augustine's *Confessions*, in which the suddenness of both the fall into sin and the upsurgence of a saving grace is what lends the text so much of its tension.

In chapter 15 of Book XI, Augustine is in search of the *fleeting* present of time; he notes that whatever can be called "present," no matter how minute, "flies suddenly out of the future into the past": *raptim a futuro in praeteritum transvolat*. This sudden flight can scarcely have escaped the notice of Heidegger the young phenomenologist—for whom, it is true, the care and concern of existence itself had not yet been expressly understood in terms of temporality. When, after those seven years have passed, he begins to sketch out *Being and Time*, and when, three years later, he refers explicitly to *raptus* as a word for the metabolic movement of time, it *must* be that both Aristotle and Augustine have been remembered.

If the key Augustinian reference to the temporality of the sudden is *raptim . . . transvolat* (XI:15), other uses of *rapere* in the *Confessions* are nonetheless instructive. Our senses snatch images quite suddenly in order to lock them away in our memory, whereby both the suddenness of the action of our senses and the perdurance of the vestiges in our memory never cease to amaze us: images *quibus sensibus raptae sint,* "seized by our senses," have a staying power that Augustine struggles to understand. Likewise, the sudden seizures by which we *learn* and spiritually grow are also ambivalent in the extreme. Their ambivalence, which is appropriate to the mystery of time as such, comes to the fore in two apparently opposed instances of rapture. First, Augustine confesses himself "ravished away by lust," seized, *rapiebat,* by the raptures of Eros; during one period of his life, theater plays propel him into ecstasy, *rapiebant* (II:2; III:2). And we know what staying power such seizures had, especially those tenacious raptures Augustine suffers at the hands of women. Second, Augustine records his long conversation with Monica at Ostia, in which the two of them review the supreme pleasures of both carnality and spirituality. Their conversation soars ever higher and flies ever more swiftly until they are seized by a singular exultation that ravishes them both, *rapida cogitatione attingimus . . . haec una rapiat* (XI:10). Whether one learns from one's sainted mother or from a ravishing woman, in either case, the learning involves rapture. Indeed, rapture comes into play even when one learns from one's father. Earlier in Book IX, Augustine marvels at how suddenly, *subito,* it became easy for him to accept the embraces of his heavenly father, embraces that released in him a flood of tears. At the end of Book IX, the son is once again suddenly seized by a fit of weeping—this time for his dead mother. Whether the torrents of joy and sorrow, the overflow of tears, *transfluebat in lacrimas,* can be tied to the ecstatic flight of time, *transvolat,* I cannot say; that the violence of mourning in particular, *violento animi imperio,* is a violence in and of time, I do suspect, and for the most excellent Augustinian reasons (IX:12). But it is time to abandon Augustine too, inasmuch as we are uncertain as to whether any of this played a role in Heidegger's understanding of the raptures of time.

Let us now look at the four instances in *Sein und Zeit* where *Entrückung* or "rapture" appears. Because the German word is the nominalization of a verb, let us translate it, not as *rapture,* but as the action or animatedness of *enrapturement,* however awkward and ugly that rendering. If we imagine Bernini's extraordinary Santa Teresa, some of the ugliness of the word may be charmed away. First, in section 68a, on the temporality of understanding, *Entrückung* is used to describe the moment of insight, the *Augenblick* that is so important to Heidegger. *Der Augenblick* is itself an ecstasis, says Heidegger (SZ 338). "It means the openly resolved, but in resoluteness the *held* enrapturement of Dasein with respect to the concernful possibilities and circumstances that Dasein confronts in its situation" (ibid.). The expression used here, *Entrückung an*, is unique, and it is odd, in that it relates the rapture not merely to the motion of time itself but to the connection between temporality and the possibilities that Dasein encounters in the world. At all events, enrapturement has to do with a very particular "situation," namely, the proper or authentic possibility of Dasein as being toward death.

The second use of the word, however, involves not appropriate Dasein, but oblivious, inappropriate Dasein. Heidegger writes, "The ecstasis (enrapturement) of oblivion [*Vergessen*] has the character of an evasion that is closed to itself, an evasion *in the face of* one's ownmost having-been, indeed in such a way that this evasion ecstatically closes off what faces it and at the same time closes off itself" (SZ 339). Now, this is very strange, doubly strange. The first use of the word has to do with open resolve, or resolute openedness, *Entschlossenheit*, although, as we noted earlier, the future ecstasis reveals itself as essentially *closed—zu*. The second use of *Entrückung* has to do once again with closure—*verschliessen* is Heidegger's word—but closure of a very different kind. *Entrückung* in this second usage is an *Ausrücken vor* . . . , an evasion in the face of something that is itself barred or locked away, and by a redoubled bolting or barring that is oblivious of itself. We confront the enigma of yet another ecstasy of closure, but this time as a self-occluding oblivion. The problem is that Heidegger's description works all too well, and we do not comprehend how such closure might be undone, so that remembrance becomes possible.

The third use of the word *enrapturement* occurs many pages later, at 68c, on the temporality of falling prey or ensnarement. Here once again the usage has to do with Dasein at its most inappropriate, as it succumbs to every temptation, every self-tranquilization, and every possible distraction that presents itself in this jingle-jangle world of ours. "However," Heidegger now cautions, "the enrapturement of existence in presentification does not mean that Dasein is detached from its ego and its self" (SZ 348). It is merely that the "I" and the "self" temporalize as alienated and oblivious. Once again we confront a sense of enrapturement in which the ecstasis seems to temporalize completely, the present now absorbing our entire future and past—as though, ever oblivious, we really do measure out our life with coffee spoons. This sort of rapture reminds us of Heidegger's analyses of "factical life" in his Marburg lectures of the early 1920s: the young phenomenologist decries our being "out there" in a distracting world, declaring that this *Aus-sich-hinaus* is "ruinous." Perhaps we should not go into ecstasies over this thing called *ecstasis*?

Finally, fourth, at the outset of section 69, Heidegger offers us his most general statement concerning enrapturement. We heard these words a few moments ago, words that caused Gertrude to alter her famous remark: "The ecstatic unity of temporality, that is, the unity of the 'outside-itself' in the raptures of future, having-been, and present, is the condition of the possibility of there being a being that can exist as its 'there'" (SZ 350). In short, the raptures of Dasein include the three "dimensions" of temporality, but they also have reference to the way in which Dasein can be snatched away by oblivion (*Vergessen*), alienation (*Entfremdung*), and evasion (*Ausrücken vor . . .*). Perhaps the fundamental aporia of the temporal analysis is the question as to how we can shift from one rapture to another; above all, how we might be snatched from a self-sealing oblivion to a moment of insight into the closed future that reveals to us our nullity.

Yet it is time, high time, to raise a possible objection to everything I have written here. For the more we try to understand how one may "move" or "shift" from the ecstases of closure in the future, oblivion in having-been, and bedazzlement in the present, or even, accepting the lesson of *Bewegtheit*, the more we want to know how we are *moved* from these "inappropriate" ecstases to the "appropriate" ones, the more likely we are to reduce the ecstases themselves to "now points" on a number line. Ecstatic temporality is not a tramway that transports us to points A, B, C, and D, no matter how badly we want to get to D. The more one "pushes" the question as to how the *Augenblick* temporalizes, the more that *how?* becomes a *when?* and, once again, the tendency to reduce the ἐκστατικόν to a programmed sequence seems unavoidable. We may be right to worry that a suppressed voluntarism underlies Heidegger's drive to the proper, a voluntarism that cannot survive the ecstatic analysis of temporality; yet this worry would have to be tempered by the worry that we ourselves, anxious to put the ecstases to work, invariably reduce them to segments of "vulgar" time. Heidegger's voluntarism or our own vulgarity? The question is not so readily answered.[8]

---

8. Michael Levine, in discussions we had at Rutgers University, developed the idea of the ecstases as a "differential structure." Not only the idea of sequentiality but also all talk of the "interpenetration" or "interweaving" of the ecstases tends to reduce time to a being, to something that *is*. Yet time *is* not; time temporalizes. Perhaps it also *temporizes*, as Derrida suspects. And such *temporizing* would be what enables some of the more mysterious manifestations of temporality, such as Freud's *Nachträglichkeit*. Only a structure that is *differential* from the outset, such that the second *e* of that word would become an *a*, can serve Heidegger's ecstatic analysis. Which would suggest perhaps that Heidegger dropped those analyses precisely because they were far ahead of their time. *Nachträglich* and *differantially* considered, they regain their significance.

Be that as it may, it is difficult to read the word *Entrückung* at any of the four places we have located and not think of suddenness. Recall again the ἐξαίφνης that Aristotle describes in *Physics* as displacement or departure in a time so minuscule that we do not sense it. Such eccentric suddenness is also a problem for Plato, or for Plato's *Parmenides*. For the notorious Parmenidean "one" appears to be both at rest and in motion, hence in transition and change, both within time and outside of time, precisely because of the "all of a sudden" (156c–e). Recall that Schleiermacher translates it as *der Augenblick*, or *das Augenblickliche*, and it is impossible to think that Heidegger, a close student of Plato's *Parmenides* from the time of the Marburg reading group ("Graeca") led by Paul Friedländer, did not know about and appreciate the translation. In a 1928–29 lecture course, Heidegger cites Plato's Seventh Letter, which emphasizes the suddenness of insight, "as though a spark of flame were to leap from the one to the other, so that the flying spark brings illumination, shedding the light in which being becomes visible" (341c; 27:221). Some years later, in another context, Heidegger asks, "Why does what is *most abyssal*—the moment—love what is also *the most fleeting*?" (94:521).

Plato also refers to the sudden or instantaneous in a more entertaining context in his *Gorgias* (523a–e). Socrates tells us that the judgment of souls used to occur on the last day of people's lives—for back in the old days people knew the day their lives would end—and they were judged by living judges while themselves still alive. As you might expect, the living judges were often swayed and even bribed by the one to be judged, so that Hades eventually complained to his brother that all sorts of unsuitable souls were showing up at the Isles of the Blessed, whereas Tartarus, Erebos, or Orkus was their fitting destination. Zeus determined that mortals would no longer know the day of their death, remembering that Prometheus, his former ally and eventual enemy, had entertained the same idea, namely, that mortals should be deprived of the foreknowledge of their death. Death would be certain, but its "when" indeterminate. The "when" would therefore come suddenly, unexpectedly, and the judgment of the soul would occur *at the very instant* it leaves the body, for at that instant, ἐξαίφνης, all possessions and influential friends are left behind.

A less entertaining story is that of *Prometheus Bound*, by Aeschylus or, more likely, by someone related to Aeschylus (ll. 247–51). The chorus of Oceanides marvels at Zeus's cruelty toward Prometheus. Yes, Prometheus stole Zeus's lightning, and so gave humankind technical power instead of the death that Zeus had planned for this botched species. Yet the Daughters of Ocean doubt whether it was the theft of fire that so angered Zeus. "Did you not go even farther in your contempt of Zeus?" they ask, whereupon Prometheus confesses, "I prevented human beings from having foreknowledge of their doom." The Daughters of Ocean ought to have expressed puzzlement over this disclosure, inasmuch as Prometheus's very name means *foreknowledge*. How could *he* have *deprived* human beings of foreknowledge? But the Daughters ask, "What sort of counterpoison did you discover for this illness of theirs?" The Greek is odd. The word νόσος clearly means illness, even though we might wonder how foreknowledge could ever be an illness; but the word for "cure" or "medicine," which I have rendered oddly as *counterpoison*, the word φάρμακον, in fact means, as you well know, both medicine and poison. It is almost as though the chorus is asking Prometheus how, in order to cure the mortals, he poisoned them. He replies, "I planted hopes, blind hopes, in their hearts." The phrase seems an oxymoron: τυφλὰς . . . ἐλπίδας, hopes beyond vision or visions beyond hope, hopeless hopes, blindness *without* insight. Perhaps the blindness of blind hopes has to do with the ecstasies of oblivion in which we all live? Perhaps it also has to do with the blinding speed at which we all live? And yet, the chorus immediately comments, "What you gave to these Earthdwellers was supremely helpful to them." The Daughters of Ocean know that pyrotechnics would get us nowhere if we did not have blind hopes in it, and they understand that our blindness, our not knowing the moment of our doom ahead of time, will be the secret of humankind's catastrophic power.

Heidegger offers five words to describe what he calls his existential conception of death, that is, the *possibility* of my own death, and we have already heard these words. Death is our "ownmost" possibility, he says, "without relation" to anyone or anything else; it is "unsurpassable," or "unpassable," inasmuch as we cannot get around it or beyond it; and finally it is "certain," and "as certain, indeterminate as to its *when*." Blind hopes sustain us all until quite suddenly something comes to enlighten us and to dash them. That something would not be death itself; it would be something like insight into the *possibility* of death, a sudden glimpse of the possibility of a future that is *closed* to us. Heidegger calls this *existence*. And he regards existence as *ecstatic*.

An even older story confirms the story of Prometheus. When Gilgamesh loses his friend Enkidu to illness, he sets out on a long journey in search of deathlessness. At long last he finds Utnapishtim the Faraway, who survived the ancient flood. Gilgamesh poses his question about death to Utnaphishtim, who replies in this way: "When the Annunaki, the judges, come together with Mammetun, the mother of destinies, they jointly decree the fates of human beings. Life and death they allot, but the day of death they do not disclose." In the end and at the end, that day, no matter how long our illness has dragged on, comes suddenly.

But enough of stories! Back to sudden death! By way of conclusion! For even if Heidegger does not discuss suddenness as such in *Being and Time*, as far as I remember, there are places when suddenness suddenly appears. The very blink of an eye, *der Augenblick*, in which we catch sight of the possibility of our being a nullity (SZ 308, 338), seems to come very fast—like the slamming door of Mahler's Sixth that twice rocks us out of our seats. And as Derrida loved to remind us, the wink or blink of an eye always involves the eyes' being closed for an instant. What a strange insight this *Augen-blink* [*sic*] must offer!

Yet here a second objection arises. No matter how suddenly the moment of insight may "leap," there is no doubt that Heidegger believes that it offers us a "hold" on our ownmost possibility, a "hold" that we can somehow carry forward, or, again remembering the lesson of *Bewegtheit*, a "hold" that carries *us* forward. True, that moment will not banish inappropriateness; nevertheless it is not simply evanescent, not merely "instantaneous." The *Augenblick* cannot be altogether *augenblicklich*. That objection being stated, however, let me continue my rhapsody on suddenness—suddenness as the conduit of finitude.

In the very word *Unbestimmtheit*, indeterminacy, which crowds the certainty of our death quite close in Heidegger's text, *gewiß und als gewiß unbestimmt*, I sense the instantaneous (SZ 258). Finally, when anxiety creeps up on me even as I flee it, so that I am breathless when it strikes—*den Atem verschlägt*, says Heidegger (SZ 186)—suddenness seems to be the key to Heidegger's insistence on the finitude of time. It is not about the cessation of time but about how time flies, at least until it hits that closed door. Derrida loved the future perfect, and his favorite future perfect was, "And life will have been so short."

Permit me one final word about ἐξαίφνης before I let you get on with your lives. Even if the classicists are dubious about any etymon for the word, it is difficult to avoid associating it with words that suggest the imperceptibility of the supremely small, the unheard and unseen, the non-phenomenal, the unappearing. Oddly, the word αἴφνης, without the ἐξ-, also means "sudden." Liddell-Scott tells us that αἴφνης is related to αἶψα, "quick," and ἄφαρ, "straightway," which seems obvious enough, but that the connection with ἀίω, "to hear" or "to perceive" in general, and even "to breathe," is "dubious"; likewise, it tells us that a relation to ἀφανής, "not appearing," which I am urging here, is also doubtful. Yet if the connection is "dubious," why mention it? Surely, because αἴφνης suggests, morphologically and perhaps even semantically, ἀφανής. That is certainly the way Plato's *Parmenides* and Aristotle's *Physics* understand it. The sudden seems to fall faster than the eye can hear or the ear can see, as it were. At all events, even the classical philologists would agree that in the word ἐξαίφνης the prefix ἐξ- is not some sort of negation. Rather, it seems to refer to something emerging "out of" suddenness—ecstatically, as it were; something occurring "all of a sudden," as we say. One is tempted to say that ἐξαίφνης parallels that odd German word *unheimlich*, which appears to emphasize, and not negate, the *heimlich* in at least one, if not both, of its senses. If the αἴφνης is indeed ἀφανής, if the sudden is the well-nigh unappearing, then ἐξαίφνης would redouble that refusal to appear, the nonphenomenality of the uncannily sudden, so to speak. Suddenness would be the outside-itself in and for the blink of an eye. Or, at least, it would refer to that instant when the eyes are closed and hence see nothing, the instant of what Derrida will call *dissimulation*. It is for him the moment dedicated not to blind hopes but to memoirs of the blind.

And now that my philological horses are out of the barn, scattering over hill and dale, you may permit me another aside, in order to conclude. I cannot help but hear, whenever Heidegger refers to *existence* and *ecstasis*, some relationship with Hölderlin's word *ex-zentrisch*. Hölderlin uses it more often than one might think, and he means much more by it than mere eccentricity. It is a crucial word for him early and late, in at least two contexts. But I have tried your patience long enough, and with matters complicated enough. Let me save for another time this wondrous complication we call *Hölderlin*, who did not hesitate to end a long text with the ecstatic words *"Nächstens mehr,"* "More, very soon."

2

Raptures and Ruptures of Time

Ecstasy comes suddenly. Its suddenness, says Aristotle, always displaces us, and such displacement and sudden departure, says Heidegger, are the very meaning of temporality and human finitude. At the end of the last lecture, I spoke briefly of Hölderlin.

Both in his poetry and in his novel *Hyperion* Hölderlin is gripped by what he calls *die ex-zentrische Bahn*. We know that he was fascinated by Kepler and by Kepler's demonstration of the elliptical orbit of the planets. The ellipse has two foci instead of one; as a result, its figure is never centered, is literally ex-centric. Something seems to be tugging at its potential round-ness and perfection, something like the force of gravity exerted by a foreign body, one might say. A human life too is never centered, but is perpetually pulled and stretched by the two foci Hölderlin's *Hyperion* calls the School of Nature and the School of Destiny. And yet a human life, however beset by calamity and however rudely disciplined by all the masters of its destiny, is determined most by birth, as Hölderlin tells us in the *Rheinhymne* (ll. 47–53):

> Denn
> Wie du anfingst, wirst du bleiben,
> So viel auch wirket die Not,
> Und die Zucht, das meiste nämlich
> Vermag die Geburt,
> Und der Lichtstrahl, der
> Dem Neugebornen begegnet. (DKV 1:329)

> For
> As you began, so you will remain,
> And as much as calamity works its effects,
> And discipline, precisely most is
> Achieved by birth
> And by the ray of light that
> Comes to meet the newborn.

A human life, caught between the push and pull of nature and culture, birth and destiny, may even be rent in the struggle between these two "schools," some lives more than others, and Hölderlin's life more than any other. Hyperion is at home in neither Greece nor Germany. Hölderlin's Empedocles desperately tries to unite the sky and earth of his love. Matthew Arnold has his Empedocles, perched at the edge of Etna's crater, announce his futile hope, "To see if we will poise our life at last." Yet poise is not attained on an eccentric orbit.[1]

Many years later, while translating Sophocles, Hölderlin uses the word *exzentrisch* again. In his "Notes on Oedipus," he speaks of Tiresias's insight into the violent power of nature, which snatches a human being out of the midpoint of its life. Tiresias continues to represent the two "schools" of *Hyperion*: he keeps watch over the power of nature, as *Aufseher über die Naturmacht*, but he is also the prophet of destiny, of the *Gang des Schicksals*. No wonder he is so elliptical! But now the second of the two foci is not merely destiny in the sense of schooling and discipline. It is death itself. Hölderlin calls the underworld, to which both Antigone and Oedipus have so fatal an attraction, *die exzentrische Sphäre der Todten*, "the eccentric sphere of the dead," again, not merely because the dead have odd mannerisms, but because life is not centered, never rounded off, not even by death (CHV 2:311). Finally, Hölderlin uses the word *exzentrisch* in yet another sense. He emphasizes throughout his notes the velocity with which the scenes of a tragedy flow, from late beginning to catastrophic end. He calls this velocity their *exzentrische Rapidität*. Odd that he would use this second Latin word, as though he wanted to refer to that root of *rapture*, the *rap-* of *rapere*. It is striking how very much Hölderlin thinks like a theater stage director: recall his remarkable insight into the caesura, both its importance for the *Darstellung* and the care one must take in locating it, not at the midpoint, but either early on or quite late in the action of, say, *Oedipus the Tyrant* and *Antigone*.

If all this seems too remote from Heidegger to merit mention, allow me to add a reference to Heidegger's 1928–29 *Introduction to Philosophy*. He is talking about the science of anthropology and its understandable tendency to anthropocentrism. The odd thing about anthropocentrism is this:

---

1. Matthew Arnold, *Empedocles on Etna*, l. 369, in *The Poems of Matthew Arnold*, ed. Miriam Allott (London: Longman, 1979), 654. For a brief discussion see Krell, *Postponements: Woman, Sensuality, and Death in Nietzsche* (Bloomington: Indiana University Press, 1986), 33, 43, 46, and esp. 110–11n6. I remain grateful to Gabriel Pearson for the reference.

True, in this kind of reflection [namely, the anthropological] Dasein comes to occupy a center all its own, but there is something strange about this so-called anthropocentric standpoint. In the anthropocentric way of observing things, we come to the insight that this essence called *Mensch*, which ostensibly stands at the center, in love with itself, is in its innermost core ex-centric [*ex-zentrisch*]. This means that precisely in accord with the essence of its existence, objectively speaking, it can never stand at the center of the being in question. (27:11)

Perhaps the secret of this off-center, eccentric, ecstatic being is its death—even if precisely most is achieved by birth. Hölderlin calls death a being snatched away, as though to stress the rape that shares the root of *rapture*; death is *Entrückung* "out of the midpoint" of one's "inner life" into "another world" (ibid.). To be sure, that "midpoint" of life was never there. Caught between the endowments of birth and the blows of destiny, human life is always elliptical, always shortfall. In any case, it would be intriguing to compare Hölderlin's use of *entrückt*, this being "snatched away," with that of his contemporaries or immediate predecessors. I can at least imagine that his *Entrückung*—like the abduction of Persephone to the realm of the dead—has a particularly harsh ring to it. Indeed, I believe that one should pursue in detail a reading of Hölderlin's notes on Sophocles, a reading that would at every moment touch on the ecstases of finite time. I am thinking of the reversal of Zeus's path, the inversion of the "eternal tendency" of divinity itself, Zeus's "more essential return" to the Earth, Zeus himself being essentially "the father of time and the father of the Earth." During his high school years, Hölderlin, like every adolescent, wondered why Zeus took such an interest in mortal boys and girls, and he did not take this to be a laughable trait of god's. Think of the great god appearing essentially as time, and human being as the moment; recall also what Hölderlin calls divine infidelity and mortal blasphemy. Think, too, of a beginning and an end that no longer rhyme, and of a "categorial inversion," after which nothing remains but pure time and space, both of which are measured in suffering, that is, in the pain of "divinely wrestling organs." Think back once again—now in a thinking that is apparently quite remote from Heidegger's—to those boys and girls who suffer Zeus's love; think back to Danaë's suffering, invoked by Antigone, which is also the suffering of the father. For, do not forget, if Zeus invades her cell as golden rain and seems to have his way with her, it is she who teaches him, the father of time, who he is and what is in store for him, to wit, the finitude of time. Hölderlin deliberately "mistranslates" Sophocles's line so that its sense will be more evident to us Hesperians:

> Sie zählete dem Vater der Zeit
> Die Stundenschläge, die goldnen.

> She counted off for the father of time
> The tolling of the hours, the golden strokes.

Do not ask for whom the bell tolls; it surely tolls for Zeus.

I will not claim that Heidegger takes any of his vocabulary or any of his existential analysis from Hölderlin, especially not from the Hölderlin who is devoted to ancient Greek tragedy. I believe that Philippe Lacoue-Labarthe's acerbic critique of Heidegger is essentially correct: in spite of Heidegger's reading of *Antigone* in his "Ister" course and in his *Introduction to Metaphysics*, Heidegger, unlike Augustine, is immune to the issues of "theatrality" that are so central to Hölderlin's life, poetics, and thought.[2] Heidegger's Hölderlin, based on a problematic reading—Kommerell calls it a potentially catastrophic reading—of a number of hymns from the period of the so-called "fatherlandly turn," is utterly foreign to the Hölderlin who is devoted to the dramatist Sophocles and to the *polis*. If I am not mistaken, Lacoue-Labarthe even dreams that if things could have been otherwise, if there could have been a Hölderlin of the theater for Heidegger, then the latter's politics would have been fundamentally different. It would have reflected the community of a *Miteinandersein* for which Heidegger was always in search, a community that is found most pristinely in the theater, among the players themselves and between theater company and audience. I reserve this particularly contentious theme for another time, another ecstasis—in part 2 of the present volume. For the moment, we have more reading to do.

What gives me the right to jump from section 65 to section 68, as I did in the first lecture and as I will continue to do here? Do the intervening sections count for nothing? In fact, they define the shape of the remaining one hundred pages of *Sein und Zeit*, so that I had best pay

---

2. Philippe Lacoue-Labarthe, *Métaphrasis* (Paris: Presses Universitaires de France, 1998), 3–5.

them some heed. Heidegger announces at the outset of section 66 that the temporality of Dasein itself imposes on us a series of tasks having to do with the repetition of the existential analysis as such; however, to the careful reader's astonishment, the tasks in question will have to do with an analysis of Dasein as existing *inappropriately*, Dasein as "inauthentic," *uneigentlich*—Dasein as lost in its everyday world. The decision seems odd. The second division has as its task "an original existential interpretation" of Dasein, and that task is fulfilled in the detailed reflections on the death of Dasein, on the open resolve that constitutes the fundament of existence itself, on the call of conscience and "guilt" or "indebtedness," in the sense of insight into the possibility of the nullity of that fundament. For each of these tasks, the everyday, vulgar, public way of understanding Dasein proves to be an obstacle that must be overcome. Each time an inappropriate aspect of existence thrusts itself to the fore, it has to be shown its proper place. Yet from section 66 on, the inappropriate reclaims its rights—not merely in the present chapter, but in all three of the three final chapters of the book, with the possible exception of chapter 5, on historicity, which we will consider in the fourth lecture of this series. That is why Heidegger is forced to *end* the third chapter of the second division with a detailed account of what is to come. Heretofore he has outlined future tasks in the *opening* section of each chapter. Oddly, both section 66, the last of this third chapter, and section 67, the first of chapter four, struggle to achieve a kind of overview of these tasks. Like the other key "methodological" sections of *Sein und Zeit*, a careful reading of these two is surely called for; yet at the risk of misconstruing the closing chapters of Heidegger's masterwork, I will focus on one paragraph alone, the final paragraph of section 66, at the end of the third chapter.

The fourth chapter will have as its theme the temporality of everydayness; the fifth, the historicity (*Geschichtlichkeit*) of Dasein; the sixth, the within-time-ness (*Innerzeitigkeit*) of Dasein, that is to say, the origin of the "vulgar" understanding of time. Everydayness, history, and vulgarity: what could be easier? Yet Heidegger begins the final paragraph in this way: "Elaborating the temporality of Dasein as everydayness, historicity, and within-time-ness will for the first time provide us with an unforgiving insight into the *entanglements* of an original ontology of Dasein" (SZ 333). The story begins simply enough: "As being in the world, Dasein exists factically with and alongside the intramundane beings it encounters" (ibid.). But it soon enough gets very complicated, so complicated that it seems we need to have read the unwritten *third* division of *Sein und Zeit* in order to understand the *second*, which is now under Heidegger's writing hand.[3]

Now comes a surprising sentence: "The being of Dasein therefore attains its comprehensive ontological transparency only on the horizon of the clarified being of beings that are not of the measure of Dasein [*im Horizont des geklärten Seins des nichtdaseinsmäßigen Seienden*], which is to say, also on the horizon of those beings that are neither handy nor present at hand, but that merely 'subsist'" (ibid.). Only much later in the book do we come to understand that what "subsists," *besteht*, is nature, or the things of nature, above all, the sun, which Heidegger will call "the light and heat bestowing star" (section 80, especially 413). There will prove to be a "world time," *Weltzeit*, that is only apparently subject to our calculation, hence, not at all vulgar—a cosmic time that belongs to the *appropriateness* of Dasein. To understand this we would have to read much farther into *Being and Time*, indeed up to the very end, focusing on the remarkable section 80. And, as I suggested a moment ago, we would have to read the division of the book that never appeared. For, as Heidegger continues,

> the interpretation of the transformations of the being of everything of which we say "it *is*" requires that an idea of being in general [*Idee von Sein überhaupt*] be adequately illuminated beforehand [*zuvor hinreichend erhellten*]. As long as this is not achieved, the temporal analysis of Dasein, which is engaged in a *reprise*, remains incomplete and trapped in a lack of clarity, to say very little of the difficulties involved in the matter. The existential-temporal analysis of Dasein demands for its part a renewed reprise within the framework of a fundamental discussion of the concept of being. (SZ 333)

---

3. I have only now written the word *unwritten* with regard to Division Three. Yet in the *Black Notebooks*, at 94:272, Heidegger makes a striking remark about the projected Third Division of Part One of *Sein und Zeit*. He writes: "Of course, the first draft of the inadequate 3d division of the 1st Part, on 'Time and Being,' had to be destroyed. A reflection of it, framed as a critical history, is in the lecture course of the Summer Semester of 1927." The lecture course to which Heidegger is referring here appears as volume 24 of the *Gesamtausgabe*, *Basic Problems of Phenomenology*, which does not surprise us. What is surprising, however, is the reference to "the first draft" of "Time and Being," and to its being destroyed. We know nothing about the contents of such a draft; nor do we know how "finished" the draft may have been before Heidegger—regrettably—destroyed it.

One begins to get a sense that fundamental ontology is an infinite task, requiring an endless analysis, so that the third division of *Sein und Zeit* would in any case never have been enough. It is as though the three divisions of Part One of *Being and Time* are themselves *ecstatically* interwoven, each one displacing us into the remaining divisions, which would be the present, past, and future of each.

With grim foreboding we may turn to section 68, "The Temporality of Disclosure in General," with its subsections a through d. Disclosure, *Erschlossenheit*, has to do with (a) understanding, *Verstehen*, related to the future ecstasy; (b) how one finds oneself to be, *Befindlichkeit*, related to having-been; (c) falling prey or ensnarement, *Verfallen*, which occurs in and through the present; and (d) discourse, which, if only because of the tenses of its verbs, touches on all the ecstases. Because the axis of appropriateness and inappropriateness divides the entire analysis, and because each temporal ecstasis includes the other two ecstases in itself, we can understand why section 68 is so long: three inappropriate ecstases, each containing all three dimensions of temporality would require nine separate analyses; the three appropriate ecstases another nine; finally, to these eighteen analyses one would have to add what Heidegger calls the "indifferent" modes of temporality based on the general structures of our being ahead of ourselves (*sich-vorweg*), already in a world (*schon-in*), alongside other beings (*sein-bei*). These "indifferent" modes of temporality prove to be of immense importance, perhaps because it is so difficult to maintain a clear division between appropriate and inappropriate. To the twenty-one separate analyses that one has a right to expect here, we have to add perhaps another nine or so, inasmuch as these last "general" structures seem to include all the others. At any rate, in order to reduce our anxiety, Heidegger assures us many times (SZ 335, 351, 365, and elsewhere) that there is but *one* temporality, that a structural unity characterizes all these phenomena, and that the unity "of the horizonal schemata of future, having-been, and present is grounded in the ecstatic unity of temporality" (SZ 365). We may still be nervous about how an "outside-itself" in and for itself could constitute a horizon and enable a unity, but let us let that go for a moment. Of these dozens of analyses, then, we will be modest and choose only two, those having to do with understanding (the ecstasis of the future) and with how we find ourselves to be (the ecstasis of having-been). I can promise you that these two will offer unforgiving entanglements enough, so that if we had to work through the entire table of ecstases, we would wish to set aside *Sein und Zeit* and return to the happy simplicity of a critique of pure reason.

Heidegger announces that he is "compelled" to alter the articulation of these structures (SZ 332), but he does not explain what compels him. The most important change is this: whereas in the first division *Befindlichkeit*, or "how one finds oneself to be," is treated first, precisely because it is the most broadly disclosive of all the structures of existence, more fundamental than all knowledge of the world and every theoretical attitude insofar as cognition and theory are *founded* modes of *being-in* the world (section 13), in the temporal analysis of Division Two understanding is treated first. Perhaps this is because understanding appears to be bound up with the future ecstasis, and the future ecstasis is said to be primary for the existentiality of Dasein and its finitude.

Understanding, for Heidegger, is not the faculty that synthesizes categories and intuitions, enabling us to *know* the world. To repeat, knowing the world is a *founded, derivative* mode of being in the world. Modern philosophy has become fixated on this particular possibility, but it is only one, and not the ownmost one. The ownmost possibility of Dasein, toward which it runs ahead, is its being toward the end, its being unto death. Yet this possibility does not disclose itself to Dasein at first and for the most part. The proper future of Dasein "must first be won . . . from the inappropriate future" (SZ 337). True, there is a general structure, or an "indifferent" mode of our futural being, the *Sich-vorweg*. Yet what dominates our everyday world is a future that is shaped by our immediate concerns and dealings; it is a future characterized by *Gewärtigen*, our being prepared for or anticipating and expecting this or that. Clearly, this very limited sense of the future is permeated by the hectic present and by what has habitually been the case: even the inappropriate future displays an intimate relation with the other two ecstases. Heidegger now (SZ 338) offers a "comparison" of how the ecstasis of the *appropriate* future presents itself: *zur Vergleichung beiziehen* is his phrase. Yet this is not quite what we want—although Heidegger might command us to be patient. Since the analysis began with the remark that the proper future has to be "won" from its inappropriate mode, however, we surely have the right to be interested in *the temporalization of the appropriate*. No mere "comparison" will give us this.

The appropriate future, however it may arrive, involves that running ahead in open resolve that discloses our situation for what it is, namely, a mortal situation. It has a way of fetching us back from the present ecstasis in which we are dispersed and distracted (*aus der Zerstreuung*). It is worth noting that such dispersion and distraction is a theme of Heidegger's from the early Marburg lectures up to the end of his life. Accordingly, it is a word that draws Derrida's attention in virtually every text he writes on Heidegger, especially his *Geschlecht* series. There is something about dispersion and distraction that dominates the entire question of the meaning of being, the history of being, and every single one of Heidegger's principal themes; it is the dispersion and distraction of human beings that Heidegger most wants to combat. They are his worst nightmare. Against dispersion and distraction Heidegger appeals to a "holding," *Halten*, that in some way is to preserve an open resoluteness, rescuing "the moment" of an appropriate present. Concerning this crucial *Augenblick* Heidegger writes: "This term must be understood in its active sense as an ecstasis. It means the openly resolved, but in resoluteness the *held* enrapturement of Dasein in those things that encounter it in the situation of its concernful possibilities." Yet the sentence ends in an odd way. The only possibility that holds us in the moment, in our appropriate present, is our ownmost, nonrelational, unsurpassable possibility, and *this* possibility has nothing to do with "possibilities to be taken care of," *besorgbaren Möglichkeiten.* The "moment" dare never be confused with the "now" of vulgar time; and yet what the "moment" gives us here is "whatever can be 'in a time' as handy or present at hand." What seems to be happening, although it is too soon to tell, is that the appropriate and inappropriate modes are eliding, the one slipping into the other, and that would be permissible if the dividing-line between these modes did not form the very axis of *Sein und Zeit,* or better, its foundation and support wall. We do not want to be so naïve as to think that either the everyday world or our inappropriate existence can be left behind once we have achieved insight into our fundamental possibility; yet what does the temporalization of that *Augenblick* bring if its revelation is not mortality but the items of our everyday *Besorgen, Zuhandenheit,* and *Vorhandenheit?* If the "unity" of the temporal horizon means that appropriateness and inappropriateness meld in this way, then not only will this temporal "repetition" of *Sein und Zeit* have to be repeated, but the reprise will have to reconstitute entirely the analyses of Divisions One and Two.

Yet matters are even worse than they seem. The ecstasy of the future also has a having-been that moves within it. Heidegger reminds us that appropriate coming-toward is also a coming *back* to one's ownmost individualized and "thrown" self. This appropriate having-been, at work in the future ecstasis, is what enables reprise or "fetching-back," *Wiederholung.* The inappropriate mode of having-been, Heidegger reminds us, is oblivion, *Vergessen.* Such oblivion is not merely a forgetting of this or that incidental item. Rather, it is a "positive" mode of having-been, a mode all its own. We have already touched on this problem in our consideration of the *second* use of the word *Entrückung,* and we have already heard Heidegger's statement, "The ecstasis (enrapturement) of oblivion has the character of an evasion that is closed to itself, an evasion *in the face of* one's ownmost having-been, indeed in such a way that this evasion ecstatically closes off what faces it and at the same time closes off itself" (SZ 339). We called such closure "strange," but it is worse than strange. In fact, it seems catastrophic. Why? Because such *verschliessen* appears to be total. Here *Entrückung* is an *Ausrücken vor . . .* , an evasion in the face of a possibility that is barred or locked away. Furthermore, oblivion is oblivious precisely of itself. What is devastating about our forgetting is that when we forget we forget that we have forgotten, otherwise we would remember to remember. Oblivion may be an automatism; remembering may suffer from an auto-immune disease. How then might a memorious retrieval or fetching-back temporalize out of oblivion? To be sure, we have to believe that it does. Merleau-Ponty writes convincingly of a memory *gardée par l'oubli*, and, of course, where else could such a forgotten memory find sanctuary but in oblivion? Heidegger seems to affirm this when he writes that oblivion (*Vergessenheit*), although it pertains to the inappropriate side of having-been, "thereby relates itself to its own thrown *being* [Sein]" (SZ 339). He continues: "It is the temporal meaning of that mode of being in accord with which I at first and for the most part have—*been*." Oblivion has ontological status. "And only on the basis of this oblivion" can the everyday world of our cares and concerns be "*maintained* [behalten]." "*Remembering* is grounded in forgetting, *and not the other way around*," says Heidegger emphatically. The *unity* of the ecstases here elaborated does not yield a horizon or backdrop for some disclosure; rather, the unity is here a bolting shut, a closing off. "The unity of these ecstases bars [*verschließt*] our appropriate ability to be and is accordingly the existential condition of our irresoluteness" (ibid.).

Now, section 68 is devoted to the temporality of *disclosure* in general. It therefore seems odd that so much has to be said there about *closure*. Yet this is not the first time that there is an emphasis on closure. In his discussion of the finitude of original time, back in section 65, Heidegger speaks of the temporal ecstasis of the future precisely in terms of closure. We have heard these words before: "The ecstatic character of the original future lies precisely in the fact that it closes our ability to be [*daß sie das Seinkönnen schließt*], which means that the future itself is closed [*das heißt selbst geschlossen ist*] and that the future as such makes possible the resolutely unclosed [*entschlossene*] existentiell understanding of nullity" (SZ 330). The ringdance of the words *schliessen, erschliessen, verschliessen, geschlossen, entschlossen* whirls in the orchestra of the ecstatic interpretation, and it is a dizzying ringdance. The ecstasy of the original, appropriate future closes off a future that is itself closed; as closed, that future opens us to the possible nullity of our existence, that is, of our being able *not* to be. This same dizzying paradox appears at the end of section 68a, on the ecstasis of the future. When one looks down the printed page (page 339) of *Sein und Zeit*, one's eyes are drawn to three words: *closes off*, "*discloses*," and then, once again, *closes off—verschließt*, "*erschließt*," *verschließt*. The middle word, *discloses*, appears within quotation marks or scare quotes. Is that because the *Erschlossenheit* in question is precisely that of "forgetting" or "oblivion," *Vergessen*? Presumably, oblivion requires that closure have the last word. After all, what ecstasy, what temporal unfolding, could unlock the "closed" theater of future possibilities, especially if self-occluding oblivion is an ecstasy all its own?

And yet. Surely we are anxious for no reason. Merleau-Ponty is surely right: of course human beings remember! All the time, over and over again. As W. C. Fields once said, reproaching the alcoholic who claimed he could not stop drinking, "Don't tell me you can't give up drinking. It's easy. . . . I've done it a thousand times." Of course there is disclosure. Benjy remembers that Caddy smells like trees, trees in the rain, although it is hard for him—and for us—to remember what event has caused him to have two names, since he is called both Benjy and Maury. Bloom remembers the lemon soap for Molly; it is in his trousers pocket. By contrast, he forgets his house key, which is in the pocket of the trousers he wore but one day preceding. The question of being, says Heidegger, "has today gone into oblivion" *ist heute in Vergessenheit gekommen*. "Today" refers to an epoch that endures for more than two millennia. If ecstasy works suddenly, its effects can certainly last.

Even if we are cautioned by the objection that the ecstases are not the "now points" of a sequential system, not a tramway to appropriateness, it is still difficult to avoid the question as to whether some sort of ecstasy will snatch us from the dispersion, distraction, and pervasive oblivion of our everyday sort of present. Last time and again today we tried the most promising of ecstases, that of the future, which is said to characterize the very existentiality of our existence. Yet the closed future does not serve the ecstatic analysis so well. Let us therefore try *Gewesenheit*, the ecstasy of our having-been, discussed in great detail in section 68b, on "the temporality of how we find ourselves to be." Indeed, if we dare translate *Befindlichkeit* as "how we find ourselves to be," this would be the very ecstasy we are looking for, the one that enables us to "find ourselves to *be*." For have we not forgotten the important role that anxiety, *die Angst*, plays in the revelation of our being? It is not intellectuality that disrupts our dogmatic slumber but a remarkable attunement or mood that can, quite suddenly, overtake us. Yet the beginning of section 68b is equally inauspicious: understanding is "equally originally" accompanied by a mood; the "there" of there-being, says Heidegger is "equally originally disclosed, or closed off, by mood," *durch Stimmung erschlossen, bzw. verschlossen* (SZ 339–40). I confess that among the German words I hate, and there are very few of them, this little *bzw.* is at the top of my list. It seems to introduce an apposition, but just as often—here, for example—an opposition. "Disclosed, or in other words, respectively, somehow or other, perhaps even by way of contradiction and negation, closed off." As if disclosure and closure came to the same! True, in his later years Heidegger will think almost exclusively about "clearing" and "concealing" as though these were, if not identical, then inextricably interlaced; even when disclosure occurs it must be safeguarded by a kind of protective concealment, *Bergen* being the root of all *Unverborgenheit.* Here, in section 68b, he reminds us of the oblivious evasion (*das vergessende Ausrücken*) that can occlude our existentiality. What seems to offer a ray of hope is the fact that forgetting is associated with fear—fear as opposed to anxiety proper. We recall the analyses of sections 30 and 40, which assert that anxiety is "an exceptional disclosedness of Dasein," *eine ausgezeichnete Erschlossenheit des Daseins.* While fear of some menacing being confuses us and darkens our world, anxiety introduces an uncanny clarity into our lives. Such clarity is expressed in the perfect coalescence of that *in the face of which* we are anxious and that *for the sake of which* we are anxious: anxiety brings us face to face with our vulnerable being in the world, and it is for the sake of that merely *possible* being-in that we are anxious—the *Wovor* and the *Worum* of anxiety dovetail.

It is now the *temporality* of this coalescence that must be shown. Is there a sequence of ecstases that will conduct us from the confusions of fear to the clarity of anxious insight into our mortality? Note that it is not simply a matter of the independent ecstases of fear and anxiety; rather, it is a matter of how, in some sense, the temporality of anxiety *as opposed to that of fear* can be described. Not that fear has to give way to anxiety, but that anxiety *somehow, sometime* temporalize, if not out of fear, then perhaps out of mourning, or joy, or even sheer boredom.

Many years ago I tried to show that the temporal unfolding of anxiety resists depiction, or at least that Heidegger is unable to show us convincingly how anxiety advenes in ecstatic time. There is one serious alteration I want to make with respect to my own earlier analysis, which back in the 1980s went as follows.[4]

---

4. See Krell, *Of Memory*, 252–53, for the following analysis.

Time is to be the horizon on which the meaning of *being* will loom. What claims Heidegger's attention in the second division of *Being and Time* is the temporal unfolding of a resolute openedness that runs ahead, not "anticipating" death, but letting that possibility come to the fore in our existence in its overwhelming power. Thus the temporal unfolding of *anxiety* becomes extremely important—anxiety as the portal to resolute openedness in the face of our mortality. If running ahead suggests the futural character of Dasein, it is nonetheless the case that the *Zu-* of *Zukunft* is also the *zu-* of *zu-rück:* as Dasein runs ahead it is cast back on its always already having been this running ahead. The *Rück* of *Entrückung* or rapture is related to the English word *rock*. The verbs *rucken* and *rücken*, for their part, suggest "sudden movement." Every forward leap into the future, toward which Dasein is "thrown," *geworfen*, is simultaneously a sudden recoil, the effect of whiplash. It is as though the waves of the future bend back over themselves even as they toss their crests ahead. Or better, it is as though we who walk into the surf of the vast seas of time are invariably cast back, sometimes head over foot, and as we go under we hear the waves laugh and announce, with Freddie Mercury, *we will we will* rück *you.*

In section 65 of *Sein und Zeit* the forward thrust of Dasein, the resolute openedness that runs ahead, bears the brunt of the wave and is tossed back onto its having-been. Rapture is a being rocked, a being thrown forward *and* back. Back onto what? Heidegger replies: "The openedness that runs ahead understands Dasein in its essential indebtedness [*Schuldigsein*]." Such understanding implies that our being indebted "assumes its indebtedness by existing and by *being* the thrown ground of a nullity [*als geworfener Grund der Nichtigkeit* sein]" (SZ 325). What this "assuming" or "taking over" can be is of course mysterious; it sounds so confident, and yet it is uttered by a nullity. Above all, the ecstatic temporality of such "taking over" has to be *shown*. In section 68, Heidegger continues to emphasize this imputed ability of Dasein to "take over" both its proper coming to itself in the future and its always already having been the thrown ground of a nullity (SZ 339). When the "ground" is "thrown," however, the effect is a radical displacement and departure, a rapture that is more a rupture.

In section 68b we confront a crucial moment of Heidegger's analysis. Here, in the analysis of the temporal unfolding of *Befindlichkeit*, "how one finds oneself to be," which is the existential structure of facticity and of having-been, Heidegger tries to show how fear and anxiety differ precisely in terms of their temporality. Fear is dazed and confused in a turbulent *present*: when the house is ablaze I grab whatever *presents itself* to me and carry it to safety. By contrast, anxiety brings Dasein back to its most proper ability to be, namely, to be the ground of a nullity. That in the face of which and that for the sake of which Dasein is anxious are one and the same. But to repeat: How does this anxious coalescence temporalize?

The answer comes on page 344 of *Sein und Zeit*. Anxiety temporalizes as a kind of *hold*—better, a being held, *gehalten*. A being held, not by things, and not by inappropriate possibilities, but by the unsurpassability of one's own death—a being held by the thrownness of one's own possibility-being. Anxiety temporalizes as a hold on the ecstasis of having-been. Such a hold makes anxiety *present*. However, even though the appropriate present of anxiety is "held," anxiety "still does not of itself have the character of the moment [*Augenblick*] that temporalizes in resolve [*Entschluss*]." The result—or lack of result—is decisive: "Anxiety only brings us into the mood of a *possible* resolve. Its present [*Gegenwart*] holds the moment when anxiety itself alone is possible, holding the moment *poised for the leap* [*hält den Augenblick . . . auf dem Sprung*]."

Anxiety attunes Dasein in such a way that resolute openedness and the moment of insight become *possible*. In anxiety itself, the *Augenblick* in which Dasein may confront its mortality becomes *possible*, but that ecstatic moment itself has not yet arrived. How does the moment temporalize? Heidegger has already identified the proper, *eigentliche* ecstasis of having-been as the possibility of reprise or repeatability, *Wiederholbarkeit*. "The future and present of anxiety temporalize from an original having-been in the sense of a bringing back to repeatability." We note the *holen* of *Wiederholbarkeit*, which must be related to the *halten* Heidegger has in mind. Yet it must also be related to the recalcitrant *Unüberholbarkeit* of our death. The problem is that having-been temporalizes as *both* reprise *and* forgetting, *both* repeatability *and* oblivion. In any case, there may be an additional problem: how are we to fetch back (*wiederholen*) a possibility that cannot be passed by or gotten around (*unüberholbar*)? How can one fetch back a possibility that we never get a good look at? If Dasein exists at first and for the most part in the thick of oblivion, but also if its ownmost possibility perpetually outruns it no matter how resolutely open resolve runs ahead, how does recovery, reprise, repeatability, or remembrance awaken? Temporal unfolding has nothing to do with "choice" or "will," unless the ecstatic analysis rests on a suppressed yet massive voluntarism and decisionism. At the top of page 344 we learn, to repeat, that anxiety "only brings us into the mood or attunement of a *possible* resolve." Toward the bottom of the page we read the second decisive statement: "But anxiety can properly arise only in a resolutely open Dasein"; "*Eigentlich aber kann die Angst nur aufsteigen in einem entschlossenen Dasein.*"

It is all about poise and leap, about how one gets poised *for* the leap. Poise is what anxiety provides, so that there may be leaping into the moment and its resolve. Yet poise can arise, properly speaking, only in a resolve that has already been attained, which is to say, poise can arise only as the result of what poise makes possible. Poise therefore occurs in midair. "To see if we will poise our life at last," says Matthew Arnold's Empedocles on the very rim of the crater into which he would leap, but Hölderlin's Manes replies to *his* Empedocles, forestalling that leap, "Are you so sure of what you see?"

The circularity of anxiety and resoluteness is a vicious—or at least a viscous—circularity. It is not a hermeneutical circle. Nor is it a mere ambiguity in the exposition. It indicates, if I am right, the moment of the gravest failure in the temporal analysis. Yet I would designate the failure differently now than I did those many years ago in *Of Memory.* Back then I argued that the failure arises from the fact that anxiety does not temporalize. But of course it does. What fails to temporalize is not anxiety but the *readiness* for anxiety. *If we were ready for anxiety, it would not be anxiety that arrives.* One cannot be ready for what comes so suddenly. In other words, and put more formally, the ecstatic interplay between an open resoluteness that runs ahead (*vorlaufende Entschlossenheit*) and the attunement of anxiety rests in utter obscurity. The revelatory power of anxiety seems to depend entirely on its appearance out of nowhere and as a nullity, such that one is never ready for it: *Bereitsein* would in fact defuse anxiety or, to keep to the language Heidegger himself will later use, "readiness" would dull, bend, or snap the point of anxiety.

The expression "readiness for anxiety" does not appear in section 68b. That is perhaps why no temporal repetition or reprise of *readiness* appears there. In section 58 of *Sein und Zeit,* Heidegger writes about our "readiness for being called upon" by guilt or indebtedness, *Bereitschaft für das Angerufen werden* (SZ 288). In section 60, where "opened resoluteness" (*Entschlossenheit*) is introduced, he argues that "wanting [or willing: *wollen*] to have a conscience" becomes "readiness for anxiety," *das Gewissenhabenwollen wird Bereitschaft zur Angst* (SZ 296). It is the temporalization of such *readiness,* I now believe, that remains not only undemonstrated but also indemonstrable.

When he first introduces the theme of *Befindlichkeit* (in section 29 of *Being and Time*), Heidegger stresses that no amount of knowing or willing can alter a mood; only another mood can shift or displace an earlier mood. We do not know why or how this happens. "And Dasein cannot know such a thing because the disclosive possibilities of knowing [*die Erschließungsmöglichkeiten des Erkennens*] do not suffice for the original disclosure of moods, in which Dasein is brought before its being as 'there' "

(SZ 134). The words "do not suffice" here try to translate the expression *viel zu kurz tragen*, which might be better rendered as "are far too short," "far too limited," "far too elliptical." For, as we recall, *elliptical* for Aristotle means falling short. Knowing falls short of the disclosive power of moods. If knowing falls short and cannot sustain the disclosive power of moods, what are we to say of "readiness" for the exceptional mood of anxiety? Is there not something here of that "factical ideal" which Heidegger fears may—and in fact, as he concedes, *does*—distort his analysis? (SZ 310). Is not "readiness for anxiety" a kind of rolling up the sleeves, a gesture that declares that I am ready for anything, that I have pulled myself together and have stiffened my upper lip, as every Puritan must? Yet what is the temporal ecstasis of this stiffened lip? Is it not the oblivious inheritance, not of acquired characteristics, but of *required* characteristics? Is not "readiness" the factical ideal inherited and internalized by every good boy and girl, every well-raised and highly capable boy and girl?

Heidegger will later in his book (in the notorious section 74) invoke the inheritance, *das Erbe*, to which every Dasein that is born is subject, an inheritance that binds "there-being" to its generation, community, and nation. What has always haunted me is that such inheritance, as far as I can see, is not subjected to a *Destruktion*, that is, to the sort of critical dismantling to which traditional *ontology* is subjected. It is as though the importance of Nietzsche's *genealogical* critique of metaphysics *and morals* has been forgotten in Heidegger's grand oeuvre. Be that as it may, there is surely something disconcerting about the nonhermeneutical circle of anxiety, open resolve, and readiness. Something in the temporal analysis breaks down. What breaks down, among other things, is the axis of appropriateness and inappropriateness, *Eigentlichkeit* and *Uneigentlichkeit*, which structures the entire analysis of ecstatic temporality. If ecstatic temporality is the surf into which we walk, then we have to concede that is difficult to preserve one's poise in the surging tide of the temporal ecstases. Perhaps this is the insight that drives Maurice Blanchot's insistence that death is not the possible impossibility of Dasein but the impossible as such. In any case, there is for Blanchot only the waiting, *l'attente*, never the readiness.

One further remark. On this same page (SZ 344) appears the *sixth* of those appearances of the word *Benommenheit*—bedazzlement or *benumbment*—on which I apparently cannot stop musing. The first five usages amount to the same: Dasein is at first and for the most part dazed and benumbed by its world, lost in a present that distracts and disperses it. Yet the sixth appearance says this about anxiety:

The possibility of the mightiness that makes the mood of anxiety so exceptional is grounded in the peculiar temporality of anxiety, to wit, that anxiety is grounded originally in having-been, in such a way that only out of having-been do future and present temporalize. In anxiety Dasein is taken fully aback, back onto its naked uncanniness, and is dazed by this uncanniness. Yet this benumbment does not merely *remove* Dasein from its "*mundane*" possibilities; rather, it also *grants* Dasein at the same time the possibility of an *appropriate* ability to be. (SZ 344)

In short, the same *effect*, namely, *Benommenheit*, is produced by the world that ensnares us *and* the anxiety that rescues us from our bedazzlement. Bedazzlement cures bedazzlement. That is odd enough. What is even odder is that two or three years after declaring that *Benommenheit* characterizes the moment of insight, the moment when we mortals stop being bewitched, bothered, and bewildered by baubles, bangles, and bright shiny beads, Heidegger uses that same word to define the essence of *animal* life. The animal, poor in world, trapped in a ring of strictly limited and limiting disinhibitions, is in Heidegger's view *essentially* benumbed. Yet why does anxious bedazzlement fail to turn the bedazzled animal into a bedazzled human animal? Heidegger later and elsewhere insists that an "abyss of essence" separates humans from animals (W 157; BW 230). Yet *Benommenheit* bridges that essence, not only once but twice. The last sentence of section 68b, a sentence that enthralled Derrida in the last of his Cerisy lectures, published as *The Animal That Therefore I Am*, ends with the following clause: ". . . how and where in general the being of animals is constituted by a 'time' remains a problem all its own" (SZ 346). Derrida devoted the final years of his teaching to the demonstration that it remains a problem for all us animals.

Allow me then to shift the discussion to that 1929–30 lecture course, "The Fundamental Concepts of Metaphysics: World—Finitude—Solitude," in which animal life is discussed in considerable detail. For the first half of the course suggests that a fundamental mood other than anxiety may be revelatory for Dasein. In that context, Heidegger says some remarkable things, some new things, about time. The new mood is in fact anticipated in section 68b of *Sein und Zeit*. There Heidegger asks about other disclosive attunements such as hope, joy, enthusiasm, and cheerfulness, moods we do not normally associate with Heidegger. He then adds another list that sounds more like him: weariness, sadness, despair, melancholy. Melancholy is especially important for the 1929–30 course, inasmuch as there Heidegger cites Aristotle's claim that philosophers are innately melancholic. Heidegger adds Novalis's observation that philosophers are homesick and crave to be at home everywhere. The mood that seems best able to disclose this melancholy, suggests Heidegger, perhaps to your and my surprise, is boredom—what in *Sein und Zeit* (345) he calls *die fahle Ungestimmtheit*, a vapid lack of mood, and in 1929–30 *die tiefe Langeweile*, profound boredom, the time that drags on a good long while.

In the lecture courses immediately following the publication of *Sein und Zeit* Heidegger tries to elaborate the unified ecstatic or "ecstematic" horizon of temporality, which he now calls *Praesenz*, but which he claims is not a temporal designation. By the end of the twenties those efforts have faltered. Perhaps a last attempt is made in the 1929–30 course. During the first half of the course Heidegger declares a new "fundamental mood" for philosophizing, setting *Angst* and *Unheimlichkeit* aside for *die tiefe Langeweile*. Profound boredom has the advantage of being the mood that seems to be shared by many at the end of the Weimar era: in all the lecture courses after *Sein und Zeit* Heidegger is searching for an account of our *Miteinandersein*, our "being with one another," an account that is free from all sentimentality and moralizing; the mood or attunement of profound boredom, close to weariness, seems to characterize the era. Heidegger can be sure that his students will know what he is talking about.

What happens when "one is bored," or when boredom drifts over one like a muffling fog? Earlier that "fog" rose as a metaphor for anxiety; now it muffles us with *ennui*, even if Durkheim is never mentioned. In profound boredom all things, whether future, past, or present, withdraw into insignificance. Heidegger's allusion to the three temporal ecstases suggests the occlusion of our *every* view on things, our dealings with them now in the present, our looking back on them in the past, and even our future intentions regarding them (*Hinsicht, Rücksicht, Absicht*). Such closing-off has something to do with time. Indeed, the occlusion or foreclosure of all beings has to do with the "uniform, universal horizon of time" *einheitliche All-Horizont der Zeit* (29/30:218). Heidegger stresses the difficulty of conceiving of such a horizon, especially with regard to time. Yet if any and every manifestation of beings occurs in and through time, then time itself may be viewed as the horizon—the backdrop or the "upon-which"—of all disclosure. In the very odd case of bottomless boredom what gets disclosed is the inanity of all disclosure. Earlier on, in *Sein und Zeit* and in his inaugural address at Freiburg, "What Is Metaphysics?" Heidegger describes the withdrawal of all beings and ourselves into indifference as productive of anxiety; now it seems that such withdrawal is so totalizing that we are left with Eliot's "Hollow Men" or Nietzsche's "Last Man," who boasts that he has invented happiness and then blinks. As formless as such a horizon seems to be, its power is overwhelming: our being-there is both *bounded by* and *banished from* the totality of beings, but also in some strange way held *spellbound* by them. Such *Gebanntsein*, one has to say, is elaborated in one of Heidegger's most telling sets of descriptions. The universal horizon of time holds us spellbound, immobile, and powerless in its grip, even if that horizon seems to be all about nothing—all about rupture rather than rapture.

Bann, in German, like *ban* and *bann* or *banns* in English, is one of those words that could occupy a researcher for weeks and weeks, as he or she pores over Hermann Paul, the Grimm Brothers, and the *OED*, undergoing repeated ecstasies of the sort only lovers of language know. What is compelling in Heidegger's descriptions is the paradoxical binding to and banishment from the disclosure of beings. Profound boredom bans beings and banishes us to a kind of wasteland; yet the *banns* of boredom can also open us, as Kierkegaard knew, by way of the point or peak of an instant (*die Spitze des Augenblicks*). If time bans us from beings, it also, in a moment or blink of an eye, ruptures the ban of time (29/30:226). Heidegger here refers his students to section 65 of *Sein und Zeit*, which does mention the moment or *Augenblick*, indeed, as the *Augen*blick, emphasizing the view on beings, the moment of *insight*, as Macquarrie and Robinson translate it. Insight into what? In 1929–30 Heidegger continues to call it the unlocking or opening view of resolve, *der Blick der Entschlossenheit*, referring not to the more general sense of *Erschlossenheit*, disclosure, but once again, as in *Sein und Zeit*, to the resolute opening of our being-there to its finitude, its being a nullity. Precisely as the fog of profound boredom closes in on us, it opens onto that final closure toward which we are heading. Profound boredom tells us about that closure in the way the witches tell Macbeth what awaits him, or the way the Delphic oracle, through the mouth of Creon, speaks to Oedipus the Tyrant. The oracle speaks in riddles, forebodingly, inasmuch as *Bann* has to do with a decree that is well-nigh occult in its power and phantasmatic in its character as both boon and bane. Heidegger summarizes all this in the following italicized passage:

> *Boredom is the bann of the time horizon, a banning that causes the moment that belongs to temporality to dwindle* [entschwinden läßt], *so that in such letting-dwindle the banned Dasein is compelled into the moment* [das gebannte Dasein in den Augenblick hineinzuzwingen] *as the proper possibility of its existence, an existence that is*

*possible in the midst of beings as a whole, beings that on the horizon
of banishment, precisely as a whole, are in default.* (29/30:230)

Heidegger's challenge as a lecturer in 1930 is to make certain that
those students in the back row are *sufficiently* bored. His problem as a German in the 1930s, which may now be our problem, as another people in
another time, is whether universal boredom and complacency will compel
us into the prickly moment or allow us to drift in the vacuous time of
massive and paralyzing oblivion. Heidegger notes the disaster that surrounds
him, and it sounds vaguely familiar to us: "Everywhere we are shattered by
crises, catastrophes, calamities: the social misery that plagues us today, the
political chaos, the impotence of science, the vacuity of art, the groundlessness of philosophy, the languishing of religion" (29/30:243). Yet nothing
seems to dislodge our needlessness and heedlessness, laments Heidegger.
And that seems to put him into a rage, a rage into which any one of us
might fall. Heidegger's rage will not diminish in the course of the 1930s,
but will wax to a point we are tempted to regard as pathological, as he
sees the tip of the sharpest moment being bent, broken, and dulled by bottomless complacency (29/30:248). His writings of the 1930s, especially his
Contributions to Philosophy of 1936–38 and his ominous *Black Notebooks*
of the same period, to be considered in Part Two of the present volume,
testify to the rage and the impotence.

Because we have heard that already in the 1930s Heidegger lets the
ecstatic analysis of temporality go, it may be well to look at one of the last
appearances of it in the years 1936–38, the years of the Schelling seminar
and the lecture courses on Hölderlin and Nietzsche. These are also the years
of what many have called Heidegger's second magnum opus, *Die Beiträge zur
Philosophie (Vom Ereignis), Contributions to Philosophy*, with the parenthetical
subtitle, *On the Event of Propriation.* There are very few references to the
ecstases of time in the *Beiträge*, but many references to *Entrückung*, indeed,
to the odd trinity, *Entrückung-Berückung-Verrückung*, which we might translate as "enrapturing-captivating-deranging." The first is related to time, as
it is in *Sein und Zeit*, but now the word refers more to the opening or the
clearing of beyng as such than to any strictly temporal interpretation; the
second is related more to space than to time (albeit always in the combination of time-space, or time-space-play), still in the sense of a sudden
entry into the region of the clearing; the third is related most often to the
wretched madness of Heidegger's own times, the age when the gods have
flown and beyng has abandoned human beings, the age when gigantism,
machination, and calculative thinking deflect every access to the openness

of beyng.[5] As for the ecstatic analysis of temporality, it is, if not dropped, then surely put into abeyance, as is every positive reference to "existential" philosophy and phenomenology. In one of the few exceptions to this general rule, Heidegger writes, referring to his use of the word *Existenz* on page 42 of *Being and Time* (*"The 'essence' of Dasein lies in its existence"*):

> At first it [the word *Existenz*] is used in reference to the old word *existentia*, meaning *not* the "what" but the "that" and the "how" of being. But this is παρουσία, presence, being at hand (the present) [*Anwesenheit, Vorhandenheit (Gegenwart)*].
>
> Here, by contrast, *Existenz* = full temporality, indeed as ecstatic. *Ex-sistere*—exposure to beings. For a long time now the word has not been used, because it can be misinterpreted— "philosophy of existence."
>
> *Being*-there as *ex-sistere*: enlisted into and standing out within [*Eingerücktsein in und Hinausstehen in*] the openness of beyng. Only on this basis is the "what" defined, i.e., the *"who"* and the selfhood of there-being.
>
> *Ex-sistenz* taken metaphysically: coming to presence and to appearance [*An-wesung, Er-scheinung*]. *Ex-sistenz* taken in terms of the history of being: an inhering enrapturement in the There [*inständliche Entrückung in das Da*]. (65:302–03)

It is not as though the intimate relation of being and time has entered into eclipse by the late 1930s; rather, the highly technical descriptions of the temporal ecstases are set aside for the sake of the most important matter. What is now vital to Heidegger is ecstasy as openness to being as such. Heidegger would affirm what Karl Reinhardt says of Hölderlin's Sophocles: "For him, time is the ecstatic; it is that in which being reveals itself."[6]

A second passage in the *Beiträge*, under the title "Beyng and Time," also refers to both ecstasy and rapture:

---

5. On *Verrückung*, see 94:276: "Not the proclamation of a doctrine to the human beings who are on hand, but the *deranging* of human beings today into the concealed need of their needlessness. Such deranging is the first presupposition if any sort of ground is to be established again."

6. Karl Reinhardt, "Hölderlin und Sophokles," in Reinhardt, *Tradition und Geist: Gesammelte Essays zur Dichtung,* ed. Carl Becker (Göttingen: Vandenhoek und Ruprecht, 1960), 387; cf. TA 330–31.

We must be able to experience "time" as the "ecstatic" play-space of the truth of beyng. En-rapturing into what is cleared means to ground the clearing itself as the open region in which beyng gathers itself into its essence. Such an essence cannot be pinpointed like some being at hand; we have to expect that its essential unfolding will be like a thrust [*wie ein Stoß*]. (65:242)

As we might anticipate, the thrust or even collision in question might make of "rapture" a rapid removal rather than some sort of arrival. In "the other beginning" toward which Heidegger is pointing, there must indeed be "extreme removal," *die äußerste Entrückung*, from beings of any kind to beyng as such (65:258). For the most part, however, Heidegger emphasizes that to which, or into which, Dasein is displaced, "with a view to its *enrapturement toward* something" (65:316). That "something," to repeat, is the clearing and concealing openness of beyng, in short, the *truth* of beyng.[7]

One might have hoped that rapture come as something other than a thrust or shove, *wie ein Stoß*. In the following chapter, the third Brauer Lecture, we will consider the dark side of Heidegger's new rhetoric, consider it only briefly, however, inasmuch as the second part of the present book will look at it in detail. The third lecture goes in search of a new beginning, a kind of renascence for the fundamental ontology of Dasein. We will "fabulate" on the push and shove of *birth* rather than death—birth as the ecstatic "other end" of Dasein.

---

7. A detailed passage on "the temporality of Da-sein as inherence [*Inständigkeit*] in the truth of being," is to be found in *Überlegungen XI*, no. 12 (95:367–69), of the *Schwarze Hefte*.

3

Ecstasy at the "Other End" of Dasein

As I suggested in the foregoing lecture, it is in the *Beiträge* as much as in the *Schwarze Hefte* that we observe the alienation and the growing truculence of Heidegger's rhetoric in the 1930s. While the rhetoric of the rectorate address of 1933 is alarming enough, it is all-too-comprehensible. I had originally reduced the following references to the *Beiträge* to a footnote, but I want to bring them into the body of my text now, in order to say something about the sudden alteration of Heidegger's style of writing and thinking in this parlous decade.

Among the many uses of ecstatic *Entrückung* or "rapture" in the *Beiträge*, we may note the following, although the list is surely incomplete: time is experienced there in a "veiled way" as "temporalization, as *enrapturing*, hence as opening"; time as "enrapturing-opening" is simultaneously "spacing," *einräumend*, "creating space" (65:191–92). Heidegger later in the *Beiträge* refers to the structures or articulations of *Entrückung-Berückung*, "enrapturing-captivating," in the "there" of time-space (65:371; cf. 383–86 on timing and spacing). He continues to refer to "time as temporality [*Temporalität*], that is, as the original unity of the rapture that clears and conceals [*der sich lichtend-verbergenden Entrückung*]," but now in the context of "the grounding of Da-sein" (65:234). Clearing and concealing, as "enrapturing-captivating, are *Ereignis* itself" (65:236). At times, *die berückende Entrückung* seems to be a motion in which the two terms have equal force (65:407); at other times, for example, when earth and world are being contrasted, Heidegger will speak of "the fairest captivation" and "the most frightful rapture," *die holdeste Berückung und furchbarste Entrückung* (65:410). The translation of *Entrückung* as *rapture* no longer seems viable; the "most frightful" *Entrückung* must be something closer to a seizure or an abduction, an arrest or an attack. Finally, a third term joins the pair *Entrückung-Berückung*: Heidegger begins to stress the need for the "*deranging* of human beings" ("Verrückung *des Menschen*") out of their complacency "into the calamity of their needlessness as utterly extreme" (65:235). Indeed, for the Heidegger of the *Beiträge*, being-there is just as much a being-gone, that is, a being lost in complacency, as it is a witness to the clearing. Hence, "if time, precisely as temporality, is rapture, then the 'end' in question here [namely, the 'end' that is the death of Dasein] means saying *no* and saying *something else* with regard to this rapture, to wit, a radical deranging [*eine völlige Verrückung*] of the there as such into the *'gone'* [*in das* 'Weg']" (65:324). Earlier on, and at the end, *der Weg* means a path of thinking; in the 1930s it means an aporia, and it is pronounced as an imperative, *Weg!* "Be gone!" Yet the rhetoric of *Entrückung*, even in the 1930s, is not always so alarming.

For *Entrückung* and *Berückung* appear also in the 1936–37 *Nietzsche* lectures in the context of an interpretation of Plato's *Phaedrus* (NI 227–28; Ni 1:195–97). There the rhetoric and the thinking are quite intriguing and really quite constructive; they offer a novel and genuinely helpful reading of Plato's text, precisely at the point where Socrates defines the beautiful. It is the beautiful that diverts our attention *from* the being that possesses beauty *to* the radiant appearing itself. It has been given to beauty alone, says Plato's Socrates, to reveal the being of beings. For the beautiful is superlative in its shining-forth and in its power to move us. His words are τὸ ἐκφανέστατον καὶ τὸ ἐρασμιώτατον, "the most radiant" and "the most erotic." Back when we were talking about the sudden, we speculated, to the classicist's possible horror, that αἴφνης, "the sudden," may be related to ἀφανής, "the unapparent" or "nonappearing," the "nonphenomenal." Here, by contrast, superlative radiance, τὸ ἐκφανέστατον, would be the appearing itself, so brilliant that it captivates our gaze and causes it to soar beyond the particular being that possesses beauty (on τὸ ἐκφανέστατον see also 95:46–47). This being swept away or enraptured, as it were, would be a facet of the *Bewegtheit* or "movedness" and "animatedness" that always fascinated Heidegger: the most radiant is also the "best beloved" or "most worthy of devotion," ἐρασμιώτατον. The combination of *Entrückung-Berückung* here is, to repeat, a worthy and even quite trenchant reading of Plato, one that speaks to the raptures of being without rocketing being off to some stratosphere of metaphysics.

I cite the Nietzsche lectures in order to contrast "enrapturing-captivating" as it is used there with the disconcerting *Entrückung-Berückung-Verrückung* that one finds in the *Beiträge* and in the *Schwarze Hefte*. Beauty's sweeping us off to raptures of radiance and Eros does not seem anything like the *deranging* of human beings to the outermost point of their complacency. Perhaps the varieties of *Entrückung-Berückung* could be measured by the contrast between the Oceanides and the Maenads? However, in either case, would Eros in Heidegger's own time really speak the language of chivalry that we hear in the *Beiträge* ("the *fairest* captivation," *die holdeste Berückung*)? And why must Heidegger insist on "the most *frightful* rapture" (*die furchbarste Entrückung*)? Such usages correspond to what Winfried Franzen analyzed years ago as Heidegger's "hard and heavy" rhetoric in the 1930s (DL 171). More troubling to me than the stern scoldings, however, are the archaisms, or the *combination* of such archaisms with the virulent and even violent language, similar to the language of *Walten* and *Gewalt* that rightly disquiets Derrida. Heidegger's discourse on "the last god" seems to me an insalubrious mix of Nietzsche (from whose *Zarathustra*, I believe, Heidegger takes the expression *der letzte Gott*) and Hölderlin (from whose late hymns Heidegger takes the sense of abandonment). All this calls for a more serious treatment than I can give it here. Yet Heidegger does take a plunge, at least to my ear and to my mind, when he lists all the things about modernity that he hates and then concludes by announcing, *denn all dieses hasset der letzte Gott zuerst* (65:406). "For the last god despiseth these things above all." Nietzsche would have asked why the *last* god still talks like Martin Luther. Or, in my translation, King James. Especially when Heidegger in these texts of the 1930s expresses scorn for the contemporary Christian churches and their faiths. Elsewhere in the *Beiträge*, Heidegger, trying to sound like Hesiod, who refers to the yawning gap of Chaos as πρώτιστα, refers to the gods' default as the *erstester Anfang*, the "firstest commencement" (65:397).

Among commencements, scarcely one is more firster than our birth. If we are alarmed by this sudden plunge in the rhetoric of the 1930s, as we well may be, can we dwell with *Sein und Zeit* a moment longer? Can we dwell on the moment when Heidegger wonders whether it makes a difference if one turns from the one end of Dasein, its *death*, to the "other end," its *birth*?

As I hope to show in the fourth and last of these Brauer Lectures, Derrida in his very first seminar on *Sein und Zeit* back in 1964–65 was struck by what he calls the "shortness of breath" or even "breathlessness" of the final chapters of that book. Perhaps that gasping for air begins with the very strange objection that Heidegger makes in section 72 to his project as a whole, the objection that the "other end" of Dasein, namely, its birth, has been largely ignored. It is as though Derrida is picturing Heidegger's masterwork reaching the end of its gestation; it is now at the far end of the bookish birth canal, contemplating perhaps with trepidation the transition from its life as a fish to its existence as a being in the world, the world of "air."

The most famous definition of philosophy comes from the mouth of Socrates in Plato's *Phaedo*. With one hand holding a cup that contains the strong medicine of hemlock and the other gripping Phaedo's toyable fair hair, Socrates declares that philosophy is "preparation for dying and being dead" (64a). Such preparation or cultivation of dying, the Greek μελέτη, endures as the self-image of philosophy up to and beyond Schopenhauer, perhaps even up to Heidegger and his notion of *Sorge*, "care." For if Dasein is *Sein zum Ende*, being toward the end that is death, how can we fail to hear Socratic-Platonic echoes?

Yet quite late in *Being and Time*, Heidegger confesses that death is but one end of Dasein. The other end is birth, and a fundamental ontology of Dasein cannot ignore it. If one were to focus on this other "end," the end that is the beginning of Dasein, one would perhaps make the discovery that Dasein is *alive*. Does Heidegger ever deny this? Does he ever doubt that Dasein, which dies, is alive? No, not really. Yet he is not comfortable admitting it. There is something about the *viviparity* of Dasein that offends—not that oviparity would help.[1]

First of all, there is all that squooshy *Lebensphilosophie* at loose among Heidegger's contemporaries, all that perfervid discourse on "life" that is based principally on the organicism of the Romantics and on superficial readings of Nietzsche. No one has lampooned such "philosophy of life" with greater trenchancy than Robert Musil, whose Walter and Clarisse are so enamored of Professor Meingast, Musil's reincarnation of Ludwig Klages. Then there is all that talk of *Erlebnis*, "lived" experience, even among phenomenologists themselves, as though other forms of experience were moribund. Heidegger polemicizes endlessly about "life" and "the living," not because he is on the side of death, one hopes, but because he is allergic to and embarrassed by all that sentimental talk of "life." Moreover, as we have already heard, Heidegger insists that "an abyss of essence" separates human being-there from all other forms of "life," especially "animal life." There is in Heidegger a strong humanism—an *abashed* humanism, a *chastized* humanism, to be sure—but an aggressive humanism, which insists on the "dignity" of human life as opposed to every other kind of life. Would attention to the *birth* of Dasein contribute to the abashment or ease it? As those of you know who have ever been born—or at least those of you who have ever given birth or even attended it—human birth is a fairly physical event.

---

1. On the themes of "birth" and "viviparity," see my discussion of Derrida's unpublished *Geschlecht III* (PO 155–56).

Many years ago, back in 1997, I believe, I presented a paper with the title "Placentality" to a distinguished group of scholars. It began with an account of Arendt and Heidegger on natality, as opposed to, or rather in relation to, fatality. It then focused on that second birth, as it were, which is so important for the health of the mother, namely, the full delivery of the placenta. Even back then I was particularly interested in the temporality of birth, and especially of this second arrival, the arrival of that nine-months' home of the fetus, to which we give the popular name *afterbirth*. The term was used as an insult when I was young, but I learned a new respect for it. Merleau-Ponty, in *The Visible and the Invisible*, quotes a remarkable phrase of Valéry, to the effect that the blue of the sea is so blue that only blood is more red, and I inverted this to say of the placenta that it radiates a red so red that only the sea is more blue. I will spare you any further details of my paper, which of course was never published, except to say that when I finished presenting it not a single question came my way. It may be that my listeners had already come to terms with the material I was presenting, so that I was belaboring the obvious, so to speak; or it may be that at the other end of Dasein things get truly messy, so that the philosophers turn aside and brood.

The pages in which Heidegger introduces the other "end" of Dasein are fascinating pages, and we might begin by reading them as closely as we can. For even if Heidegger soon lets the end of birth go and persists with and in being toward the end we call *death*, we might be allowed to engage in a speculative adventure, which would ask: What might change in the two divisions of the existential-ontological analysis that we possess under the title *Sein und Zeit* if one were to think principally of birth, and not death, as the "end" of Dasein? Recall that Hannah Arendt, who found the inspiration for her *Vita activa* precisely in these pages, felt that such a shift in emphasis would have enormous political implications, inasmuch as each new birth promises renewal in and of the public space. Yet the implications, she would agree, go far beyond that, if there is any "beyond" to political community. First of all, however, let us read Heidegger's own text—at the outset of section 72, "The Existential-Ontological Exposition of the Problem of History."

Odd that history should imply birth as opposed to death, especially if one thinks of the "New Angel" of history contemplating all the death and destruction of the past. One recalls Bloom's words, "It's no use, force, hatred, history, all that," spoken just before the Citizen shies a beer tin at him. And we remember Dedalus's response to Mr. Deasey, "History is a nightmare from which I am trying to awake." It is also odd that I am

breaking with my purported focus on ecstatic temporality in sections 65
and 68, neither of which mentions birth. Yet it may turn out to be the
case that there is something ecstatic and even rapturous about the birth
and early years of Dasein.

Augustine would not have thought so, perhaps because of the dubious
neighborhood in which birth takes place. In fact, he tells us that his birth
and early years, because he can remember nothing about them, seem not to
belong to him at all. Indeed, he declares that they do not pertain to him.
Because he cannot remember them, and because the spirit of his father—not
Patricius, his absurd worldly father, but the other one—demands that spirit
forget the flesh, Augustine imagines that those years of oblivion that begin
with birth really pertain to someone else. One wonders whether Monica,
his mother, would agree. In any case, Heidegger begins his discussion of
history by summarizing what the history of his own book has been up
to now. His book is in search of the meaning of being, taking as its clue
the *understanding* of being that only Dasein seems to have. By this time
the book has discovered that *temporality* structures the *care* and *concern* of
Dasein; it also structures the nexus (*Zusammenhang*) of death, indebtedness,
and wanting to have a conscience, as the *whole* of Dasein—Dasein in its
appropriate completeness. "Can Dasein be understood more originally than
in the projection of its existence proper?" asks Heidegger (SZ 372). The
answer should be a resounding *No*. And yet . . .

Heidegger is struck by a severe doubt, *ein schweres Bedenken*. He does
not doubt that his book has grasped the whole of Dasein in its being unto
death or, more properly, its being toward the *end*. Yet now his text says
something that at first sounds silly. "However, death is only the 'end' of
Dasein; taken formally, it is only the *one* end that encompasses Dasein. Yet
the other 'end' is the 'beginning,' 'birth' " (SZ 373). Heidegger seems to be
playing with the word *end*, confusing the singular *termination* of Dasein
with one of two *bookends*, as it were. What matters to Heidegger and to
his book, however, is what lies between the two bookends, the "between" of
birth and death. And this "between," even though it seems to be completely
accounted for by the analyses of its inappropriate and appropriate being
toward death, appears now to be "one-sided." Heidegger places the word
"*einseitig*" in quotation marks or scare quotes, for it does seem that he is
citing Hegel, who always manages to push a recalcitrant dialectic along by
saying that the results so far appear to be "one-sided." Then Heidegger says
something that sounds even sillier. He says that so far his book has interpreted Dasein merely as "facing forward" ("*nach vorne*"), as though it had
left all its having-been—hence, its history—behind it. His book must now

confront *das Sein zum Anfang,* "being toward the beginning," and above all it must give an account of the "stretching" of Dasein "between" birth and death. Only in this way will Dilthey's *Zusammenhang des Lebens,* "the nexus of life," be saved. There is nothing silly about all this, in Heidegger's view, and it calls forth from him one of his most understated yet most stringent remonstrances: "In the field of these investigations it is perhaps already a gain if we learn not to take the problems so lightly" (ibid.).

Just as death is not some event out there in a future time that consists of "now points," the point of death being not yet reached, so birth is not some point in our past, an item that had its importance back then but now is irrelevant, finished. The stubborn vulgarity of our way of reading time causes us to drain both death and birth of their significance. It also causes every analysis of the "between" to suffer shipwreck, *scheitern* (SZ 374). Dasein is not only stretched between birth and death as its end points, but is also in some sense *self-stretching,* and the consequences of this self-stretching are not what we may at first think, namely, that Heidegger is here succumbing to the ancient ontological notion of self-movement, *autokinesis,* as though Dasein *could* be autonomous, *selbst-ständig.* No, it is rather that Dasein somehow always already bears the weight, import, impact, or impress of its birth and death in every moment of its life. "Understood existentially, birth is not, not ever, something past [*ein Vergangenes*] in the sense of something no longer present at hand, just as little as death would be described appropriately as having the mode of something still outstanding, something that is not yet present at hand but is approaching" (ibid.). Now comes a more positive way of expressing the same point, more positive but less transparent: "Factical Dasein exists birthingly [or: by way of birth, *Das faktische Dasein existiert gebürtig*], and birthingly it is already dying, in the sense of being unto death" (ibid.). There is in effect nothing surprising about this, perhaps, except for the odd word *birthingly, gebürtig,* which simply means "by birth." It seems to refer to *nationality,* or what is *native to* someone or something, *natal* in a strong yet not clearly defined sense. Heidegger has already indicated something essential about these two ends of Dasein by citing *Der Ackermann aus Böhmen.*[2] The Bohemian peasant is

---

2. See Alois Bernt and Konrad Burdach, eds., *Der Ackermann aus Böhmen* (Berlin: Weidmannsche Buchhandlung, 1917), 3 and 45–46. Heidegger refers to lines 19 and 20 of chapter 20 of *Der Ackermann* at SZ 245. I have expanded a bit his reference. Although the text was once held to be anonymous, it is now attributed to Johannes von Saaz, aka Johannes von Tepl.

cursing death for having taken his young wife, and death defends himself.
First, the peasant speaks:

> *Grimmiger tilger aller leute, schedelicher echter aller werlte, freis-*
> *samer morder aller menschen, ir Tot, euch sei verfluchet!*

> Malevolent subverter of all persons, thoroughly malign to all
> the world, murderous devourer of all humankind, thou Death,
> my curse upon you!

Death, offended by the peasant's vituperation and in defense of his office,
replies:

> *Weistu des nicht, so wisse es nu: als balde ein mensche geboren*
> *wird, als balde hat es den leikauf getrunken, das es sterben sol.*
> *Anefanges geswisterde ist das ende. . . . [A]ls schiere ein mensche*
> *lebendig wird, als schiere ist es alt genug zu sterben.*

> If you knew it not before, so know it now: as soon as a human
> being is born it has drunk from the proffered chalice, and so it
> is to die. The end is akin to the beginning. . . . The instant a
> human being comes to be alive it is old enough to die.

Birth and death are siblings between whom there should be no rivalry:
Anefanges geswisterde ist das ende. In an early lecture course at Freiburg,
Heidegger cites Luther's commentary on *Genesis* to the same end, or to
both "ends," of Dasein: *Statim enim ab utero matris mori incipimus.* "For as
soon as we abandon our mother's womb we begin to die" (61:182). Or, as
another distinguished phenomenologist once put it, "Therefore, everyman,
look to that last end that is thy death and the dust that gripeth on every
man that is born of woman for as he came naked forth from his mother's
womb so naked shall he wend him at the last for to go as he came."[3] And
Heidegger now admits that this kinship of birth and death is decisive for the
"between," whether or not we become properly aware of it. Once again he
uses that irritating abbreviation *bzw.*, *beziehungsweise*, as though there were
really nothing that might distinguish propriety from impropriety, nothing
that might chastise a "flighty" Dasein that would rightly be put to shame

---

3. James Joyce, *Ulysses* (London: The Bodley Head, 1960), 503–04, "Oxen of the Sun."

by a Dasein that "runs ahead" on its own two resolutely open feet: "In the unity of thrownness and a being unto death that is fleeing or, *beziehungsweise*, that runs ahead, birth and death, when it comes to Dasein, 'hang' 'together'" (SZ 374). Yet appropriateness *does* make a difference: Heidegger now appeals to that *Ständigkeit des Selbsts*, that consistency and constancy of self, which he seems to find so reassuring and which I find so unexamined and so problematic.[4]

Perhaps this is the point at which we can abandon our close reading and commence with a far-flung fantasy. Imagine that the focus of our newly fashioned *Sein und Zeit* would be birth—birth and the extended period of latency, of a puberty and an adolescence that do not figure as themes for existential analysis—rather than death. For a moment, let us set aside adult Dasein, with its hammer and nails, its turn signals, its shoes for

---

4. Allow me to insert a philological remark concerning *Selbst-ständigkeit*. Decades ago, during the final years of Heidegger's life, his assistant, Friedrich-Wilhelm von Herrmann, was helping Heidegger to prepare the collected works, the *Martin Heidegger Gesamtausgabe*, to be published by Vittorio Klostermann. Of special importance was the new printing of *Sein und Zeit*. A number of changes were introduced into Heidegger's text—*without footnoting*. And yet the new Klostermann edition was said to be "unaltered" except for the marginal notes by Heidegger himself. Among the changes that either Heidegger or von Herrmann or both urged the publisher to introduce—in this case in vain, however—was the word *Ständigkeit* for *Stetigkeit* and *Stätigkeit*. The proposal was made to alter (at SZ 390–91) the word *Stätigkeit*, used three times, to *Ständigkeit*, in conformity with earlier and later usages. There was no proposal to change Heidegger's use of *Stätigkeit* at SZ 398, where it seems to mean a "persistent" effort to interpret (and to confront critically) Dilthey's sense of history. At SZ 423 Heidegger uses the expression *die Stetigkeit der Zeit, Stetigkeit* with an *e*, not an *ä*; at SZ 424 he employs the word *Stetigen*. Yet there was no move to alter these expressions. The contexts make it clear that in 1927 Heidegger wants to distinguish in some way the permanence of things present-at-hand (*vorhanden*) from the permanence and autonomy of the self in Dasein. Heidegger's complaint about the Cartesian, Kantian, and Hegelian interpretations of the self is that they slip unawares into categories that are inappropriate to Dasein. Perhaps already in 1927 Heidegger is anxious about the possibility that such confusion might arise with his own insistence on *Selbst-ständigkeit*. Certainly from the 1930s onward Heidegger defines the metaphysics of presence, from which he would take his distance by means an "other" beginning, in terms of its *Ständigkeit* [or *Beständigkeit*] *des Anwesens*, "permanence of presence." To repeat, the danger would be that Heidegger's own use of the word *Selbst-ständigkeit* in *Sein und Zeit* might be taken as a lapse into Cartesian or even medieval metaphysics and morals (see SZ 117, 308, 322–23, 375, 410, and 423–24).

trudging through the furrows of fields and its tools for writing fundamental-ontological tomes. Let us set aside even that Dasein that runs ahead resolutely to meet its mortality.

Dasein, when grown up, revolves about or is involved with its own being. *Dasein geht um sein Sein.* About what does Bébé Dasein revolve, if not about its own being? On what possibilities does it project itself? For there can be no doubt that Dasein at any age is thrown (*geworfen*—one could almost say *littered*) into possibilities of being, whether or not it projects itself understandingly on them: *Seinkönnen* is as applicable to Bébé Dasein as it is to any mature Dasein, middle-aged Dasein, or dotard Dasein. As I learned from my colleague Will McNeill, there is a lecture course in which Heidegger at least for a moment envisages an infantile Dasein. In a moment we will look at Heidegger's 1928–29 *Introduction to Philosophy*, which briefly entertains Bébé Dasein, yet not before engaging in our own flight of fancy—a rewrite of *Sein und Zeit* from the point of view of what we might call Childe Heidegger. Childe Heidegger is much younger than Lord Byron's Harold, however, and much closer to Spanky and Our Gang. Heidegger and the Little Rascals, then. A more scientific fantasy would doubtless compare the existential analyses of *Sein und Zeit* with Jean Piaget's *La Représentation du monde chez l'enfant* (1955), along with a great deal of the more recent pedagogical and child-development literature. I will be significantly less scientific than that, however.

Das faktische Dasein exisiert gebürtig. How might the force of this statement, if one were to take it with the utmost seriousness, alter the analyses of *Sein und Zeit*? Some things would not change, of course. "Handiness," *Zuhandenheit*, would be the way in which the infant and the young child encounter their world, confronting it far more primordially than they will later on in the theoretical perspective or in terms of that "presence at hand," *Vorhandenheit*, that their teachers insist on at school. Space would be understood, not in terms of Galilean-Cartesian coordinates, but as the very *Da* of Dasein. In fact, the word *da!* is constantly on the lips of Bébé Dasein when you carry him or her about, the word he or she utters, pointing that little index finger imperiously in one direction after another, *da—da—da—da!* *Da-Sein* indeed.

Both Bébé Dasein and Childe Heidegger would take special interest in section 11 of *Sein und Zeit*, which treats what some might call "primitive Dasein." The adult Heidegger does not accept such a rubric. Indeed, he is well ahead of his time in criticizing contemporary ethnology for its reportage of so-called primitive societies, but also in criticizing philosophers who use such reportage to construct a neo-Kantian interpretation of "mythical thinking." The reference is of course to Ernst Cassirer.[5] In the adult Heidegger's view, third-world societies, and especially those whose "traditional" mode of life appears to represent a much earlier stage of "development" in "civilization," may in fact offer a "more extensive self-interpretation" of Dasein than our own; indeed, they may have a much less cluttered relation to "being" than we sophisticated latecomers. Although Childe Heidegger would certainly want to avoid the trap of conflating traditional societies with childhood, he might be willing to hope that a rewriting of *Sein und Zeit* could at least aim toward a comprehensive account of the child's world, wherever that child may be at home. To be sure, the adult Heidegger would find much to criticize in the presuppositions behind Piaget's psychological investigations into early childhood, his and those of countless others since. Yet Childe Heidegger might be astonished to discover in the research of educators and child psychologists a novel appreciation of the role of the *body* in the child's learning-by-doing. I will say nothing here of the infant's desire—and its remarkable ability—to respond to music with dance, its remarkably early sense of rhythm, and nothing about its ability to respond to both *world* and *earth* in its artwork. Yet I cannot remain silent about Bébé Dasein's thumb and Bébé Dasein's mum. Bébé Dasein's existence, his or her very being, seems to revolve about the mother. Bébé Dasein *geht um* ihr *Sein*, we might say, with a special focus on her breasts, which I can understand in spite of my maturity and even dotage. Yet when she is not available, Bébé Dasein revolves about its thumb or the two middle fingers of its hand. The existentials of *Zuhandenheit* and *Vorhandenheit* do not seem to be applicable here, in spite of the hand's having fingers and a thumb.

---

5. See SZ 50–52, esp. 51, footnote 1. A far more detailed confrontation with Cassirer—not at Davos, but much earlier, in Hamburg in 1923—is reflected the little-discussed but truly remarkable review by Heidegger of Cassirer's second volume of *Philosophie der symbolischen Formen*. See Heidegger's review in the *Deutsche Literaturzeitung*, 49:21 (1928), 999–1012. The review appears as an appendix to *Kant and the Problem of Metaphysics* in volume 3 of the Martin Heidegger *Gesamtausgabe*, ed. F.-W. von Herrmann (Frankfurt am Main: V. Klostermann, 1998), 255–70. A detailed study of this review would be rewarding. Compare with the Cassirer review SZ 313, which emphasizes the way in which Dasein *lives* its myths, cults, and rites, at least in those societies we call "primitive." Finally, compare Heidegger's treatment of ethnology with that of Georges Bataille and the entire College of Sociology. See Denis Hollier, *Le collège de sociologie (1937–1939): Textes de Georges Bataille, Roger Caillois, René M. Guastalla, Pierre Klossowski, Alexandre Kojève, Michel Leiris, Anatole Lewitsky, Hans Mayer, Jean Paulhan, Jean Wahl, etc.* (Paris: Idées/Gallimard, 1979), *passim*.

In any case, this focus on the thumb and on what psychologists call "transitional objects" is remarkable, and, to repeat, it seems to call for renewed focus on the human body, or on human bodies in the plural. This would be what is newest about our new edition of *Sein und Zeit*. Bébé Dasein, we said a moment ago, *geht um* ihr *Sein*. One would have to forgive the confusion of our French colleagues, for whom the word *Sein*, pronounced as *sē*, means "the breast." Should Division Three of our new *Sein und Zeit* be translated as "Time and the Breast"? While some may raise cries of horror, Bébé Dasein does not flinch.[6]

Other analyses of Heidegger's masterwork would not need to change. Childe Heidegger would certainly understand the thesis of section 13 of *Sein und Zeit*, to wit, the thesis that knowing the world is a founded, derivative mode, and that our schools—from crèche to university—often overestimate its importance. The child, at least when at play, is aware of a broader-based *Sein-in-einer-Welt*, a dwelling in the world that is more bedazzled than ambitious to master and subdue. Indeed, the fascination with play that phenomenology and philosophy generally developed throughout the twentieth century—think of Benjamin's fascination with toys and socks, and indeed with an entire "Berlin Childhood"; Wittgenstein's fascination with spontaneous games; Huizenga's *Homo ludens*; Roger Caillois's ethnological researches into and Gadamer's essays on play; think too of Eugen Fink's wonderful book, *Spiel als Weltsymbol, Play as Cosmic Symbol*—a book that has never received the attention it deserves. All this—and so much I am failing to mention—suggests that Childe Heidegger is on to something here. But now it is story time:

Memita's mum bought her two little wooden chairs, and Memita promptly named them after her two favorite preschool friends, Tobias and Matthias. (She was into boys.) Memita would spend the day instructing,

---

6. Preeminent among those French colleagues is Jean-Luc Nancy: see his *La Naissance des seins, suivi de Péan pour Aphrodite* (Paris: Galilée, 2006). My thanks to Silvia Cernea Clark for the gift of this reference. I am also grateful to Thomas Schestag of Brown University for directing me to Heidegger's correspondence with Emil Staiger concerning Eduard Mörike's poem "Auf einer Lampe." The Brothers Grimm tell us that one of the older meanings of *die Lampe* is the nipple of the breast. Unexpectedly, therefore, Heidegger's *Seinsdenken*, and not only when one crosses the Rhine, takes us to one of Freud's primal scenes, perhaps the most primal of all his scenes, namely, that of the newborn in search of the breast. See my remarks on Freud's "Scientific Project" of 1895 in OM, chapter 3.

entertaining, and comforting her two little friends. One day, I absentmind-edly upset one of the chairs. Memita screamed and dashed to assuage Tobias's pain. I apologized. A day or so later, early on a summer morning, Memita was outside with Matthias and Tobias when her mother called out, "Pan-cakes!" Memita, in her mad dash to the kitchen table, sent both little boys reeling. I rushed to pick them up, and I did not fail to chastise her:

—Memita! I cried, look what you've done to Matthias and Tobias!

She turned in the doorway and gave me a very strange look, almost sad, and certainly condescending.

—Papi, they're only *chairs*.

The child's way of *knowing* the world is actually a great deal more complicated than our own; that world's *Bewandtnisganzheit*, the totality of its references and relations, may well be far more intricate and multilayered than our own. It certainly merits ontological investigation.

I could go on like this, but time is of the essence, ecstatic time. So let me stop, but not before remarking, now that the word *ecstasy* has fallen, that there is something about the prevalence of ecstasy in the child's world that is precisely the point of my entire speculation. The child is *out there—in* the world, but almost always *out there*. The child is moved, *bewegt*, in an emphatic way, a way that Heidegger was constantly struggling to explain to the adults. The intensity of the child's ecstatic existence baffles us. We cannot tell whether the budding ecstasy is primarily futural, since the future *is* theirs; or primarily bound to having-been, even if, trailing clouds of glory, they have so little past; or primarily present, since sometimes they seem to be rapt to the moment, as though they were Buddha. They seem to exist equiprimordially in all three ecstases at once, which is precisely what Heidegger claims we all do, even later on. It is just that our adult present either gets crushed by the need to plan and execute or sinks into nostalgia about the good old days.

Yet life is not always kind to the children—life in the form of grown-ups and even other children. This is an aspect of the *Da-*, the *Da-* of *Da-Sein*, that is even more transparent to Childe Heidegger than it is to the later phenomenologist. True, for the latter, *Miteinandersein* is a problem—not the same problem it was for Husserl, to wit, the problem of empathy, nor for Buber's *I and Thou*, but nevertheless a problem. For the child and even the infant, being-with-one-another is the original endowment, *das Mitgift*, which is also *das Gift*, perhaps hemlock. Being together with others is the original *Ereignis*, which is always *Ent-eignis*—no propriation without expropriation, even in the case of that Other who is so central to the infant's existence. In section 69 of *Sein und Zeit* Heidegger comes to see that the *Da-* of *Da-Sein*, as *Existenz*, is the clearing of being, *die Lichtung des Seins*. Yet Childe Heidegger, focusing on that recent end of its birth, develops an interpretation of the clearing of being in the *Da-* of *Da-Sein* that is quite close to Freud's famous analysis of another childhood game, the game he claims is the very first game. Whenever the mother, Sophie, unaccountably disappears, perhaps to go shopping for a new set of maternity clothes, Bébé Ernst tosses his toy—a bobbin on a string—out of his crib, while still holding onto the end of the string. He then cries *O O O O!* This is not an exclamation of grief or surprise but the effort to say *fort*, that is, to say that both mother and toy are "gone," *weg!* as it were. Both mother and toy have withdrawn into concealment. Bébé Ernst, after having tossed the bobbin out of his crib, now pulls on the string, so that the bobbin reappears. The accompanying cry is *A A A A!* or perhaps even the complete ontological determination, *da da da da!* This is uttered as an incantation, as though by sympathetic magic *die Anwesung* or coming to presence of the toy will produce in its wake the desired presencing of the mother. However, as we know, but as Bébé Ernst has yet to discover, it is possible that one day the mother will disappear forever; this might happen during an influenza epidemic, although it might happen an infinite number of different ways, life is that fragile. And then the magic no longer works. "Pulling strings" will not bring Sophie back.[7]

It is as though every infant, factically *gebürtig*, will come to realize either late or early on that the *Da* on which it is grounded, which is to say, the mother and all other caretakers, including the father, is the ground of a nullity, that is, the ground of the possibility of the radical and irreversible impossibility of *Da-Sein*. *Da-Sein* is *Fort-Sein* is *Weg!-Sein*. One of the most shattering dramas or traumas of existence is that in which Childe Dasein either gradually or quite suddenly encounters the fogbank of death and the grim necessity of mourning. According to Freud and to experience, that

---

7. See Krell, "Pulling Strings Wins No Wisdom," a plenary address at the conference "Freud After Derrida," University of Manitoba, Winnipeg, on October 6, 2010. The Proceedings have been published in *Mosaic*, 44:3 (September 2011), 15–28.

drama begins when Mum, and perhaps even Dad, for whatever reason and for however brief a time, leaves the house.[8]

In the 1928–29 *Einleitung in die Philosophie* Heidegger suggests that even Bébé Dasein, and perhaps Bébé Dasein above all, well before the rest of us, has an inkling of the shaky ground on which our thrown being in the world stands—or wobbles. Heidegger begins by warning us that the "other end" of Dasein, birth, is even more resistant to analysis than the end we call *death* (27:124). Yet, if we observe the very first moment of the infant's "earthly Dasein," *Erdendasein*, he writes, as though there were any other kind, we hear its cries and we see its "fidgeting" or the "wriggling" movements of its limbs directed chaotically out into the world. Heidegger speaks of the infant's *zappelnde Bewegung in die Welt* (27:125), the word *zappeln* reminding us of Gregor Samsa's limbs, precisely at the instant of his second birth, as it were, his *Transformation* or even *Deformation—Die Verwandlung*.[9] The jerking, well-nigh spastic movements are at first and for the most part goalless and bootless, and yet they seem to be "directed toward" something, *gerichtet auf*. . . . They may be seen as either intending *toward* or *away from* something, even if that something remains undisclosed to the newborn and to us. Heidegger continues:

> What determines this Dasein at first is quiet, warmth, nourishment, sleep, and a kind of twilight-state [*Schlaf- und Dämmerzustand*]. It has been concluded from this that such Dasein is at first at least to some extent folded in on itself and enclosed within itself, that the subject is still entirely sequestered in itself. This very presupposition is fundamentally skewed, insofar as the reaction of the child—if we may orient ourselves with the help of this word—has the character of shock, of fright [*des Schocks, des Schrecks*]. Perhaps the first cry is a very particular kind of shock.

---

8. All the more reason to praise two remarkable books by Françoise Dastur, one for grownups, the other for children: *How Are We to Confront Death?* translated by Robert Vallier (New York: Fordham University Press, 2012), and *Pourquoi la mort?* (Paris: Gallimard Jeunesse, 2009), not yet translated—yet why should English-language publishers be less courageous than the French? And why should our children be kept in the dark?

9. I am grateful to William Shinevar of Brown University for discussion of these translations of Kafka's title.

I interrupt here in order to introduce a second witness of this birth shock. I am not thinking of Otto Rank, although one certainly might, or of the fictional hero of a story of mine titled "The School of Birth Analysis," but of Luce Irigaray. Her wonderful book, *L'Oubli de l'air chez Martin Heidegger*, begun the morning she learned of Heidegger's death on May 26, 1976, has a remarkable passage on birth. She envisages birth as the critical passage from amniotic existence to the chill of air—air that, like being, is often forgotten even by great thinkers, perhaps because air is both essential and at times painful, even shocking. Indeed, there is something ecstatic about that first blast of air. Irigaray writes:

> The air remains—it is what resuscitates life, yet at first under the form of an absence: nothing is there but what it is, and it does not appear. This provenance of life, this mediation and milieu of life—these give themselves without appearing as such. The first time they give themselves, they are felt as pain. The open air represents the possibility of life, yet it is also the sign of the loss of that which—or of her who—gave everything without distance, without hesitation, and without chagrin. The air, the open, is in the beginning the limitless immensity of mourning. There all is lost.[10]

One needs to take a breather after that account of birth. Yet we have not the luxury. Let us continue with Heidegger's analysis of "the other end." Fright results from the sense of disturbance. The infant's being startled or disturbed is a primal form of hesitation, of letting something go, but also of being plunged into something and being struck by it (*Be-stürztsein, Betroffenheit*), even if the "it" is entirely concealed. Heidegger now makes his essential point: the sense of fright, of being plunged into something, of being struck, is a primal *Befindlichkeit*. It is how we find ourselves to be, even before there is any cognizant self there in the twilight zone of the newborn, and long, long before there could be anything like an autonomous, independent self standing resolute and foursquare on its two feet. (Four in the morning, two at noontide, three in the evening, as the Sphinx of Thebes knows.) This primal *Befindlichkeit* is essentially related to *Angst*,

---

10. Luce Irigaray, *L'oubli de l'air: Chez Martin Heidegger* (Paris: Minuit, 1983), 43 and 145. Irigaray's text has been translated by Mary Beth Mader and published by the University of Texas Press.

which here is felt to temporalize early on, perhaps at the very onset of our *Erdendasein*—however one may identify the indeterminate *when?* of that onset. If in the past we have been troubled by the difficulty of understanding how anxiety temporalizes, perhaps that is only because we are so remote from our birth—even if we do continue to be natives of birth. Needless to say, our new trouble about how one might be *ready* for anxiety, *ready* to embrace it with open resolve, will not be a trouble that Bébé Dasein can assuage. And while Childe Heidegger can be stubborn, even bull-headed, and throw temper tantrums, we may be reluctant to speak of its "resolute openness." That portion of the book *Sein und Zeit* will have to be rewritten, as will the chapters dealing with "conscience" and "indebtedness" or "guilt," *Gewissen* and *Schuld*.

Once again in the 1928–29 course, Heidegger refers to the "disturbance" of our initial twilight state. Anxiety itself may be the remnant of this initial disturbance, and Heidegger uses the word *Unbehagen* to describe it, *Unbehagen* being a word that is so important for the work we mistranslate as *Civilization and Its Discontents*, namely, *Das Unbehagen in der Kultur*. The malaise in question, the disquiet and the discomfiting *Unbehagen* of the infant, evokes some very early signs of defense, the effort to avert and to parry, if only by the uncontrolled wriggling of our limbs. For Heidegger, those uncontrolled movements are clear signs that we are confronting here what the grownups will call *being in the world*:

> It is not the case that the child during its first few weeks emerges from an enclosed subjectivity to confront objects; rather, it is already—and not first of all when it is torn out of its twilight zone—directed outward toward something. It is already out there alongside things. Some sort of being [*Ein irgend Seiendes*] is already manifest, even though there is no comportment toward this being as yet, no direct turning toward it. Aversion and defense, along with this internally centering need for quiet, warmth, and sleep, possess a peculiarly negative character. Before such phenomena as defense, aversion, and resistance are made clear in their ontological structure, we cannot even begin to interpret the condition of the child in its essence. (27:125–26)

The newborn is "always already" alongside beings or with beings; its temporal structure is already ecstatic, its existence already out there in a world. It is only that the day is overcast, waiting for George to sing "Here Comes the Sun." Yet the infant is closer than we are to the "peculiarly negative character" of human existence, the grownup situation that will be called "being the ground of a nullity." In a final step of his analysis, Heidegger distinguishes infantile aversion from the notion of defense. Aversion is circumvention in the face of something (*Ausweichen vor . . .*) precisely as unknown. Here, once again, Heidegger falls back on his analysis of anxiety, which is the principal object of grownup evasion. Every aversion, every attempt to evade, has an "against which" (*ein Dagegen*), albeit not by way of "active," well-informed opposition. To understand infantile turning away or aversion, one would have to understand the "intentionalities" of *Gegenwehr, Gegenbewegung, Entgegenstellen*. These analyses would aim to understand the "first situation in which such a Dasein finds itself to be, its initially helpless delivery over to the world," *anfänglich hilflosen Auslieferung an die Welt* (27:126). This last phrase calls to mind a very similar one from the adult book we know as *Sein und Zeit*. There Heidegger refers almost in passing to the fact that Dasein is handed over or abandoned to a world that it will never master, *Dasein in seiner Überlassenheit an eine "Welt," deren es nie Herr wird* (SZ 356). There are some things that do not change for Dasein from one end to the other. Being a nullity is one of them.

That said, the later Heidegger, the grownup, as we have seen, has considerable confidence in the idea of the "self." Independence or autonomy of self, *Selbst-ständigkeit*, is an ideal inherited from the tradition. Some call it *Mündigkeit*. And even if the grownup Heidegger wants to avoid the solipsism of the cogito, it is clear that a resolute Dasein, radically individualized and isolated in its ownmost possibility, is *solus ipse*—indeed, more *vereinzelt* and *vereinsamt*, more "individualized" and "solitary," than ever: *solus ipsissime*. Childe Heidegger is more keenly aware of the snares of such narcissism. He knows that there is no self except in attachment to, and even inherence in, the *Anlehnungstypus*, the caring nurturer or nurturers. Bébé Dasein may even be apprised of the happenstance that whatever "self" he or she possesses has been imbibed with its mother's milk, perhaps even with its father's cooing. Merleau-Ponty has a wonderful "Working Note" titled "Ἐγώ and οὔτις," "I and No One," a title that calls to mind the wily Odysseus. Its first sentence reads: "I, truly, that is no one, it is the anonymous" (VI 299). If there is an "I," it is the ego not of the cogito but of the nurtured and tended body. The oldest stream in the world and the most continuous, the Okeanos of the self, flows from this galactic *Zärtlichkeit*, or "tenderness." In the fragment of an essay on religion and community, Hölderlin invokes "the more tender relations" (*die zärtlicheren Verhältnisse*), as being of the essence to the community. The phrase Hölderlin uses to evoke community is none other than *der Zusammenhang des Lebens*, "the nexus of life." The word *zärtlich* does not appear in *Sein und Zeit*. Yet three other Heideggerians may help us here, three very famous ones in their own right. The first is Merleau-Ponty, whom I cited an instant ago.

I decided early on in the preparation of these lectures to refer to Maurice Merleau-Ponty's long chapter on temporality in the *Phenomenology of Perception*. Before rereading that chapter, I read through his "Working Notes" for a book he intended to write, to be called *A Genealogy [or: The Origin] of Truth* or *The Visible and the Invisible*, notes his death in May 1961 cut short. I will proceed chronologically, however, even if I want to expand upon one or two of Merleau-Ponty's late "Working Notes."

Concerning the chapter on "Temporality" in Merleau-Ponty's *Phenomenology of Perception*, let me say only a few things. Much of the chapter revolves about Husserl's notion of "passive synthesis." Time is in flux, yet phenomenological "evidence" can be found only in the moments and the montages of the flux. Time is therefore both continuous and punctual. Yet it is the "field of presence" that draws Merleau-Ponty's attention, a field not simply of the present but the result of a larger synthesis of what Merleau calls "centrifugal movements" toward my own past and future. Such a synthesis is not cogitative or cognitive. It derives from what Heidegger calls the "transcendence" of being-in-the-world, which of course Merleau-Ponty understands as a *bodily* being-in-the-world, one that does not depend on the intellect or reason for its syntheses (PP 478). The present itself, ironically, "is nothing other than a general flight outside the self, the unique law of these centrifugal movements, or, as Heidegger says, an 'ek-stasis' " (PP 479–80). And Merleau-Ponty raises the question we expect him to raise: "How is it that the temporal *ek-stasis* is not an absolute disintegration, in which the individuality of the moments would disappear?" (PP 480). His reply echoes Heidegger's, and indeed cites Heidegger (SZ 350, 373) to the effect that time temporalizes completely in each of its ecstases, such that both the *cohésion d'une vie (Zusammenhang des Lebens)* and the centrifugal force of each ecstasis are preserved. Merleau-Ponty does not pursue Heidegger's response to the question of disintegration, namely, the claim that temporalization occurs as the self-stretching stretch of existence, which is the "between" of birth and death. Yet he does say that the "dehiscence" of the present toward the future (and presumably also toward the past) is the very "archetype of the *self's relation to itself*" (PP 487).

The sole criticism of Heidegger's ecstatic analysis offered by Merleau-Ponty is worth noting, in part because it will be repeated by Derrida in his 1964–65 seminar on Heidegger, the question of being, and history. The criticism focuses on "resolute openness," *Entschlossenheit*, which in *some* of Heidegger's descriptions seems to promise "rescue" from dispersion and inappropriateness or inauthenticity. Merleau-Ponty writes:

> Heidegger's historical time, which flows from the future and which by way of resolute decision *has* its history, thus rescuing itself once and for all from dispersion, is impossible in terms of Heidegger's own thought: for, if time is an *ek-stasis*, if present and past are two results of this ecstasis, how could we cease altogether to see time from the point of view of the present, and how would we ever definitively exit from the inauthentic? (PP 489)

Our decisions are made in the present, and if the present ecstasy involves everydayness as much as "the moment of insight," the possibility of inappropriateness—as Heidegger most often concedes—is a constant companion from birth to death. The present is not presence in the sense intended by modern philosophy: rather, it is presence to the world, presence by way of ecstasis (PP 490). Finally, Merleau-Ponty emphasizes that ecstatic openness to the world is guaranteed by the "lived" body, one's *own* body, across the dimensions of space and time. Precisely why and how this is so would have been questions to which his future work on *ontology* would have responded.

The first of the "Working Notes" to *The Visible and the Invisible* to catch my attention bears the title "Time and Chiasm." The latter word becomes one of Merleau-Ponty's most telling words for what he calls the "interlacing" of perceiving and perceived, a word for what he also calls *la chair*, "flesh," meaning not only the living body but also, remarkably, "the flesh of the world." As the word *flesh* suggests, Merleau-Ponty is always concerned not to forget the role of the human body in the sundry syntheses of what we like to call *meaning*, although oblivion is where the well-trained philosopher usually prefers to keep the body. As one perfervid believer in *The Life of Brian* urges us all, "Do not concern yourself with the things of the body, but with the things of the face and head!" He meant to say "mind," of course.

The question behind my turning to Merleau-Ponty, spurred by Hölderlin's mysterious reference to "the more tender relations" in the community, was whether the ecstases of temporality could be interpreted, beyond Husserl's notion of "passive synthesis," precisely as a corporeal synthesis, a synthesis that has to do with the "body schema," as interpreted in the studies of Lhermitte and Schilder. Heidegger's question as to whether animal life too is bound up with temporality, unfortunately followed by his general closure of questioning concerning the human organism—recall again his reference in the "Letter on Humanism" to the "absymal kinship" of the human body with the beast—made me want to refer in some detail to Merleau-Ponty's notion of corporeal synthesis. Merleau-Ponty's note, "Time and Chiasm," reads:

> The *Stiftung* [institution] of a point in time can be transmitted to other points without "continuity," without "conservation," and without fictive "support" in the psyche from the moment we understand time as chiasm[.]
>
> Thus past and present are *Ineinander* [within-one-another], each one both enveloped and enveloping—and that very thing is flesh[.] (VI 321)

One may wonder whether the *Ausser-sich* may be described as an *Ineinander*, yet the mutual "enveloping" of past and present at least suggests something like the ecstasis of each. Indeed, the main thrust of the "Working Notes" is their call to resist the immanence (with an *a*) and the interiority of which modern philosophy is so proud. Merleau-Ponty, like Heidegger, prefers to emphasize the fact that "transcendence" is our perpetual situation in the world. It is not merely the intermediate stage of the path to absolute spirit.

A second working note, an earlier one, makes this a bit more transparent. Merleau-Ponty refers to the "institution" (*Stiftung*) "not only of an instant but of a whole *system of temporal indices*—time (already as time of the body, the taximetric time of the corporeal schema) is the model of these symbolic matrices, which are our opening to being" (VI 227; cf. 244, 248). "Taximetric" refers to zoospores that move toward or away from a stimulus, hence to an observable tropism across space. It would not be inaccurate to refer to the temporality of Heidegger's *Bewegtheit* in this respect. One of the implications of this "taximetric time" is that "serial time," the mathematical time-line consisting of now-points that a consciousness would hold together, is replaced by what Merleau-Ponty here also calls "mythic time," mythic not in the sense of "unscientific" but in the sense of an overarching ontology of what he calls "*l'Être sauvage*," "wild being." It is not all that "wild," however. Merleau-Ponty's best example of taximetric time is his perceiving this or that aspect of his apartment as he wanders through it—across both space and time.

What one might hope for is that thinkers and researchers repeat the lessons of Merleau-Ponty's *Phenomenology* regarding our perception of space by shifting attention to our perception of time. One would try to avoid both the "objective thinking" that reduces our experience of time to the clocked time of the laboratory and the "intellectualist" approach that has the mind doing all the (impossible) work of time. The key to taximetric time would still be *le corps propre*, the "proper" perhaps now offering us a new way to understand Heidegger's *eigentlich*, which otherwise capitulates to "factical ideals" and even to "jargon." The body proper is the "lived body," as the English translations say, the body that is not just yet the "fresh cadaver" so beloved of Descartes and every machinist to follow. At the center of his *Phenomenology*, Merleau-Ponty writes: "The body proper is in the world as the heart is in the organism: it maintains continually in life the spectacle of the visible, animating and nourishing it from the inside, forming a system with it" (PP 235). Such *maintenance*, even as it nourishes "from the inside," occurs across time and space *in the world*. If Merleau-Ponty's project induces him to stress the ecstasis of *the present* in perception—as does Heidegger's project in the lecture courses immediately subsequent to *Sein und Zeit*—it is precisely a present that displaces itself ecstatically toward both future and past, and does so, not by some "natural geometry," but by the syntheses of the lived body itself (PP 237). How this occurs would be one of those secrets buried deep in the heart of nature—nature and the "native" or "natal" rather than the mind or soul—but it would surely involve the body's diurnal and seasonal rhythms, the measure of its *menses*, the sensitivity of its pineal and other glands, and the complex effects of the entire endocrine cocktail.

The twilight zone of sleep and dreams, as of our gradual or sudden waking and getting oriented each morning, along with that quite remarkable horizontal life of lovers that Merleau-Ponty describes so well as the "strange statue" that is the "outside of its inside and the inside of its outside" (VI 189), would merit as much attention in a phenomenology of taximetric time as our clock time. No doubt, scientific investigations would play an important part in this ecstatic-corporeal phenomenology of time, but Merleau-Ponty's critique of "objective thought" and of naïve empiricism would retain its force.

Allow me to revert, by way of conclusion, to those "more tender relations" to which Hölderlin refers us. Sartre once complained that Merleau-Ponty's childhood was so golden that he never left it behind. For a taximetric phenomenology and an ontology of Bébé Dasein, however, that could only be an advantage. Would that advantage eventually accrue to the politics of our public spaces, our theaters and our assemblies? May one still dream of renewal in the community, not by means of a thrust or shove, but precisely in terms of Hölderlin's "more tender relations"? In the face of what may well be universal skepticism, I leave the question open.

The second well-known Heideggerian, to be introduced next time, says nothing about tenderness, which is not his style, but he has a great deal to say about the vulnerability that is akin to tenderness. You will recall the fundamental teaching of "The Mirror Stage as That Which Forms the Function of the Ego." That is where we will begin next time, stepping like that other childe, Alice, through the looking-glass. And if we dare follow Alice, why not rise to the occasion of reading a third Heideggerian, Derrida, right alongside Lacan?

Nächstens, therefore, *noch mehr.*

4

Dasein Through the Looking-Glass

"The Mirror Stage as That Which Forms the Function of the Ego." What essay would or could Heidegger have hated and feared more? And to think that a dedicated Heideggerian penned it! The essay announces at the very outset that it is engaged in combat against every philosophy derived from the Cartesian cogito; as Heidegger knows, that means *all* of modern philosophy, whether analytic or hermeneutic. The Lacanian tale of ego-formation, a tale very different from that of the *ego cogito me cogitare*, goes something like this. And let us hope, for Heidegger's sake, that this tale of ego formation has nothing to do with our "autonomous" "self."

Between six and eighteen months of life, a period before the infant can walk, or walk well, it experiences its body movements as uncontrolled, chaotic, well-nigh spastic efforts. Indeed, you have seen how eighteen-month Childe Heidegger, legs churning, arms akimbo, bent forward at an angle of forty-five degrees, careens dead ahead until he meets a wall. That is how he stops. At a still more dire moment of your own life, you have seen a newborn or at least newly transformed or deformed Gregor Samsa lying on his back, limbs in the air, *zappelnd*. These spasmodic movements are mirrored by strongly felt needs inside, needs that themselves produce spasms of hunger and painful irritation. Taken together, these uncontrolled movements and spasms seem to rend the infant's very existence into morsels, sheer fragments of οὔτις in the mouth of an ogre. These are precisely morsels and fragments of *time*, a disjointed time, a time out of joint.

Somewhere along its inept way, however, the infant confronts a mirror. It looks into the mirror and is astonished, bedazzled. That first look, the infant's gaze fixing the silhouette of its self, is soon met ludically and with jubilation, says Lacan. The grownup Heidegger will associate such jubilation with the birthing of a god, the last god; the grownup Lacan knows that the birthing of the last god is actually the most recent event at the lying-in hospital. It features not Demeter or Semele or Danaë, but Mina Purefoy. Be that as it may, the very joy that the infant takes in its silhouette, which is what the Greeks call an εἶδος, the εἴδη constituting the realm of ideas, is seductive and deceptive, inasmuch as the infant never coalesces with its image, never fills out to the full its well-defined specular outline. Only Alfred Hitchcock can do that; but he is a magician. For the rest of us, that ludic image is in fact an uncanny double, an alien posing as the autonomous self, a spectral projection. To recognize myself as Ἐγώ in the image is always already to have failed to live up to it, to be equal to it, to *be* the being that is disclosed to me before there is any "me" there. To be sure, the specular image is also my threshold to the visible world, it is Merleau-Ponty's seeing *and* being seen, but again the world only as an effect of doubling. This is the genuine sense of what a much younger Heidegger (not quite a child but much younger than the Heidegger of *Sein und Zeit*, even though Heidegger used this word also in his magnum opus) calls *Reluzenz*, that is, the proclivity of Dasein to interpret itself in the reflected light of categories that have to do with things out there in the world, things "not of the measure" of Dasein, thus botching its self-understanding to the point of unrecognizability. The mirror image is the primal scene of a relucence that never ends.

The matrix with which the mirror stage confronts the infant is irreparably split: on the one side, a seductive Gestalt, exteriority, the stature of a statue, the permanence of an "I"; on the other side, a chaos of pressing needs, pangs, and frights, an interiority that poses as the "I" behind my eyes, a turbulence of spasmodic movements, the production of an alien automaton, the permanence not of autonomy but of alienation. In short, the uncanny relation to "self," as of "self" to world, will remain *un rapport ambigu*.

The growing child's sense of beauty, especially at puberty, will be homeomorphic with this projected mirror image; the child will try to occupy fully that same form, the form of the same, the form of absolute perfection—τὸ ἐκφανέστατον καὶ τὸ ἐρασμιώτατον—in an other. Yet the same primordial discord will frustrate this fulfillment as well, as the spasms and uncontrolled movements once did; perhaps new spasms will come to disperse and distract the child, he or she fully expecting that someday one will be equal to the orthopedic totality one has beheld—Gregor Samsa's sister Grete on the tram stretching her young body so alluringly in and for the closing lines, the most horrific lines, of Kafka's tale. For the proper function of the ego is not to gather cogitative experience but to serve as "the knot of servitude to the imaginary" (É 100). And whatever dreams Hegel or Kojève may have dreamed, no dialectic will grant the ego mastery; no logic-chopping will untie or cut the knot. Needless to say, dreams of *readiness* for anxiety and fantasies of a *resoluteness* that would rout dispersion will continue to be dreams. Luckily, anxiety will still crowd us close. "Luckily," since anxiety alone will enable us to see what is advancing toward us as our closed future.

The primordial discord or disjunction within ego formation creates the symbolic matrix into which the "I" precipitates prior to any conscious identification with others, prior even to language; that original disjunction also introduces all the future possibilities, every *Seinsart* or mode of being and the entire *Seinkönnen* or ability to *be* of the *Da*, namely, the possibilities of inversion, neurosis, psychosis, paranoia. One might have hoped for other possibilities for possibility-being, some other abilities for the being that is able to be, some capacity for renewal—certainly Arendt would insist on this, and one can imagine Derrida hoping for it as well. Yet Lacan is adamant. The precipitation of the disjunctive ego is irreducible and will never be outgrown. It is, one might say, ownmost, nonrelational, and unsurpassable. And, yes, certain. Is it then indeterminate as to its when? Six to eighteen months, says the master. And the precipitation occurs, says the master, here as mysterious as he always is, *dans une ligne de fiction*, on the vector of a kind of fiction. It is as though the principal discourse of the *Da* will be phantasmatic, fabulous, fabled, storied, somewhere between the glorious language of literature and the idle chitchat of the streets. Schelling says that whatever is known must be *narrated*. Such *Erzählung* is difficult for science and philosophy, and every bit as difficult for *thinking*. It is also unpredictable for the therapist. For the specular ego frustrates not only the analysand but also the analyst. The final words of Lacan's remarkably ecstatic essay are these: ". . . psychoanalysis can accompany the patient to the ecstatic limit of the '*that is what you are* [Tu es cela],' where the cipher of the patient's destiny as a mortal is revealed to him or her; but as practitioners it is not in our sole power to lead the patient to the moment when the veritable voyage begins" (És 100).

Lacan, as you see, like any good Heideggerian, or like any worthy priest of an ancient mystery religion, can be exceedingly modest. At the conclusion of his *Ethics of Psychoanalysis*, Lacan confesses that he continues to eat the scroll of psychoanalysis, the scroll that a dubious angel by the name of Siegmund, or perhaps Schlomo, delivered to him, a scroll that is sweet in his mouth but that produces cramps and spasms in his belly. The patient's destiny as a mortal is mirrored in the mortality of the analyst—this is the true countertransference. And the *that is what you are* is a silhouette that neither patient nor analyst fills with completude. Why? Because the limit, as you have only now heard, is *ecstatic*. In and for itself it is outside itself. We mortals pass through the looking-glass precisely as being-in-the-world. Yet that does not mean that we reach the "other side" of our specular self, getting behind or beyond our phantasms, fables, and foibles to the Wonderland of the real; rather, these revenants accompany us every step of the way, from the end called "birth" to the end called "death." Certain aspects of the grownup Heidegger's *Sein und Zeit* will survive our rewrite. Others not.

At this juncture allow me add two postscripts to our discussion of the theme of birth, the "other end" of Dasein. The first postscript has to do with the question of the relation of Dasein to illness. Heidegger's existential conception of death and of our being toward the end, except for that fleeting reference to Nietzsche's *Zarathustra*, takes neither illness nor senescence into account when it comes to the possibility that is ownmost, nonrelational, unsurpassable, certain and as certain indeterminate as to its *when*. It is as though Dasein, which we now know is both natal and fatal, had no fundamental relation to the possibility of birth defects, infection, organ failure, cellular superfetation—whether benign or malignant—cellular mutation and cell death. To say nothing of autoimmune diseases. However, both Bébé Dasein and Childe Heidegger know that illness is a constant companion of their mortality—they have long since felt those belly cramps and spasms of which the angels and the doctors speak. To suppose, as the adult Heidegger seems to, that illness is an ontic affair, consigned to the sole purview of biologists, physicians, and pathologists, is to miss its existential-ontological import. If Childe Heidegger should come to rewrite *Sein und Zeit*, the possibilities of contagion and illness would surely play the central role they played throughout Schelling's thinking, from the 1799 *Erster Entwurf* to the much later Erlangen lectures and on through his final lectures during the 1840s in Berlin. Attention to illness and to what Yeats calls "dull decrepitude" would alter the existential concept of death; it would also complicate the otherwise arbitrary and prejudicial distinctions Heidegger introduces between human "dying," animal "perishing," and a generalized "demise."

The second postscript: I have said nothing about the sex of Bébé Dasein. Would it be possible, and would it not be necessary, to repeat the analyses of *Sein und Zeit* with a view to feminine and masculine worlds, female and male beings, and perhaps something beyond these dualities that nevertheless would not be neutral, not neutered? Indeed, can the neutrality of the neuter *das Dasein* be maintained? This was Derrida's question in *Geschlecht I*, you will remember. And his question in the *Animal* book, you will also recall, was whether and how one can take up the question Heidegger said was "a matter all its own," namely, whether the being of animals—and which ones? since there are many of them besides us—may be understood as determined by "time." I even know some philosophers who are beginning to think, as already Goethe may have thought, that trees and plants too are in some sense ecstatic. Hegel despised them because they cannot walk—they cannot walk because their mouths never stop sucking the earth and their nether parts never stop exposing themselves to the sky. Yet may not one still pose the question of ecstasy with reference to our heliotropic friends? And to our sexed and gendered friends?

The question is not so much whether I am now, with these childish preoccupations, trying your patience. The question is: How much patience and persistence can we children bring to such questions?

Yet it is neither to the Derrida of the animals nor to the Derrida of *la vie-la-mort*, nor to the Derrida of the four generations of *Geschlecht* that I now want to turn. I want to read with you some portions of Derrida's very first seminar on Heidegger, taught at the École Normale Supérieure in 1964–65, when he was thirty-four years of age. The course has the title: "Heidegger: the Question of Being and History."[1]

What ameliorates the abruptness of my shift from Lacan to Derrida is that it is section 72 of *Being and Time*, on historicity, that contains Heidegger's reference to birth, the reference that sent me to Lacan's looking-glass in the first place. This same section is crucial for Derrida's seminar as well, albeit for very different reasons. A second amelioration is that Derrida quotes Lacan twice during the seminar, both times with unstinting approval, these references having to do with the fact that the symbolic, or language in general, creates humankind, rather than humankind creating the symbolic. Derrida cites Lacan's "Function and Field of Speech and Language

---

1. Jacques Derrida, *Heidegger: la question de l'Être et l'Histoire*, ed. Thomas Dutoit and Marguerite Derrida (Paris: Galilée, 2013), referred to by page number in the body of my text. An English translation by Geoff Bennington is under way. I have incorporated into my own translations here the many corrections of the French text that Bennington has found. My thanks to him for these corrections. And, speaking of translations, I should note that throughout his seminar Derrida himself translates many long passages from *Sein und Zeit*. Readers may recall that at the time only the first division of the book had been translated into French. As one would expect, Derrida's translation and his commentary on issues of translation are thought provoking throughout.

in Psychoanalysis" and his seminar on Poe's "The Purloined Letter," both
to the same effect: the human being speaks, but only because the symbolic
has made him human; the human being does not constitute the symbolic,
but the symbolic constitutes the human (97; 124). Here too, as in the case
of Heidegger, Derrida does not pause to declare his differences with Lacan.

"Heidegger: the question of Being and History" is the title of Derrida's
seminar. The words *Being* and *History* are capitalized for two related reasons:
first, Derrida's topic is Heidegger's meditation on *Sein*, and while it focuses
on Heidegger's *Being and Time* the scope of the seminar is Heidegger's
thought in its entirety, including the texts of the so-called turn; second,
Derrida's special interest is the relation of *Sein* to *Geschichte*, albeit not to
the discipline of "history" (*Historie*) as such. The enormous range of the
question he has chosen has to do with Derrida's growing awareness of the
importance of Heidegger's notion of the "history of being as presence," a
notion that he believes responds decisively to both Hegel's phenomenology
of spirit and Husserl's transcendental phenomenology of consciousness. As
close as Heidegger often appears to be to Hegel's spirit and letter, the difference between them is decisive. And even though Heidegger owes much
to Husserl, identifying himself still as a phenomenologist, Heidegger's *Sein
und Zeit*, in Derrida's view, is the beginning of the end of phenomenology—indeed, the end of phenomenality as such. Yet Derrida is also aware
of the problematic nature of Heidegger's notion of a history of being as
presence, problematic principally because Heidegger sometimes appears to
stand outside of such a history and at other times well within it. Yet what
is most remarkable about Derrida's seminar is its sympathetic treatment of
Heidegger. In this first confrontation, one may fairly say that Derrida *gives
himself over* to Heidegger's text more completely than he ever will again:
the generosity, the *Hingabe*, of the interpretation is truly astonishing. An
example, and a surprising one: Derrida acknowledges Heidegger's "adherence
to Nazism," yet he does not allow himself to be distracted from his theme;
he offers his seminar participants neither a *caveat* nor a condemnation (98,
275, 283, 288). The implication throughout is that even in section 74 of
Sein und Zeit, and precisely there as it turns out, there is nothing that would
compel Heidegger's political choices to be our own—or even to be *his* own.

Because of my own emphasis on ecstatic temporality, I want to trace
the references in Derrida's seminar to *ekstasis* and *ek-sistence*. One of our
ongoing discussions involved my concern that Derrida was not focusing
sufficiently on Heidegger's ecstatic interpretation of temporality and my
sense that his own concerns—presence, the "living present," the "absolute
past," the trace, spacing, effraction, the undecidable frontier between inside

and outside, and many others—required him to do so. Moreover, I felt that when one takes seriously the *"outside itself* in-and-for-itself" it complicates Derrida's principal complaints in his published writings on Heidegger, namely, the *proximity* of Dasein to being and the tendency of Heidegger himself to *gather* all differences into a unity. Is not proximity rocked by ecstasis? And does not something happen to gathering, *Versammlung*, when one takes ecstasy seriously? However that may be, I will focus of the sixth, seventh, and eighth hours of the seminar and touch on only three of Derrida's many areas of inquiry.

First, Derrida discusses the theme of birth in a context quite different from the one I have chosen to pursue. For Derrida, it is at the moment when "the other end" of Dasein is introduced that the finitude of Dasein becomes clear, and such finitude means nothing less than the end of the metaphysics of presence.

Second, Derrida notes the way in which, in these final "breathless" sections of Heidegger's magnum opus, the enigmatic past assumes preeminence over both present and future. What Derrida finds decisive in the overcoming of Hegel's self-present spirit and Husserl's "living present" is Heidegger's treatment of "the present," not as the site of experience and phenomenality, but as "the past of a future" (276, 309), a phrase on which Derrida does not elaborate, but which we may perhaps read as "the (absolute) past of a (suddenly passing, utterly finite, and 'closed') future."

Third, Derrida analyzes the enigma of the past in terms of Heidegger's notions of transmission and transmissibility, *Überlieferung* and *sich überliefern*. Derrida interprets these on the basis of what Heidegger's *Kant and the Problem of Metaphysics* calls "the pure auto-affection of time."

Each of these three topics is obstreperous enough. Students back in 1964 who were expecting a gentle introductory course on Heidegger must have been stunned—especially when they learned that they would be reading *Sein und Zeit* in German. Let me begin with some general remarks about the course, however, inasmuch as it is not yet well known. The question of being and history in Heidegger is not a question of ontology, Derrida argues, inasmuch as Heidegger's abandonment of fundamental ontology and phenomenology is already foreshadowed in *Sein und Zeit* itself. Heidegger wants not merely to deconstruct or dismantle metaphysics and ontology but to destroy it in a stronger sense: not to annihilate it, or simply to walk away from it, since both annihilation and abandonment are impossible for philosophy, but to *solicit* it, as Derrida prefers to say; that is, to expose all its vulnerabilities and to cause all its assurances to tremble. One of the most intriguing aspects of the seminar is Derrida's attention throughout to philosophy's resistance (from Plato's *Theaetetus*, *Sophist*, and *Timaeus* on through the opening pages of Heidegger's *Sein und Zeit*) to "telling stories about beings." Those stories are always family stories, children's stories, family romances, and Derrida is already thinking of things that will appear later in "White Mythology" and in *Glas*. The issue of "metaphor" is preeminent among those things: Derrida is struck by Heidegger's declaration at the end of section 7 of *Sein und Zeit*, apologizing in advance for the awkwardness of his word choices and even his grammar, that "it is one thing to develop narratives about this or that being [*über Seiendes erzählend zu berichten*], and another to grasp beings in their being" (SZ 39). After citing this passage, Derrida writes two words into the middle of his page, words he then underscores: *Métaphore ontique* (57). A fruitful way to read the published text of Derrida's seminar would be to trace the idea that what Heidegger calls "ontological difference" is for Derrida the question as to whether the language of *Sein* is inevitably and inextricably a language of *Seiendes*—ontic metaphor struggling in vain to become ontological conceptuality, as it were. Derrida's remarkable training in both philosophy and literature, and in both logic and rhetoric, is what makes his reading of Heidegger so extraordinarily rich. It is also what obligates him to read *Sein und Zeit* from the vantage point of Heidegger's analysis of "the grammar and etymology of the word *being*" in his 1935 *Introduction to Metaphysics*. And it is also what enables him to see Heidegger's celebration of speech over writing as "more than Platonic," something he will show a few years later in "Plato's Pharmacy." Finally, it enables him to cast a critical eye on Heidegger's insistence that *logos* is essentially a *gathering* into One. The latter issue, *Versammlung*, will preoccupy Derrida from the *Geschlecht* series of the 1980s, through *Of Spirit*, to his final seminar, *The Beast and the Sovereign*. But now to the three *topoi* that are related most closely to the theme of ecstasy.

During the sixth of the nine sessions of the seminar Derrida reaches the center of his inquiry. Here he reads section 72, "Temporality and Historicity," *Zeitlichkeit und Geschichtlichkeit*, which introduces the fifth chapter of Division Two of *Sein und Zeit*. What is remarkable about this chapter is that it has to do with Dasein as *properly* historical. Whereas the chapters preceding and following this chapter return to the analysis of Dasein in its everydayness and inappropriate being-within-time, the chapter on *Geschichte* will try to say something about Dasein in its proper mode, the mode of its being toward the ends of both birth and death. Yet Heidegger's analysis of the *Geschehen* of *Geschichte* is short of breath: it falls back on the analysis of ecstatic temporality without adding much that is new to that analysis. Or, if it does add something new, that new material does not seem to attach firmly enough to what precedes it. Every reader of *Sein und Zeit* experiences shortness of breath, perhaps even a gasp, when Dasein suddenly discovers its heritage, chooses its hero, and joins its generation, community, and people or nation—in this case the German *Volk*—in struggle, *Kampf*, in order to confront its proper destiny, *Schicksal*. These things do pertain to that "other end" of Dasein called *birth*. Yet Heidegger's choices reflect—for reasons that are not transparent—the particular epoch into which Heidegger is born; "epoch" therefore means both a determinate time frame and a certain "suspension" or *epochē* in a history that is otherwise ongoing and remarkably diverse. Part of that suspension into which any given Dasein precipitates through birth is what Derrida will later call "philosophical nationality and nationalism."

Derrida begins to read section 72 by referring to the 1938 essay, "The Time When All the World Becomes an Image," *Die Zeit des Weltbildes*. (The rubric *Weltbild* suggests that we have not abandoned the theme of "relucence" and the mirror stage.) His question is how one can come to see an epoch *as* an epoch, and his suspicion is that only if one occupies a position *between* epochs, with one coming to an end and the other incipient, can something like "epochality" emerge. "Epochality," you may recall, is the fourth of those themes that form the weft or *Geflecht* of Derrida's 1987 *De l'esprit*. The thesis of Heidegger's "World Image" essay, however, is that for philosophy from Plato to Husserl there is but one epoch. In Derrida's words: "There are no conceptions of the world in history; there is one epoch that has a conception of the world, and that is the epoch that forges the concept of a conception of the world" (197). As a result, "the world *is* altogether in the epoch; there is nothing else" (199). Whether or not there is or can be one epoch only, we surely have to note the differences within such an epoch. For example, we would have to take into account, as Heidegger does, the still undecided battle between the ancients and the moderns in that one epoch. Nevertheless, Heidegger invariably stresses the unity: "In spite of the differences among the Greek, medieval, and modern epochs, there is a unity, the unity of one grand epoch of the world that is commanded by philosophy as the destiny of Europe and that sees the deployment of the world as objectivity [*objectité*, Heidegger's *Objektität*] from Plato to Husserl" (199–200). In spite of the differences—for example, when, as Heidegger says, medieval "security in sanctity" becomes the modern "security in certitude"—the need to secure the world as imaged object prevails throughout the single and singular epoch of metaphysics.

Derrida insists that Heidegger's analysis is not reactionary, nor is it a cranky condemnation of modernity. What that analysis reveals, perhaps in spite of itself, is that the historicity of being is no longer enclosed in a single epoch, that the epoch devoted to securing an image of the world, that is, of beings as a whole, is entering into its end. True, that end may well be technological catastrophe and, true again, that catastrophe may take considerable time even as its plummeting accelerates. Nevertheless, this is the end—"of our elaborate plans the end, of everything that stands the end." And what is commencing? The possibility of an inquiry into or meditation on being as such, whatever that may mean.

Only at this point does Derrida turn to section 72 on historicity. He reminds us that the prior analyses of appropriateness and inappropriate-ness, of care, falling prey, being unto death, and anxiety will all come to bear on this section. He makes a special point of saying that a new way of conceiving affectivity, namely, Heidegger's analysis of *Befindlichkeit*, will also come to bear—and how could it not, if the existential structure of "how we find ourselves to be" is associated with facticity and thus with the past or the having-been of Dasein, hence with its history? (203). He reminds us too that the "whole being" (*Ganzsein*) of Dasein for which Heidegger is in search has to do with "the ecstasy of the future, as being toward the end and being toward death," such that "the *very being* of Dasein" reveals itself "as finitude" (204).

It is above all the structure of *Jemeinigkeit*, of existence as "in each case my own," that in Derrida's view impels Heidegger's turn from the end we call *death* to the end we call *birth. My* birth, as Derrida emphasizes. If my *death* resists every effort to envisage its possibility, so much so that Heidegger prefers the expression *Sein zum Ende*, perhaps the "other end" of Dasein may be more accessible? As we have seen, Heidegger quickly denies this, but Derrida speculates that it is perhaps this other end of Dasein that will enable us to understand and accept once and for all that Heidegger is not talking about forms of consciousness or self-consciousness, *Bewusstsein* or *Selbstbewusstsein*. Rather, as Merleau-Ponty emphasizes, it is the nexus of life, *der Zusammenhang des Lebens*, with which Heidegger is concerned (205). The nexus or stretch of life has to be thought "without hurrying toward the horizon of a consciousness or a cogito," says Derrida, but also without turning that stretch of life into presence at hand, as though the stretch or the self-stretching were a possible object of scientific inquiry.

Having mentioned the self-presence of consciousness and the presence at hand that at least seems to be opposed to it, Derrida now develops his main thesis: "The *root* of the problem is what we will now touch upon, or at least brush up against. Everything—everything, that is to say, not only this or that gesture of the destruction of metaphysics but the totality of the destruction and the sense that commands it in its entirety—turns about the sense of the *Present* and about the privilege accorded by all philosophy to *the present*" (207). To put it paradoxically, the two "ends" of Dasein that engage it to, and remove it from, the nexus of life do not occur in the living present of a consciousness that would constitute "experience." With his reference to birth Heidegger intends to "solicit" (in the sense of "subvert") the privilege of the present as "evidence" and "assurance," and thereby to shake the foundation of the totality of metaphysics, "which is to say, philosophy itself" (209). Heidegger's audacity in this regard, his desire to devastate what Derrida calls, in a striking phrase, *philosophical invulnerability*, becomes clear when we reflect on the fact that we live in the present, experience in the present, remember and anticipate in the present. And if Husserl's "living present" is a tautology, it will at least continue to give itself out as a priori certain. Recall that when Schelling wished to write a book about *The Past* his nightmare was that he could never escape the living present in order to gain genuine access to his topic. Although Husserl's nightmare is different, haunted as it is by ghosts that flit about the zero-point of recollection, his is nonetheless the nightmare of impossible presence.

Derrida's detailed analysis of "the living present" in both Hegel and Husserl cannot detain us here, and yet it is fascinating to see in the seminar an early form of one of the most telling chapters of Derrida's *La voix et le phénomène*. The outcome of the analysis is the insight that for Hegel, the "discoverer" of history, and for Husserl, especially the Husserl of the *Krisis*, for whom history is said to be of the essence, the form of historicity itself depends on a moment of *non*history: historicity for Hegel and Husserl is rooted in the putative instant (outside of both time and history) when spirit is altogether with itself, *ganz bei sich*, and ideal objects are transmitted successfully as self-identical. The transmission of ideal objects such as geometric demonstrations and the self-possession of spirit are alike impossible without the *dissimulation* of presence within the present. Such dissimulation is not an error or an oversight by a bemused subjectivity; it is "the very form of historialization, which constitutes [itself] by dissimulating itself in the very *presence* of appearance" (213).

Heidegger's audacity is surely matched by Derrida's. Here one would have to recall Derrida's account of the voice—although there is not a hint of it as yet in the Heidegger seminar. For it is the voice that *gives itself out as*, that is, *dissimulates* the perfect presence of spoken signs to their intended significations. Thus there is something—or everything—that is unsurpassable, *indépassable*, about the epoch of metaphysics as presence. Remarkably, this is the very word, or a translation of the word, that serves Heidegger as one of the existentials of my death, which is forever *unüberholbar*. But if one also cannot get around the history of metaphysics as presence, which is as inevitable as death, how can either Heidegger or Derrida descry it, and descry it as dissimulating? Derrida confesses that there is no getting around this problem. "Nevertheless," he adds,

> one can pose the question of evidence and of presence and ask oneself whether the evidence of the presence of the present does not revert to a sense of experience for which historicity, that is, the character of the past, would be precisely that which—its meaning being determined within the presence of the present—itself radically and definitively escapes from the form of the present. In other words, experience would have a meaning that would essentially never let itself be phenomenalized in the form of the living present. Such a meaning—which would never phenomenalize in the form of the living present—would not ever phenomenalize and would not ever come to experience as such. (214)

To this astonishingly rebarbative paragraph Derrida adds the word, as he so often does, *Commenter*. "Comment on this." The paradox seems to be this: if both being and experience give themselves out as the presence of the present, there is something about historicity, something about the passing and the pastness of the past, something about what Nietzsche calls the "it *was*," that will forever escape our grasp. The *es war* is (in) the *Imperfekt*. The result? "One would in particular never think *origin* and *end,* birth and death, as such . . ." (214). *My* birth and *my* death, but also *origins* and *ends* in general, that is to say, the very objects of metaphysics, its ἀρχαί and its τέλοι, would not be able to appear in the form of presence; or if they were to appear, they would appear precisely as that which *cannot* appear in the form of presence, hence as dissimulation. "The certitude of the living present, as the absolute form of experience and the absolute source of meaning, presupposes as such the neutralization of *my* birth and *my* death" (ibid.). In an analysis that anticipates what he will later assert concerning the *testamentary* ego and the signature as *mortgage*, Derrida here notes that the metaphysics of presence requires that I think "the possibility of a temporalization without me," whether that "me" be empirical or transcendental. "In any case," Derrida concludes, "to hold onto the present as a foundation and as the source of meaning is to affirm infinity and eternity as the foundation of meaning and eventually the foundation of the historicity of meaning. In its essence, the present is that which would not come to an end. It is in itself ahistorical" (ibid.).

To break the hold of the living present, Heidegger can only insist on the finitude of Dasein. In the first of my own lectures, I spoke about the difficulty of demonstrating finitude, especially when the thesis concerning the primacy of the future ecstasis is shaken. Derrida responds to this, as it were, by citing two later passages, both from section 74, that now declare finitude to be bound up with historicity. Heidegger writes, and sets in italic, *"Only temporality proper, which at the same time is finite, makes something like destiny, and that means proper historicity, possible"* (SZ 385). However, he then reaffirms the primacy of the future ecstasis, even and precisely in the matter of historicity, and adds: *"Proper being toward death, that is, the finitude of temporality, is the concealed ground of the historicity of Dasein"* (SZ 386). To break the hold of presence is vital to the rescue of history proper. Against both Hegel and Husserl, Derrida affirms, "There is no history if temporality is not finite" (215). Yet *how* does one break the hold of "the presence of the present" if the dissimulating present gives itself out as the horizon of all experience? Surely, Heidegger's appeal to a recognizable destiny, *Schicksal*, drags both past and future, through retrospective and prospective illusion, into the presence of the present? Surely, his ostensible envisaging of the "concealed ground" of historicity is dissimulation itself? Derrida's answer, to put the matter simply, is this: the hold of presence can be broken only if one insists on ecstatic *ek-sistence*, as the later Heidegger will do, *ek-sistence* rather than *experience*, especially when experience is Hegel's science of the experience of *consciousness*. As Derrida puts it, "to replace the notion of experience with that of *ek-sistence* unto death" is to destroy the determination of being as presence and thus "to shatter the epoch" (224).

It is only at this point, late in the sixth session, that Derrida introduces the passage in which Heidegger defines Dasein as *gebürtig*—factical Dasein existing "birthingly," as I rendered it, or less absurdly, "natally." Derrida, who is translating all these passages himself, adds a bracketed comment after this uncanny word *gebürtig*: *"[comme native—comme ce qui a une naissance—nature?]"* (225). Dasein as *natal*, we might say, *natal* as well as *fatal*; Dasein as having a birth; Dasein as *natus est*, hence as *nature* itself. Dasein beneath the light-dispensing and warmth-giving star.

In the closing moments of the session, Derrida introduces a word that will be a mainstay in his later thinking. He refers to Emmanuel Levinas's effort to invoke a past to which one has only a tenuous relation. It would be a past that has never been present and that therefore cannot be presentified, an *absolute* past, as it were. To invoke such a past would require that one abandon the traditional structure of sign and signified and "elaborate a thematic of the *Trace*" (227).

As the seventh session goes on to show, the past, for a thematic of the trace, is an *enigma*. It is here that the notion of ecstasy, precisely as ecstasis—displacement, departure, withdrawal—becomes important. Once again, *dissimulation* is the conundrum. "The present, that is to say, phenomenality, manifestation, is the dissimulation of originary historicity itself, which therefore may not be thought as another present; rather, it must be thought as an origin that has passed, in a sense that is not to be thought as a past present" (256). If the present is dissimulation, then all manifestation becomes the "withdrawal of an origin that never possessed a present phenomenality" (ibid.). This in turn requires "an absolute exit, a radical *ek-stasis*, originary and without return" (ibid.). The language here is already that of the *Grammatology*. And it is here that Derrida responds—or will have responded—to my insistence that he take up the theme of ecstatic temporality. He writes, "It is *ek-stasis* and not presence that is the fundamental origin of temporality" (ibid.). He knows full well that the words *fundamental* and *origin* are paleonymic, and even that they will have to be crossed out or erased as he writes them, one hand correcting the incorrigible other hand. Ecstasis is the *dérobement*, withdrawal, that can only be *traced*, never signified as such. Furthermore, the *unity* of the temporal ecstases is itself ecstatic, precisely as Heidegger insists it is, and hence not on the horizon of presence. In a sense, but a sense that is very helpful, Derrida shows that Heidegger himself dethrones the present ecstasy, that is, the ecstasy most likely to promise a horizon of *Praesenz*, merely by defining it as "the past of a future" (276, 309). That is to say, the ecstatic present incorporates all that is unforeseeable about the future, the imprevidibility of the future as such, along with all the secrets, complicities, and complexities of the past. In order to *know* the present, one would need both a fortune-teller and a hundred-eyed historian, a sweet-tempered Argos Panoptes, such as we have never known. For the past is constituted as "a future that has been" (ibid.), a future that is already bygone, a future for which not even clairvoyance suffices.

At this point Derrida raises a significant objection to Heidegger's ecstatic analysis, an objection that Merleau-Ponty had already raised. By emphasizing the primacy of the future, Heidegger grants a certain privilege to *Entschlossenheit*, and if such resoluteness falls back on certain metaphysico-moral "factical ideals," then the metaphysics of presence will continue to determine the project of *Sein und Zeit*. During the seventh hour of his seminar, Derrida shows why and how recognition of the *dissimulation* of presence causes the axis of appropriateness, *Eigentlichkeit*, to tremble and the confidence in resolve, *Entschlossenheit*, to be shaken. Drawing on Heidegger's own later analyses of the untruth within truth and the withdrawal of being within all presencing, Derrida writes,

> If dissimulation of being means the revealing of being, and the other way around, it follows that all the concepts derived from them, which doubtless means practically all the significations of the discourse, signify the same and their contrary. From now on, one would no longer be able either to say or to live a *simple* signification; and *Entschlossenheit*, the condition of authenticity, will also be precisely precipitation toward inauthenticity. Whence the passage from the initial *Entschlossenheit* to the *Gelassenheit* of the texts at the end. (249–50)

It is Heidegger himself, Derrida assures us, who stresses the riddlesome or enigmatic quality of the past, or of having-been, which historicity proper seems to privilege (257; SZ 381). No amount of resolute openedness or open resolution will banish the enigma of our access to the past. It is not merely that history presents us with puzzles. It is that the past and the passivity that adheres to it play a crucial role in the very *Bewegtheit* of Dasein, and that the origin of that past withdraws from us as resolutely as the future suddenly thrusts itself upon us. Early on in the seminar, during its second hour, Derrida invokes the importance for Heidegger's fundamental ontology of the "always already" in our understanding of being:

> Without this familiarity with the meaning of being or this pre-understanding of the *sense* of being, the explicit question of the meaning of being could not even arise. There is thus an *already* to the question of the meaning of being, a reference to an *always already*, to a past always already flown yet still efficacious, which allows the question to become more radical, freer, more independent, more concrete, first and last. The weight of the *already* in the *originary* signifies *already* the absolute and originary historicity of the question of being; it signifies that the question of being is fully and originarily and thoroughly historical. (79)

True, such an "already" will prove to be but a "trace." To give an account of it, to tell its tale, to tell stories about the "always already," one will have to revert to *mythos* rather than *logos*. Or, rather, that very distinction, prevalent since Plato, will have begun to tremble. Such an account or tale would be an αἶνος, a narrative or story that is inherently dark or riddlesome, enigmatic. Only now does one become aware that when Derrida raises the *question* of *being* and *history*, which is the title he chooses for his first seminar on Heidegger, that last word, *l'histoire*, means not only a history but also a story, precisely as the word *Geschichte* would have meant to Heidegger—one has to imagine it—a mere story, a tale. In that case, section 72 would be raising the question of the temporality not only of history but also of narrativity, hence of discourse as such:

> Enigmatic, therefore, is this discourse—and the enigma is always, as its Greek name, αἶνος, indicates, a discourse and even a story [*une histoire*]—enigmatic, therefore, is the discourse on history [*sur l'histoire*] at the moment it becomes necessary to talk about the *past*. Enigmatic is discourse on the past, enigmatic is the past as origin of discourse, enigmatic is historicity as discursivity. The time of the past in discourse and the past of time in *ek-sistence* are the enigma itself. They are not one set of enigmas among others but the enigma of enigma, the enigmatic source of enigma in general: enigmaticity. (257)

The reversion to *mythos*, that is, to multilayered discourses on the "always already," invariably takes us back to the earliest Greek thinkers, poets, and writers. "The Greeks were drawn to enigmas," writes Roberto Calasso, who then immediately poses the question, "But what is an enigma?"[2] It is far more than a "mysterious formulation" or a "problem." An enigma does not surrender its uncanny nature to any response we may make to it. Calasso himself reverts to the classic enigma, the riddle posed by the Sphinx to Oedipus: "What is the being that has but one voice [*una unica voce*] and yet sometimes has two feet, sometimes three, sometimes four, and is progressively weaker the more feet it has?" (ibid.). Oedipus's answer, ὁ ἄνθρωπος, *der Mensch*, *l'uomo*, remains as enigmatic in its unique voice as it does in its four-legged morning, its two-legged afternoon, and its three-legged, limping evening. His answer is as riddlesome as his own destiny, as enigmatic as the destiny of any woman or man born. Calasso comments:

---

2. Roberto Calasso, *Le nozze di Cadmo e Armonia* (Milan: Adelphi Edizioni, 1988), 384; translated by Tim Parks as *The Marriage of Cadmus and Harmony* (New York: Alfred A. Knopf, 1993), 343–44.

Resolving an enigma means shifting it to a higher level, as the first drops away. The Sphinx hints at the indecipherable nature of man, this elusive, multiform being whose definition cannot be otherwise than elusive and multiform. Oedipus was drawn to the Sphinx, and he resolved the Sphinx's enigma, but only to become an enigma himself. Thus anthropologists were drawn to Oedipus, and are still there measuring themselves against him, wondering about him. (Ibid.)

Anthropologists of all stripes—not to mention psychoanalysts and philosophers—continue to riddle on the riddle. In early lectures and essays of his, written just after the publication of *Being and Time*, Heidegger was fond of repeating the ironic phrase, *Was der Mensch sei, weiß jedermann* (W 82). "Everybody knows what human being is." Yet what about that "unique voice" of the human being?

Back in the second lecture I cited the four subsections of section 68, "The Temporality of Disclosedness in General," noting only that the subject of the fourth subsection, "discourse" or "speech," *die Rede*, touches on all the ecstases—if only because of the array of verb tenses in any given language. I neglected to note that Heidegger grants a special privilege to the present and to presencing, *Gegenwärtigen*, in discourse, even though he is careful to postpone the entire discussion until such time as "the problem of the fundamental nexus of being and truth [*Sein und Wahrheit*] is developed on the basis of the problematic of temporality" (SZ 349). This would have been the task of the third division, *Zeit und Sein*, which was never completed and never published. Yet what one must now stress is Derrida's resistance to "presencing" as the privileged ecstasis of discourse. Especially here the force of the *always already* is felt: for Derrida, as for Schelling, the *Geschehen* of *Geschichte*, the latter word meaning both *history* and the *recounting of a story*, the enigmaticity of the past and of all discourse on the past prevails.

Several times in his seminar Derrida depicts the enigma of the *present* ecstasis in a way that may help us to deal with the dissimulating present of metaphysics. To repeat, he defines the present, not as the horizon of all experience and the backdrop of all evidence, but as "the past of a future" (276). If earlier on in these lectures I expressed a worry about Heidegger's *Gewesenheit*, the present-perfect form of having-been that he prefers over *Vergangenheit*, the simple past or *Imperfekt*, Derrida assures us that having-been "is not a past present, a past now"; even if we call it present-perfect, the perfection of its imperfect present is nothing more than "the past of a future" (309). Likewise, the past object becomes "something possible [only] by returning to take its departure from a future that is bounded by death" (ibid.). That is as ecstatic as Derrida will ever get, enigmatically so. He would have admired the lyrics of a song popular these days on the German alternative rock and rap scene, a song by "Cro," who dons a panda mask whenever he performs, proclaiming somewhat wearily, *Heute war gestern schon morgen*. "Yesterday today was already tomorrow," or "Already yesterday today was tomorrow."[3] Which reminds me of an American ditty about the man who tries to take a train to the town of Morrow in the great state of Ohio. The station master tells him, "You cannot go to Morrow anymore today, 'cuz the train that goes to Morrow is a mile upon its way." In both cases, presence is no more than the irretrievable past of a closed future. And if ditties and pop songs are not enough to drive the point home, here is a passage from the opening of Martin Walser's *Der springende Brunnen*:

> As long as something is, it is not what it will have been. When something is over, one is no longer the one to whom it happened. True, one is closer to that one than to the others. Although the past was not there whenever it was present, it now imposes itself on us as though it had been there in the way it now imposes itself. Yet as long as something is, it is not what it will have been. When something is over, one is no longer the one to whom it happened. Whenever that concerning which we now say that it was *was*, we did not know it is. Now we say that it was such and such, even though back then, when it was, we knew nothing about what we are saying now.[4]

---

3. Thanks to my friend Joe Kemming for the reference to Cro the Panda.

4. "Solange etwas ist, ist es nicht das, was es gewesen sein wird. Wenn etwas vorbei ist, ist man nicht mehr der, dem es passierte. Allerdings ist man dem näher als anderen. Obwohl es die Vergangenheit, als sie Gegenwart war, nicht gegeben hat, drängt sie sich jetzt auf, als habe es sie so gegeben, wie sie sich jetzt aufdrängt. Aber solange etwas ist, ist es nicht das, was es gewesen sein wird. Wenn etwas vorbei ist, ist man nicht mehr der, dem es passierte. Als das war, von dem wir jetzt sagen, dass es gewesen sei, haben wir nicht gewußt, dass es ist. Jetzt sagen wir, dass es so und so gewesen sei, obwohl wir damals, als es war, nichts von dem wussten, was wir jetzt sagen." Martin Walser, *Ein springender Brunnen* ([Roman] Frankfurt am Main: Suhrkamp, 1998), 9. I am grateful to Gerhard Richter for the reference and for our detailed discussions on the (difficult!) translation of the Walser passage.

Which brings us to our third and final topic, the transmission of the past as heritage. The transmission of heritage, in Derrida's view, is itself an *ecstatic* process. Derrida develops this most difficult of his analyses in the penultimate session, the eighth, of the seminar. The most telling sign of the shortness of breath that characterizes the final sections of *Sein und Zeit*, he argues, is the paucity of description concerning the *Geschehen* of *Geschichte*, the "occurrence" or "happening" of history. The only two new terms introduced, according to Derrida, are "heritage," *das Erbe*, and the manner in which heritage is to be transmitted, *überliefert*; better, the way in which tradition transmits itself, *sich überliefert*. Derrida nominalizes this last as *Sichüberlieferung*, translating it as *auto-transmission* and relating it to a concept that will fascinate him up to the time of his death, namely, *pure auto-affection*. This last notion he traces back—or forward—to a very difficult moment of Heidegger's 1929 *Kant and the Problem of Metaphysics*. And that book, as always, will send us back to the first Critique, where all hope of ease of comprehension is lost.

"Auto-transmission" itself seems to promise ease, precisely because the transmission is automatic. Sheer *Fahrvergnügen*, one might say. Yet Derrida hastens to say that for Heidegger the transmission of heritage is not the movement of *consciousness* as presence to self, as it is for both Hegel and Husserl. Rather, auto-transmission takes the form of "an *ekstase, sortie de soi . . . and not presence to self*" (265). The familiar notion of repetition or reprise, *Wiederholung*, which is the fetching back of something that has been, a theme that Heidegger develops at great length in *Sein und Zeit* as the *proper* mode of the ecstasis of *Gewesenheit*, is anything but the command, "Play it again, Sam." If one thinks of the elements of a heritage as Husserlian "retentions," one must say that no living *present* embraces them, enabling us to reel these elements back as "evidence." Paradoxically, it is the unfolding of time itself that complicates the fetching. "Auto-affection and auto-tradition," writes Derrida, "are the very movement of the temporalization of time" (ibid.). So far, so good. If time and tide wash onto the shore bits and pieces of what has been, bleached and sanded down perhaps, but otherwise in good shape, then heritage is simply a matter of waiting and then beachcombing.

That this is not so Derrida tries to show by referring to section 34 of *Kant and the Problem of Metaphysics*, "Time as Pure Self-Affection and the Time-Character of the Self" (KPM 182–89). Here Heidegger comments on the B edition of the "Transcendental Aesthetic" of the first Critique, "Concerning Time" (B 66–70). The controversy has to do with Kant's effort in this second edition to think through the pure form of inner intuition, time, as a self-affection of the *Gemüt*—that impossible word that is not exactly the "mind," not exactly the "heart of hearts," but very much the core of the self. Kant's words, over which Heidegger and Derrida alike ruminate, are these: "*die Art, wie das Gemüt durch eigene Tätigkeit, nämlich dieses Setzen ihrer Vorstellung, mithin durch sich selbst affiziert wird, d. i. ein innerer Sinn seiner Form nach,*" which we might render, tremulously, as follows: "the way in which the *Gemüt* by means of its own activity, namely, this positing of the representation [of its relations, *Verhältnisse*, or of its own form, *Form der Anschauung*], is consequently affected by itself, that is, by an inner sense in accord with its form" (B 68). The issue is whether intellectual intuition is possible, or whether human intuition is always derivative. Kant repeats twice in the next few lines the phrase concerning self-affection ("*so muß es dasselbe [das, was im Gemüte liegt] affizieren . . . wie es von innen affiziert wird*"), so that it clear that "self-affection" is not self-love and not a pure presence to self but a being impacted, mediated, altered, *affected* from the inside by time itself. At the end of the paragraph, which neither Heidegger nor Derrida cites, Kant's meaning comes through: the *Gemüt* cannot represent itself as "immediately self-acting," but only "as it is affected from within, hence as it appears to itself, not as it is," *folglich wie es sich erscheint, nicht wie es ist* (B 69). For Heidegger, the conclusion is inevitable: whereas he believed, while writing *Sein und Zeit*, that Kant failed to provide "an analytic of the *Gemüt*" (SZ 25), by 1929 he is satisfied that the core of finite Dasein is finite time—and that already Kant knows this. If time affects itself and transmits itself, then at our core we are not self-activating, and we no longer need the ecstatic interpretation of temporality to demonstrate the finitude of Dasein. *Bewegtheit* suffices. Accordingly, in the long and detailed account of fundamental ontology with which *Kant and the Problem of Metaphysics* concludes, Heidegger disdains to mention ecstatic temporality—as though it had never been central to his effort. Derrida accepts this omission. It is enough if one recognizes that "all affection is a manifestation by which a being already given [*un étant déjà donné*] announces itself" (266). What affects me, even from within, is precisely what I have not created or constituted; I, thinking of myself thinking, come to myself always too late for that. Ultimately, for both Heidegger and Derrida, the result of such auto-affection is once again an enigma. Derrida writes: "time, being nothing, cannot as such affect anything else"; time is affection *of* itself *by* itself; time is auto-affection, "a concept as incomprehensible as is, in truth, the movement of temporalization" (ibid.). The only thing that is pellucid is that the self—which, as ostensibly "autonomous," *Selbst-ständig*, gave me trouble at the outset of these lectures—has no unmediated access either to the world or to itself. Affectivity is the transcendence of finite Dasein toward the world (267). Derrida stops just short—as Kant certainly also does—of calling such affectivity *dissimulation*. Yet if the "I think" never gave itself out as, never dissimulated itself as, pure presence to self, Kant would never have had to write about the most stubborn of those well-nigh inbred and even "destined" semblances, illusions, and subreptions that lead reason by the nose. Kant introduces the "Paralogisms of Pure Reason" by saying that "illusion" is "unavoidable but not indissoluble," a fairly tight distinction, you will agree (A 341; B 399).

Derrida continues to identify the transcendence of Dasein as "this exit from the self," *cette sortie hors de soi*, and as "its properly ecstatic movement," *son propre mouvement extatique* (272). He emphasizes, as Heidegger himself does, that an analytic of Dasein can say nothing about which aspects of one's heritage one in fact appropriates, nothing about how one elects one's heroes. He also emphasizes, as Heidegger does not and cannot, that any and every thinking of *Entschlossenheit* risks becoming a "voluntaristic radicalism" (273). And if resolute openness "runs ahead," as we have heard over and over again, Derrida has a novel translation for such *Vorlaufen*: he calls it *precursory* (276). Here the upper lip is not so stiff. As for choosing one's heroes, let us say only this: Childe Heidegger knows, but the adult Heidegger may have forgotten, that adolescence is the time when heroes are chosen, and it is they who choose us, precisely by auto-affection, not we who choose them. Or at least let us say that for an ecstatic being, it is always a question of elective affinities that are always already in play out there in the world.

I will have to cut short this consideration of the eighth session, which goes on to discuss auto-transmission precisely in terms of *Entschlossenheit* and the (unlikely) possibility of a recognizable ethics and politics in Heidegger. What there is in Heidegger is a new way to understand the present, not as perfect proximity and pure presence, but, to repeat, "as the past of a future" (276). This means that we must "live the present not as the origin and absolute form of experience," but as *ek-sistence*, which is to say, "as the product, the constituted, the derived, constituted by way of a return that takes its departure from the horizon of the future and the ecstasis of the future" (ibid.). The future proper can be encountered only precursorily, only as "the finite to-come," the *à-venir fini*, "which is to say, on the basis of the unsurpassability of a possible death" (ibid.). Such is our sole opening onto the future, "in which what we call the present is constituted in passing," *en passé*, the present itself "never appearing as such" (ibid.). Perhaps this is what Heidegger means when he stresses the *closure* of the future and the *oblivion* of the past?

Having begun with Lacan, and having then moved to Derrida, what else is left for me but to return to Schelling in order to conclude? Why not end enigmatically? In his *Ages of the World*, written three times and set three times in print, in 1811, 1813, and 1815, but then each time withdrawn from publication, Schelling tries to gain access to what he calls "the elevated past." He finds it impossible to escape from a present that is not so much living as of the living-dead; if as the Old Book says, there is nothing new under the sun, then it is time to change solar systems. It is also time to change philosophy, advancing from logic and dialectic to what Schelling calls narrative, *Erzählung*. The introduction to all three versions of the unpublished *Ages of the World* tells us that even when the past is known, the known remains to be "narrated." *Das Gewußte wird erzählt.*[5]

What sort of story have I been recounting about ecstatic temporality? In the first lecture, I asked how Heidegger's sense of the finitude of time can be preserved if not the future but having-been, *Gewesenheit*, becomes the "primary" ecstasis for analysis. In the second, with help from Aristotle's ἐξαίφνης, Augustine's *raptim*, and Hölderlin's *ex-zentrische Rapidität*, I asked whether the suddenness of the ecstases left traces of finitude. In the third, discovering in our "having-been" the "other end" of Dasein, the natality of our existence struck us as the very enigma of having-been. Bébé Dasein and Childe Heidegger gave our analysis of ecstasy a new lease on life, as it were, even if the attunement of anxiety remained at the heart of their life story. And even now, today, the seemingly confident cry, "You *are* that," betrays considerable anxiety. The ripple effect of our enigmatic past and problematic future—the aporia that we are not *present* to the experience of our birth and the phenomenon of our death—leads to the sudden collapse of "philosophical invulnerability." Tales of ecstatic temporality remain as vulnerable as all narratives must be. Yet our own time, careening dead ahead, and therefore unbeknownst to itself vulnerable through and through, in my view very much needs that narrative.

In the course of his meditation on the "oldest narratives" concerning "The Past," Schelling offers what he tenuously calls a *genealogy of time and of times*; even though he never uses the word *ecstatic* here, there is certainly something ecstatic about his genealogy and his narrative. Here too it is a matter of birth, albeit not of an absolute beginning, "since every beginning of time presupposes a time that already has been" (DW 75). Each moment of time and every epoch, eon, or age is thus born solely by way

---

5. For the source, and for further discussion, see chapter 4 of TA, "God's Trauma."

of what Schelling describes as a "polar holding-apart" of the entire mass of past and future, *nur in diesem polarischen Auseinanderhalten* (ibid.). Newborn moments in each case presuppose scissions, or *Scheidungen*, which are themselves compelled by love. Love is a search, *ein Suchen*, says Schelling, remembering the longing and languishing implied in the word *Sehnsucht.* Love is a search for the beginning and a being unable to find it, *Suchen und Nichtfindenkönnen des Anfangs* (ibid.). Time is generated from neither end nor beginning, therefore, but *in medias res*: "Thus time originates in every moment [*Augenblick*], indeed as the *whole* of time [*als* ganze *Zeit*], as time in which past, present, and future are dynamically held asunder, yet at the same time thereby held together" (74). Time opens up in the middle, as it were, between contraction and expansion, systole and diastole, the self-absorbed father and the prodigal son. Is time then a tale of fathers and sons alone? Or who is that there in the middle?

Love, especially the love of fathers and sons, is not the last word, not where birth is concerned. And as the word *search* has already suggested, the longing and languor of *Sehnsucht* becomes the word, even the Word. And the word *Sucht* in *Sehnsucht*, as Schelling knows full well, has as its etymon *Seuche*, hoof-and-mouth disease, or any dire, death-dealing epidemic. The longing of love can be like that. Observe young Werther stretched out languidly on his divan, languorously languishing for love, lingeringly extinguishing for love. Stretched out? Heidegger says that Dasein, between birth and death, is an ecstatic self-stretching, *Sich-erstreckung*. Derrida calls this notion of Heidegger's a "beautiful invention" (205).

You yourselves have already marveled over the self-stretching in that terrible final moment of another narrative that is not so old: you see her through the tram window that reflects the spring sunlight as though it were a looking-glass; you see Gregor Samsa's sister, Grete, who in the course of the story undergoes her own deformations. You see her now, in a present that is nothing more than the absolute past of an occluded future, her young body stretching languorously on the streetcar that later, elsewhere, is called "Desire." And that would be enigma enough for one eon.

Interlude

Some Indefensible Ideas About Polemic and Criticism

Note: This Brauer Lecture was delivered at Brown University in autumn 2012, that is to say, two years before my lecture series on ecstatic temporality in Heidegger and also two years before the publication of Heidegger's Black Notebooks. *The lecture has not been published previously, and I thought it would provide a gentle introduction to this second part of the book, which otherwise makes for very unpleasant reading, to say the least. The theme of the interlude is polemic and criticism in general, to which I oppose the idea of* Hingebung, *literally, "giving-over," in the sense of a devotion to someone or something that seems to eliminate critical distance. Whether one can devote oneself to anything and everything, "give over" to anyone and everyone, is of course the spanner in the works, as the English like to say. On the more positive side, the lecture argues for the magnification of what is great in past efforts at artistic creativity and thinking. Once again, I have not tried to alter the lecture style, and I have edited the material only slightly for publication here. The easy familiarity of the style gives an impression—a correct impression—of the hospitality of the faculty and students of Brown University, where polemic, at least in my experience, plays no role at all.*

Every genuine philosopher would rightly insist that an idea is not an idea if it cannot be defended: an idea must have contours—otherwise it is no εἶδος—and these contours must either arise from or produce something like walls, and walls must be defended against siege, or else there is no idea to speak of. There is instead some messy intuition, some vague notion unworthy of a public airing. Yet I stand before you the victim of certain convictions, held for a long time now, certain ideas and beliefs about polemic, criticism, and what I will call "giving-over," ideas that seem to me both convincing and indefensible, and I have decided to talk about them this evening. To come out of the closet. In my new clothes.

Perhaps these indefensible ideas are mere quirks and tics of mine, mere symptoms of my own private hysteria. Yet I have been acting on these ideas for decades now, as though they were my compass in a snowstorm. With your indulgence, I would like to try to formulate them here, refine them if I can, even hone them. Not defend them, however, because I suspect they are indefensible. Each idea has a story or two behind it, and while philosophers do not countenance storytelling, there are surely no philosophers present, and I myself have largely retired from the field.

First story, and first indefensible idea. I attended a conference on Heidegger in Berlin back in the 1980s, in the midst of one of the endless series of Heidegger scandals. The sponsors had invited me to attend, I believe, for the sole purpose of my sitting next to—and thereby babysitting—the famous critic whom they had invited as plenary speaker. The critic had dabbled a bit in philosophy, and that was enough to permit him to pontificate on Heidegger. Over the entire weekend I was forced to listen to the scathing remarks—more often personal than professional or scholarly—that the critic hissed into my ear as each nervous presenter spoke, doing his or her best, but to no avail. By the end of the weekend I was so full of poison, so full of his venom, that I vowed I would never read a word of his work. Indefensible idea number one: a vicious person cannot do good critical work; it may look like good work, and it may be based on a mastery of ancient Greek, Latin, and all contemporary European languages; but it can only *look like* good work, so that one may in fact ignore it without peril. Ortega y Gasset once observed that a colleague of his was able to bore everyone in nineteen different languages, and I rejoin that glossolalia, if it is venomous, is best avoided—and that it can be avoided with impunity.

Surely, this idea is indefensible. A remarkably spiteful person can be a competent scholar, can he or she not? Some of our most gifted authors and artists seem to have been obstreperous and sometimes highly unpleasant characters. Breakfast with Joyce? High tea with Beckett? How about a friendly chat with Jackson Pollock? But I rejoin, rather desperately, that if Joyce and Beckett had been as rancorous as my charge, they would not have written *Portrait of the Artist* or *Company*, and Pollock would not have painted. No, I stick with my idea, febrile in theory (since it is indefensible) but potent in practice: I am now as I was then innocent of all knowledge of this critic's two dozen books, some of which treat directly themes that concern me closely and on which I have written and published my own meager books—without reference to him. Shame on me, you may say. I reply that if my idea is wrongheaded, indefensible as it is, I prefer to quit the scholarly world and go back to my first job, which was mowing lawns, or my second, which was driving a taxicab nights in Pittsburgh, Pennsylvania, where there's a pawn shop on the corner, since after all life is at bottom powerful and pleasurable yet also short and therefore not to be wasted.

Is it simply cornball to expect that a healthy dose of humanity—of humaneness or simple courtesy—accompany intellectual acuity? Does heart really have to accompany head? Is it indeed the case that all thinking, as Empedocles of Acragas speculated, is "pericardial," that is, carried by the blood that flows through and around the heart, not the brain? Is one a sentimental fool to insist on at least a minimal flow of liberality even in our critics?

There are so many stories I could tell that go in the opposite direction of my babysitting story. For example, the story of Hannah Arendt insisting that I stop at a pharmacy on our way to Heidegger's house in Zähringen ("One does not go with a runny nose to see the greatest thinker of the twentieth century"), in spite of the fact that she raised the most relentless criticisms against that thinker's fatal mistakes and flaws. Stories also of the elderly Heidegger's many kindnesses to me, although he was a very old man by then, but even so, kindnesses and acts of genuine generosity. Stories of Jacques Derrida, who whenever we met never failed to ask after the health and well-being of my mother and my wife and children, naming them all by name, exercising always and everywhere a generosity well beyond anything one might have expected. My favorite Derrida story is caught on film. A flustered undergraduate in California approaches him after his lecture and says to him, "I just wanted to say that I read one of your novels and I really loved it," and he replies, without a hint of irony or condescension, "Thank you, you are very kind."

In short, throughout my perhaps excessively sheltered and fortunate life, the great minds that I have met and at least to some degree worked with were persons who had what horse breeders call "depth through the heart." I recall in all of them their capacity to make sharp judgments; it isn't that they were beautiful souls and milksops. We were looking at a proposed English translation of Heidegger's Hölderlin lectures when Hannah Arendt brushed the manuscript aside with the remark, "This translator has wooden ears." And that, as they say, was that. Yet by and large the errors that thinkers have made, at least in my presence, have always been on the side of generosity.

A second, but related, indefensible idea. In a late lecture course (from the Winter Semester 1951–52), Heidegger talks about polemic. I am interested in his remarks because Heidegger himself, in his lecture courses during the 1920s and '30s, could be mordant, even sardonic. *(In his private notes from the 1930s, as we shall see, he could be much worse than that.)* He was no stranger to polemic. Yet in 1951, as he was thinking about what it is we call thinking, and what it is that in our time *calls on us* to think, Heidegger says that polemic never rises to the level of thinking. "Every kind of polemic fails from the start to attain the stance of thinking. The role of an opponent is not the role of thinking. For a thinking is indeed thinking only when it pursues what speaks *for* a thing" (WhD? 49). Only what magnifies the greatness of a prior thinking rises to the level of thinking. Such magnification may make look lackluster when we would prefer to be terrifically—and bitingly—original. Nevertheless, however servile the magnification of past efforts may make us seem, and however much we relish the pizzazz of the trenchant critic, I believe in this need for magnification, even if I am not sure if I ever achieve it, since it takes so much hard work. Of course, I also worry about the claim that one can identify with assurance the "greatness" of past works of art and thought, those that are "worth" our magnifying them. There is a presumption there that needs to be kept at bay. Even so, magnification of what one, whether rightly or wrongly, takes to be magnificent seems to me the fitting task always and everywhere.

If I ever did achieve magnification, it must have been in the old days, when I taught American and English literature at the University of Freiburg. (I was given the job because I was a native speaker, not because I knew anything about literature.) Whereas my colleagues were genuine *Literaturwissenschaftler*, real scholars of literature, whose critical abilities always amazed me, and from whom I learned most of what I know about literature, I was just a fan. But perhaps the finest teaching I have ever done, and not only in my own estimation, since a number of my German students from the 1970s are still in close touch with me, involved my merely selecting passages from the works of Melville, Whitman, Dickinson, Emerson, Yeats, and Joyce, and saying, "Hey, listen to this," then reading aloud to them. Without much commentary, without having much of critical importance to say. What more is there to magnify if one speaks briefly about the meanings of the word *antique* and then recites Dickinson's "The Bible is an antique Volume"? It is not that I scorned the relevant critical literature or the methods of rigorous stylistic and rhetorical analysis. Far from it. It is that I was ignorant of them. Indefensibly, I preferred and still do prefer this ignorance over the danger of obstructing the reader's contact with the text in question.

On rare occasions (I *hope* rare), I have engaged in polemic, for instance, when the structure of a conference or the agenda of a discussion seemed either hopelessly inane or excessively dogmatic. In those instances I played all the nasty tricks I had learned in "forensics" during my high school and college years, seeking to humiliate and devastate an opponent, causing him or her to self-destruct before an audience. But I wasn't *thinking* at those moments. I wasn't saying, "Hey, listen to this." I was begging, "Please, stop this. Just stop." Or perhaps, at my sympathetic best, *O Freunde, nicht diese Töne! Lasst uns angenehmere anstimmen, und freudenvollere.*

Allow me to mention some instances of polemic that particularly horrify me. Hegel, in his lectures on aesthetics, castigates the Romantics, especially Friedrich Schlegel, the author of *Lucinde.* He also has a go at the admirable Friedrich von Hardenberg, "Novalis," although Hegel concedes that Novalis is a nobler spirit than Schlegel. Novalis, like Keats, died at age twenty-nine, leaving behind him an astonishing amount of work in poetry, fiction, philosophy, and science—for he was a mining inspector as well as a writer. His fiancée Sophie von Kühn had died at age fifteen of tuberculosis; Novalis too died of consumption a few years later. Novalis once noted that God must be heavy metal—otherwise oxygen would hollow out his lungs. Hegel, in his lectures on aesthetics, declares with obvious scorn that the characters and situations of Novalis's literary works are "hollow"; unsatisfied with this, he diagnoses Novalis himself as suffering from a "consumption of the spirit," *Schwindsucht des Geistes.* I remember feeling vaguely ill when I read those words of Hegel's. The polemic did Novalis no harm, to be sure. Yet what a slur against spirit, against Hegel's *Geist,* perhaps against *Geist* "as such," if one may say so: to mock another man's mortal illness in order to win a few points on the "wit" scale. What damage to Hegel himself and to his vaunted system!

At the risk of offending the sensibilities of my friend Gerhard Richter, I want to mention another instance of polemic, this time in one of Gerhard's heroes, namely, Theodor W. Adorno. As a music critic, Adorno is endlessly polemical, even with the composers he admires. Perhaps the worst instance of his polemic is his apoplectic response to Jean Sibelius in 1938. Wolfgang Rihm has meanwhile done us and Sibelius the service of showing that Adorno is wrong with respect to virtually every one of his complaints, but that does nothing to ameliorate the ugliness of Adorno's attack. A brief extract:

> Here is how matters stand: any old completely formless and trivial sequence of tones is constructed, tones that usually are not even fully harmonized, presented unisono with points of organ pedal, soporific harmonies and whatever else the five lines of a musical staff can produce in order to avoid a logical progression

of chords. These sequences of tones soon enough experience a setback, somewhat in the manner of a suckling babe that falls off a table and injures its spine. They cannot really walk. They remain stuck where they are.[1]

Now, whatever one may think of Sibelius, and whatever one may hear or fail to hear in Sibelius's music, suckling infants should not be allowed to fall, injure their spines, and be crippled for life. Adorno's polemic is barbaric, as barbaric as the very things he is always so prepared to call barbaric. Nonetheless, his polemic has its unintended comic side: how many listeners have complained concerning Adorno's own heroes—Schönberg, Berg, and Webern—that their sequences of tones are formless (except for the sterile logic of avoidance that is the serial twelve-tone row) and unharmonic. One can only hope that these critics of the second Vienna school (and I insist that I am *not* one of them) at least leave the suckling babes of both Vienna and Helsinki unharmed. If polemic in philosophy never rises to the level of thinking, polemic in music criticism is more often than not the proclamation, as the old song says, "I won't dance, don't ask me." But the refusal to trip the light fantastic is not a critical virtue, and it may not be a sign of critical acumen at all; it is most likely an incapacity of the heart. How much of our criticism rests on such incapacitation? A proud young Inca tour guide, showing some modern tourists the massive, solid walls at Machu Picchu, announces as he points toward those walls, "Los Inca." Then, pointing to a dilapidated wall built by the conquistadores, a wall now in ruins, he announces, "Los Inca-paces." How can we form for ourselves a culture that builds instead of tears down, a culture of capacities instead of incapacities? By *capacity* I do not mean some "faculty" or "power" or "agency," but an enhanced receptivity coupled with enormous energy for work. We rightly dream of such a culture.

And yet. How much in our world, so regularly inane and predictably vicious as it is, cries out for polemic! Even if the satisfaction we get from polemic wilts as soon as it escapes our lips, do we not justifiably crave such satisfaction? And even if we overcome the worst aspects of our professional academic deformation, do we not need polemic in order to survive the *Dummheit* that surrounds us? How should one respond to Fox? What can we say of the U.S. House of Representatives—other than what Samuel

---

1. T. W. Adorno, "Glosse über Sibelius," in Adorno, *Gesammelte Schriften*, 20 vols. (Frankfurt am Main: Suhrkamp, 1982), 17:247.

Langehorn Clemens has already so scathingly written? Some suggest that even in our universities polemic is called for. . . . Are not some wars just wars, as Aquinas, Kant, and Carl Schmitt all agree? I leave the question in suspense.

One further word about polemic. A word from Novalis, who often has wise things to say. In the following "Logological Fragment" (CHV 2:313), he indicates how often polemic fails to stand the test of time. More often than not, he says, it merely displays some battle we are still fighting with ourselves, or *were* fighting, but a battle that now seems superfluous. He writes:

> In every philosophy one has to be able to distinguish between the contingent and the essential. To the contingent belongs a philosophy's polemical side. In later times these earlier opinions, devoted to refutation and shunting aside, seem to us oddly out of place, like wasted efforts—. Actually, such polemic is a battle we are still fighting with ourselves [*noch eine Selbstbekämpfung*]—as though the thinker who has outgrown this earlier phase is still disturbed by the prejudices of his school years, a disturbance that in more enlightened times he can really no longer comprehend, since he feels no need to seek safety in opposing them.

Polemic, then, is the comet's tail among heavenly bodies, evoking our applause, but only briefly. Or, vulgarizing the image, we may say that polemic is the belated outburst of a feisty adolescence, one that has already had its fling.

Allow me to insert a "last word" about polemic. Long after I had read and cited Adorno's "Glosse über Sibelius," I had the occasion to read a passage in Adorno's Ästhetische Theorie *that shows how very unpolemical Adorno can be. I had just completed the second pass of proofs for a book on Derrida's unpublished* Geschlecht III, *which itself is a detailed reading of Heidegger's second essay on Georg Trakl, "Die Sprache im Gedicht: eine Erörterung von Georg Trakls Gedicht." My book, under the title* Phantoms of the Other, *concludes with a chapter on Georg and Gretl Trakl, the tragically fated brother and sister whose "magnetism," both for one another and for Derrida and Heidegger, I was trying to understand. To my astonishment, I found the most remarkable account of this magnetism in Adorno's aesthetic theory. The context is Adorno's striking analysis of enigmaticity,* Rätselhaftigkeit, Rätselcharakter, *in the work of art; such enigmaticity, he argues, removes the work to a distant terrain that not even the sturdiest hermeneutical vehicle can cross. Adorno's prime examples*

*are taken from music, as always; yet at a certain point he shifts from musical
composition proper to the use of musical metaphor in poetry. His example is
Trakl's use (in "Psalm") of the word* Sonaten, *the sonatas (probably by Schubert,
if one succumbs to the temptation to try to identify them) that Georg hears
his sister Grete playing in the next room. Allow me to cite the passage in full,
because it is a prime instance not of polemic but of magnification of greatness
in the work of art:*

> The word *sonata* in Trakl's poems attains a value that comes to it
> there alone, by means of its sound [*Klang*] and the associations
> to which the poem itself guides us. If one wished to imagine a
> particular sonata on the basis of these diffuse sounds, one would
> miss what the word wants to do within the poem; one would also
> quite inappropriately conjure up the *imago* of this or that sonata
> and the sonata form in general. Nonetheless such conjuring up
> would be legitimate, since it would build upon fragments and
> shards of sonatas, and the very name *sonata* reminds us of the
> sound that is meant and that the poem itself awakens. The term
> refers to highly articulated, thematically elaborated motifs, the
> unity of which is comprised of markedly distinct manifolds, with
> development and reprise. The line, "*Es sind Zimmer, erfüllt von
> Akkorden und Sonaten*" ("It is rooms reverberating with chords
> and sonatas"), does not bring all that much with it, but it does
> achieve the feeling that children have when they pronounce
> the name; it has more to do with the misnomer "Moonlight
> Sonata" than with the composition as such, and yet there is no
> contingency here. Without the sonatas that the sister played
> there would have been no articulated sounds, sounds quite apart
> [*die abgeschiedenen Laute*], in which the melancholy of the poet
> seeks refuge.[2]

This was everything the seventh and last chapter of my Phantoms of the
Other *tried to say, and the fact that Adorno said it without my knowing the*

---

2. Theodor W. Adorno, *Ästhetische Theorie*, ed. Gretel Adorno and Rolf Tiedemann
(Frankfurt am Main: Suhrkamp-Taschenbuch Wissenschaft, 2000 [1970]), 186. My
translation differs somewhat from that of Robert Hullot-Kentor, which is nonetheless
admirably clear. See Adorno, *Aesthetic Theory* (Minneapolis: University of Minnesota
Press, 1997), 122–23.

fact leads me to a final remark, as I hope, about polemic, which is that we are seldom in a place where we can afford to be polemical. So much for the "we." As for me, I learn—or fail to learn—over and over again that I am never in a place that permits polemic.[3]

Let me set polemic aside, therefore, and turn to more general questions of criticism. A disclaimer: I do not want to set criticism and creative capacities in too stark an opposition. The oldest cliché concerning the critic is that he or she is a "Rafael without hands," a dancer without rhythm, a singer without a voice. Think of all those students of musicology who could not master their instrument, all those students of drama who could not act, all those poets who could not write—what else is left for them to do? Abandoned as they are to pursue a love that will never be requited, how dare we raise a voice against them? How can we expect their life be anything other than a protracted exercise in *ressentiment*? Of course, in addition to *ressentiment* there is always the possibility of sheer incompetence. Recall Mr. Curdle, Dickens's Shakespeare critic in *Nicholas Nickleby*. Curdle, writes Dickens,

> had written a pamphlet of sixty-four pages, post octavo, on the character of the Nurse's deceased husband in Romeo and Juliet, with an inquiry whether he really had been a 'merry man' in his lifetime, or whether it was merely his widow's affectionate partiality that induced her so to report him. He had likewise proved, that by altering the received mode of punctuation, any one of Shakespeare's plays could be made quite different, and the sense completely changed; it is needless to say, therefore, that he was a great critic, and a very profound and most original thinker.

Several pages later, when Curdle is asked to define the "classical unities" on which he is forever expatiating, he wheys in (sic) with the following: "'The unities, sir,' he said, 'are a completeness—a kind of universal dovetailedness with regard to place and time—a sort of general oneness, if I may be allowed to use so strong an expression.'"

---

3. Allow me to add one more point about the complexity that always defeats polemic, in this case my remarks above about the applicability of Adorno's criticisms of Sibelius to the practitioners of the serial twelve-tone row: it appears that Adorno himself comes very close to such a critique of seriality, at least the "recent" use of it, insofar as seriality may be a mere mathematization of composition. See Adorno, *Ästhetische Theorie*, 214–15; English translation, 142–43.

As I said, however, such pomposity and incompetence constitute the oldest clichés concerning the critic, not entirely indefensible, but hardly fair. Criticism? What *is* it? Are there not sundry *kinds* of criticism, and is not anything we say about it in general indefensible? It seems that the polemic one might wish to aim *against* criticism is reducible to the bons mots of weak criticism itself. Some of these bon mots, to be sure, are truly *beaux.* Here is Jean Paul: "Among all the instruments the kettledrum is hardest to tune—the kettledrum and the book reviewer." And here is Nietzsche, from the second part of *Human, All-Too-Human: "To the Credit of the Critics.*—Insects bite, not out of malevolence, but because they too want to live: just so, our critics; they want our blood, not our pain" (KSA 2:445). Yet on occasion these reflections so critical of criticism reach far beyond the quip; they go deep down into the origins of those cultures that have been shaped by philosophy and science, down to the very seedbeds of criticism. In his very first book, *The Birth of Tragedy from the Spirit of Music,* Nietzsche defines "Socratism" as the degeneration of creative instincts, the instincts of an Aeschylus or a Sophocles, to criticism, that is, the transformation of artistic creativity into a form of consciousness, *Bewusstsein.* Socrates becomes "a true monstrosity—*per defectum,*" and the otherwise childless Greek spawns all the rest of us academicians. True, the modern critic is no Socrates, who has his own undeniable if eccentric Eros. Here are some extracts from an unpublished fragment of Nietzsche's, a note on modernity as shaped by *Kritizismus:*

> *"Modernity"* viewed via the simile of nourishment and digestion. . . . [T]he plethora of disparate impressions is greater than ever:—*cosmopolitanism* of foodstuffs, literatures, newspapers, forms, tastes, even landscapes.
>
> The tempo of this stream is *prestissimo;* the impressions erase one another; one defends oneself instinctively against taking something in, letting it go deep, becoming something one would have to "digest"[.]
>
> The result is a *weakening* of the digestive force. A kind of *adaptation* to this surfeit of impressions occurs: the human being loses the power to *act;* he or she merely reacts to extrinsic excitations. *Expends his or her energies* partly in *appropriation,* partly in *defense,* partly in *refutation.*
>
> *A profound weakening of spontaneity:*—the historian, the critic, the analyst, the interpreter, the observer, the collector,

the reader—all these are *reactive* talents—they are *all* science [*Wissenschaft*]!

Artificial *adjustment* of one's nature to that of a "mirror"; interested, but only epidermically interested, as it were: a fundamental coolness, an equilibrium, a temperature *kept low* under the thin surface, the surface on which there is something warm, something moving, some "storm" and surging surf.

Contrast between this *external* animatedness to a certain *profound heaviness and weariness.* (KSA 12:464)

These incisive words of Nietzsche's recoil on the one who writes them. (How do we imagine Nietzsche discerned these things about modern criticism? It was by the same inculcated discipline through which he knew about Protestant Christianity—it's always all in the family.) Surely it is indefensible, untenable, unjustifiable, to say that a life of learning—which would be criticism at its very best—remains a reactive strategy, preeminently a form of surfeit, exhaustion, *ressentiment*, or what Melville likes to call *dyspepsia*? Besides, criticism without teeth seems itself to be an indefensible idea. Creative criticism (not "constructive" criticism, which often merely masks its rancor), criticism arising from a truly creative surge—do we ever find it? Of course we do. At the moment I think of André Bleikasten's splendid books on Faulkner's *As I Lay Dying* and *The Sound and the Fury*; surely every major writer and artist has found his or her Bleikasten. And Shakespeare criticism is not always "curdled." Not surprisingly, we often find that the best criticism comes from the hands of artists and writers who in addition to their criticism have their own lives to lead, as it were. Allow me four examples, which reflect my own very limited experience: Sergei Prokofiev on Rachmaninov, Maurice Blanchot on Kafka, Jacques Derrida on just about everyone, and, my personal favorite, D. H. Lawrence on Walt Whitman.

How could one expect Prokofiev—with his daring leaps of melody and harmony, his modulations to a new key after almost every measure, his dissonances, and the rhythms that drove Diaghilev's dancers crazy—to have a sympathetic word for Rachmaninov? Rachmaninov limits himself to the smallest possible range of variations in tone, harmony, and rhythm; compared to Prokofiev, Rachmaninov seems condemned to produce a very cramped sort of music. Yet the only word of criticism I know from Prokofiev, who concedes all that I have just said about the last great Romantic composer, is this: "And yet, sometimes he managed to fit amazingly beautiful themes into that small range." For those of us who love Rachmaninov in spite of all the repetitions and the apparent lack of experimentation, love him simply because his melodies and harmonies invade our emotional ear and work their effects on us willy-nilly, Prokofiev's words are a source of comfort, even if we have to replace his "sometimes" with "almost always." And Prokofiev's generosity causes us to admire him in turn, and to love him as much for his *Cinderella* as for his second symphony.

Blanchot on Kafka? Endlessly, throughout his life, Blanchot was reading Kafka and writing about Kafka, always magnifying the greatness of Kafka. Yet at the same time always elaborating his own idea of the narrative voice, the neuter and neutral voice of narrative, precisely with the aid of Kafka's tales. Kafka holds Blanchot's writing hand as it performs the critical gesture. Never enough night when one is writing, says Kafka, and Blanchot responds by speculating on what he calls "the *other* night." When matters become critical, and they become critical when Blanchot writes about Kafka's response to the feminine world, one will often have to demur; one will dare to say "no" to Blanchot. But it will be a halting "no," unsure of its own desires and resistances, a "no" very much in the form of an indefensible idea. It seems we can and must on occasion say "no" even when the criticism is very much on target.

Derrida on just about everyone, I joked a moment ago. Yet the joke is on us. So much of the invective showered on deconstruction and its "founder," or better, its "finder," arises simply from the universal astonishment at the breadth and depth of the man's reading. One can devote one's life to gaining expertise in a certain field, one can be the world's greatest Proust expert, or the world's second-greatest Proust expert, and then read one relatively brief essay by Little Mister Sunshine, and the hierarchy is upset forever. Another little story. My first contact with Derrida was through intermediaries, some American commentators who seemed to me mere jugglers with words. I resisted, and I polemicized, until a former teacher of mine came to visit me in Germany. He pressed into my hot little hands a book Derrida had written on Nietzsche and Heidegger titled *Éperons: les styles de Nietzsche.* Now, I had written my doctoral dissertation on Heidegger's *Nietzsche,* all eleven hundred pages of it, and I was engaged at that time in editing and translating those pages; as far as I was concerned, the conversation involved Nietzsche, Heidegger, and *me.* How alarmed I was when I read Derrida's *Spurs.* The conversation had changed; the circle had expanded. What was Derrida's secret? It lay in what he called a "double reading." No one talks or writes about this anymore—we prefer simpler methods nowadays, we are so weary—so let me say just a word about it, not with regard to *Spurs* but concerning the project Derrida called *Geschlecht,* referring to Heidegger's cryptic and rarely read utterances on lineage, generation, gender, and sex.

Heidegger and sex? That too must be a joke. Virtually every postwar thinker, especially if he or she was French, showed that sex was nonexistent in Heidegger's *Existenz*. In an article called *Geschlecht I*, Derrida uncovered some remarkable asseverations by Heidegger on sexuality, which is one facet of *Geschlecht*, and he announced a plan to produce three more generations of this *Geschlecht*, all the way down to Heidegger's exceedingly challenging readings of the Austrian poet Georg Trakl in the 1950s. In the inaugural article, *Geschlecht I*, Derrida took very seriously the traditional (French) critique of Heidegger, showing in greater detail than any prior reader of Heidegger how suspect, how banal, how *metaphysical* Heidegger's pronouncements concerning human embodiment and sexuality in fact seem to be. The first half of Derrida's *Geschlecht I* is therefore devastating: one wants to help Heidegger up off the floor, call him an ambulance. And then comes the second half of the double reading. What if all this talk on Heidegger's part—of the prepotency of sex in a neutral and neuter Dasein, which is *das* Dasein after all—actually opens the possibility of multiple sexualities and multiple sexes and genders in our time? What if Heidegger's were not one of those endless discourses on sexuality about which Michel Foucault complains in the first volume of *The History of Sexuality* and against which Herbert Marcuse inveighs in *One-Dimensional Man* but the startling announcement of something unheard-of, something never proposed by a thinker before Heidegger?

With a single writing hand, as it were, Derrida demolishes the Heideggerian text, uncovering all its hopeless and hapless strategies and painful obfuscations, and then, using the other hand, he celebrates the possibility that, whatever weaknesses may have marred this thought, *thinking of the highest order is going on there*, a thinking that has to be magnified rather than belittled. Derrida never mocks, it seems to me, no matter how trenchant his readings can be. He never strikes a match to burn a book or an author. For there is always that second half, that more generous half, of his reading—the complimentary complement, as it were.[4]

After Derrida, D. H. Lawrence looks positively curmudgeonly. So cranky he is! Many of you know Lawrence's text on Whitman, know it much better than I. But I wonder if you can imagine the shock I felt when

---

4. For further discussion of this theme, see my *Phantoms of the Other: Four Generations of Derrida's* Geschlecht (Albany: SUNY Press, 2015), *passim.*

I read for the first time *Studies in Classic American Literature*. I have read it over and over again in the intervening years, not only for Whitman, but for Melville and all the others, and I have repeatedly quoted and paraphrased it in my own writing.

In the cruelest possible way Lawrence begins, as though to outdo Hegel and to give Adorno lessons in polemic. Whitman is fat, Whitman is greasy, Whitman *leaks*. His poetry dribbles all over the page and out into the universe. Whitman's leaves are parchment, that is, saturated sheep fat. Whitman, the emoting bore, the arrogant democrat, heart on sleeve, slobbering over his poems, squandering his self. On and on it goes, Lawrence's invective, Lawrence's contumely. For example, this:

> Post-mortem effects. Ghosts.
>
> A certain ghoulish insistency. A certain horrible pottage of human parts. A certain stridency and portentousness. A luridness about his beatitudes. . . .
>
> Your self.
>
> Oh, Walter, Walter, what have you done with it? What have you done with yourself? With your own individual self? For it sounds as if it had all leaked out of you, leaked into the universe.
>
> Post-mortem effects. The individuality had leaked out of him.
>
> No, no, don't lay this down to poetry. These are postmortem effects. And Walt's great poems are really huge fat tomb-plants, great rank graveyard growths.
>
> All that false exuberance. All those lists of things boiled in one pudding-cloth! No, no! (. . .)
>
> This awful Whitman. This post-mortem poet. This poet with the private soul leaking out of him all the time. All his privacy leaking out in a sort of dribble, oozing into the universe.[5]

Lawrence goes on like this for pages, not merely paragraphs: his polemic is vitriolic, merciless, accurate. Every lover of Whitman, abashed, quashed, tries to save his hero, concedes, *yes he's a bit overweight, but let's say he's pleasingly plump, he's had a stroke for god's sake, lay off! And yes, he's all heart on sleeve and on trousers and on a Manhatto bus, and yes his lines go*

---

5. D. H. Lawrence, *Studies in Classic American Literature* (Harmondsworth, UK: Penguin, 1971), 171, 173–74, and 179.

*on for forever, like Bob Dylan's, never quite fitting into the music, yes, it's all
true, I confess it abjectly, I love a failed poet.* Lawrence forces this confession
from us. And then? Then comes a paragraph break, a simple paragraph
break like all the others, giving not a hint of the shift that is imminent.
Whereupon we read the following:

> Whitman, the great poet, has meant so much to me. Whit-
> man, the one man breaking a way ahead. Whitman, the one
> pioneer. And only Whitman. No English pioneers, no French.
> No European pioneer-poets. . . . Ahead of Whitman, nothing.
> Ahead of all poets, pioneering into the wilderness of unopened
> life, Whitman. Beyond him, none.

I have used Lawrence's lines, "Ahead of Whitman, nothing, beyond
him, none" with respect to the great poets of my own private and indefensible love life, above all, Hölderlin. Ahead of Hölderlin, nothing and no
one! Such exclamations are always indefensible, even if ideas of a rough and
ready sort urge them, and even if one is in very good critical company. It
remains true, however, that one loves the poets one loves. And love, as we
know, is indefensible.

What is the secret of capable and honest criticism? After all, we do
not read a critic to hear litanies of adoration. We read our writers and we
hear our musicians themselves and we worship in private. If we read critics
at all it is to enlarge our sensibility and to learn new modes and motets
for our liturgy. What is the secret? I was driven by this question to write
a short story called "At Bottom—Life." The story is about a critic who at
the beginning of the story is found dead in his drab apartment. The dead
critic was clearly a pervert: a policeman finds him with his head leaning
against the sacroiliac of a female mannequin that is seated at a piano. The
corpse is decomposing; the scene is unpleasant. It's the pits, in fact; it's rock
bottom. Yet, at bottom, there's life. The policeman discovers a document
beside the corpse, an account of the dead man's relationship—real or imag-
ined, we do not know—with a famous French pianist, a pianist of the most
extraordinary talent and beauty. I will not bore you with further details,
although I'd love to read you the story sometime. I simply want to stress
the undeniable—and indefensible—happenstance that the critic (for in an
earlier life he was a music critic for an important Chicago daily) has failed
to know the dancer from the dance. That is to say, he has fallen hopelessly
in love with the artist as well as with her music. He has *given over* entirely,
he has sacrificed every brain cell and every fiber of his erstwhile vibrant

life to this woman who plays the piano. She plays it very well, no doubt. And the critic knows enough about music to convince the reader—even a policeman—that her talent and dedication reveal the essence of the best. We may mock his enthusiasm; enthusiasm, as Kant demonstrates, always invites mockery. We scoff, we *insist* that one distinguish between the dancer and the dance. Yet, as Paul de Man says, *no one* can tell the dancer from the dance, no one can rigorously distinguish between them, and this inability is precisely Yeats's point. True, we hate those effete groupies who sip their very expensive wines and who, coming and going, talk of Michelangelo or Rachmaninov, confusing biography for work, worshiping the artist while oblivious of the art. We want very much to be one of those critics who can tell the dance from the dancer, critics who retain "critical distance," an expression that encapsulates our faith and our hope as it abolishes our charity. We do not want to die at the backside of a mannequin. We do not want to be slain by a statue, as Nietzsche's Zarathustra says. And yet. There is something about this "giving-over," the surrender of criticism to a languor that in my view allows for greater devotion to creativity, and I want to dedicate the rest of my indefensible remarks to it.

"Giving-over" tries to translate, in an all-too-literal way, the German *Hingebung* or *Hingabe*, usually rendered as "devotion" or "devotedness." It is a word that fascinated Hegel. For him *Hingebung* is the essence of phenomenology, inasmuch as the phenomenologist must give him- or herself over to appearances in order to cultivate the science of the experience of consciousness. When philosophy remains intransigent, stolid and stiff, it exhibits the dogmatism that criticism always wants and needs to disrupt. The problem for Hegel, however, is that *Hingebung* is a word most often attributed to what women do when they fall hopelessly in love. It is a word used very often by Friedrich Schlegel in his novel *Lucinde*, although Schlegel perversely attributes *Hingebung* to Lucinde and Julius alike. That is why Hegel hates this novel more than any other text. A man's job, in Hegel's view, is to prevent the "weaker sex" from giving over too soon. He's got to get her to the altar as quickly as possible—Oh, get her to the church on time! he pleads—in order that the "natural" order of events is reversed, nature being a sort of trap, and sexual congress *follow* rather than *precede* marriage. It's all about the horse and carriage, this love and marriage affair. Women are allowed to give over, all right, but only if the man has given himself over to her—not emotionally, because that too is a lure of nature, but legally, ecclesiastically, publicly.

I do not want to focus on Hegel's problems, although Hegel has lots of problems and they are always gripping. I want to take up this notion of

Hingebung, however sexually charged it is, however "gendered," because I sense that my own resistance to polemic and to the less inspired forms of criticism has to do with their failure to give-over. Giving-over is perhaps by definition indefensible, however. It leaks all over the place, out into the universe and onto the page. If not fat, it is rotund, and maybe orotund. Hoping to be pleasingly plump, it can be, as the German says, *plump,* crass, vulgar, coarse. Why should giving over be necessary? It is so undignified.

Part of the impulse for what I am saying or trying to say here comes from an unexpected source. A medical researcher, Hans Selye, many decades ago ended his book *The Stress of Life* with a chapter on "gratitude." It was the oddest thing. Dr. Selye felt that we could reduce the amount of deleterious stress in our lives if we could more often give ourselves over to thankfulness. How sweet to see a chemist go sentimental! At last, a doctor with bedside manners! As much as one wanted to mock, however, there seemed to be some wisdom in the wizened doctor's prescription. Criticism feeds on tension, the tension of the bow invoked by Heraclitus, the bow that is life itself (βίος) and the bow that kills (βιός). Criticism thrives on the tension that separates us from the work of art. Such tension mounts, for example, as we watch Derrida showing how maudlin Heidegger's ideas about the prepotent sexuality of Dasein seem, or as we hear how postmortem Whitman's leakages appear to be. At a certain point, however, that critical tension can snap and release something very unexpected, something we might call "giving-over." The terms of surrender, or in any case the result of the peace pact, would be a certain generosity. Another story about Derrida.

For years I argued with my late friend Michel Haar about the importance of Derrida's work. This was after I had been forced to read *Spurs.* Dear Michel resisted. His reasons were not foolish, but they were unreasonable. In March 1987, we went together to hear a lecture by Derrida on Heidegger, which was one of Michel's specializations, as it was one of mine, a lecture called "Of Spirit." We sat together in the Amphithéâtre Poincaré and heard the extraordinary lecture, which was many hours long. Afterward we left the hall in the dark of night and headed toward the Place du Panthéon on our way home. We were crossing the square; the traffic was normal. That is to say, cars were whizzing by us chaotically and at utterly insane speeds. A life on foot was not worth a plug centime. Michel stopped in the middle of the square. I tried to urge him on, vehicles careening by us, honking, threatening multiple deaths. Michel stood stock still. His head dropped to his chest, and I heard him mutter, more to himself than to me, *"Bon, bon—il est un génie."* "Okay, okay, so he's a genius." Michel had finally given over, and the cars hadn't even noticed.

It isn't that Michel Haar lost his brains there at the Panthéon, the traffic notwithstanding. Neither he nor I would ever stop writing in the margins of all our Derrida books "Non! Non!" It isn't that the fine points, namely, the points that Derrida himself always disputed, had lost their import. It was rather that a certain kind of resistance had given way, a certain fight given up, a certain acknowledgment rendered. Grudgingly, as acknowledgments sometimes have to be made; one must never give over too quickly, timing is everything. Maybe criticism can be—even *has to be*—the prolegomena to this "giving-over." Critique, κρίσις, κρίνειν—these words mean the capacity to distinguish, to differentiate. What good is giving-over if the giver cannot separate the strands, make careful judgments? Sartre says that what we desire of a lover is his or her *freedom*. But do we want that freedom to be stupid? Or could giving-over be the situation of lovers who, in search of fusion, discover that their being two, not one, is not their grief but their good fortune? Even so, there may come a moment when insisting on one's own seems pointless.

If Hegel is right, and giving-over is "womanly," perhaps we should never be afraid of becoming what a human being, if she or he is lucky, can become. That same pericardial Empedocles once said, thinking of his past lives, "I was both boy and girl, and bush and fish." Perhaps the demands we make on our own lives are too small. It is doubtless indefensible to insist that criticism take up such things as our identities as woman and man, girl and boy, bush and fish, and, above all, that it demand giving-over. Yet, as I said, I'll mow the lawn, I'll drive the taxi, if it ain't so. As indefensible as the idea of *Hingebung* seems, especially in its gendered nature, it strikes me as a clue concerning both the creative process and what we hope criticism can become.

By way of conclusion, I commend my indefensible ideas to you for either discussion or, as in *The Life of Brian*, a public stoning. "Two flat ones and a packet of gravel," as Brian's mom demands. Stated baldly, these ideas are:

1. That works of criticism by an author who is saturated with *ressentiment* may be safely ignored, *should* be ignored.

2. That only what magnifies the efforts of others to think and to create merits the name *thinking*.

3. That polemic, while sometimes unavoidable, does not think.

4. That a giving-over that cannot differentiate, cannot perform κρίσις, is useless.

5. That nevertheless the finest moment of criticism, a moment
that may advene at the very beginning of the process or,
more likely, very late in it, is the moment of *Hingebung*.

In the end, I think of that dancer I always confuse with the dance.
The endless hours of warm-ups and rehearsals, a lifetime of sore joints
and aching feet. The sheer effort fills me with overwhelming admiration,
to which no amount of gratitude on my part—much less criticism—can
respond adequately. I am sometimes, and I believe at my best, overwhelmed
by gratitude. This indefensible surrender may be mere pathos or even bathos
on my part, I don't know. And, sometimes, I don't really mind what it is. I
do not want to be always looking ahead and looking behind, alert and vigilant, judicious and coolly skeptical. Sometimes I need to reduce the critical
distance, allow the temperature beneath my epidermis to rise, expose myself
to the storms that are playing across the surface, give over and ride the
waves. No, not *ride* them, but *be cradled* by them. Hölderlin, in his hymn
to memory, *Mnemosyne*, intones a sort of singsong, a kind of barcarolle:

> Vorwärts aber und rükwärts wollen wir
> Nicht sehen. Uns wiegen lassen, wie
> Auf schwankem Kahne der See. (CHV 1:437)

> But forward and backward we will not want
> To look. Let ourselves be cradled, as
> On the swaying skiff of sea.

Part Two

On the *Black Notebooks*
(1931–1941)

5

Does Rescue Also Grow?

Wo aber Gefahr ist, wächst
Das Rettende auch.
But where danger is, grows
Also the rescuing.

—Friedrich Hölderlin, "Patmos"

There is little excuse, in a book that presents a series of lectures on the ecstases of time, for me to comment on Heidegger's *Schwarze Hefte*, the first three volumes of which (there will be nine altogether) have recently appeared.[1] True, Heidegger does appeal in the *Notebooks* to the "ecstatic character" of his analysis of "existence" in *Sein und Zeit*, which, he says, makes it clear that his magnum opus has nothing to do with *Existenzphilosophie* (95:35–36). Why the "ecstatic character" of existence has this singular—and purely negative—clarifying power Heidegger does not say. He merely reiterates, "The *ecstatic* character that is attributed to everything 'existential' makes impossible from top to bottom every effort to conjoin an essentially subjectivistic 'illumination of existence' and the 'existential analytic,' which pertains solely to the question of being" (95:36). Yet one may safely avow that in Heidegger's thinking after *Being and Time* the

---

1. Martin Heidegger, *Überlegungen II–VI (Schwarze Hefte 1931–1938*, Martin Heidegger *Gesamtausgabe*, vol. 94 (Frankfurt am Main: Vittorio Klostermann, 2014); *Überlegungen VII–XI (Schwarze Hefte 1938/39, Gesamtausgabe*, vol. 95 (Frankfurt am Main: Vittorio Klostermann, 2014); and *Überlegungen XII–XV (Schwarze Hefte 1939–1941, Gesamtausgabe*, vol. 96 (Frankfurt am Main: Vittorio Klostermann, 2014). The editor of these volumes, Peter Trawny, notes that eventually nine volumes of the Martin Heidegger *Gesamtausgabe* will contain the material of these notebooks, namely, volumes 94–102. The *Schwarze Hefte* cover a period of some forty years, roughly, 1931–1971.

ecstatic is still for him an eminent designation the human being's standing out into the open, that is, into the clearing or the truth of being (94:272).

In its simplest terms, the transition in the use of *Ekstase, Existenz,* and *Entrückung* from *Sein und Zeit* to the 1936–38 *Beiträge* and other writings of this period, including the *Black Notebooks,* amounts to this: whereas existence is characterized in the earlier work as temporal in the sense of the three temporal ecstases, namely, future, having-been, and present, and whereas "rapture" in the earlier work refers to the rapid motion and interplay of these three equiprimordial ecstases, in Heidegger's later thinking all these words refer to the unified and singular thrust of human existence into the clearing and openness—the truth—of beyng. Heidegger now most often writes *Seyn* with a *y*, presumably not in order to imitate the early modern and Romantic spelling, but to express "the other beginning" in the history of *Sein* that he envisages. Why that other commencement must spell archaically is a mystery, as is the identification of that commencement with the regression to a "last god."

However, I did not turn to the *Schwarze Hefte* in order to learn more about ecstasy in Heidegger's later thinking. The truth is that the appearance of these *Black Notebooks* in March 2014 interrupted my preparation of the Brauer Lectures at an early stage, and for a considerable period of time they wreaked havoc with my plans to lecture on Heidegger. The *Schwarze Hefte* were "received" with much controversy and even fury: the initial reviews were so jarringly negative, so polemical, that I decided I had better interrupt my work in order to read them.

I cannot say that I am happy I did so. And I have to begin with a confession: I began to read with my eyes, but after many hundreds of pages I had to read with my index finger running down the middle of the page, the middle of *every* dreary page, it is true; there are surely things I will have overlooked. Yet I will not be returning to these pages, nor are the as yet unpublished volumes of the *Schwarze Hefte* in my future, should I have one. Why? Because there is, in my view, precious little of philosophical or "thoughtful" importance in the three volumes I have read. They do present a dire view of Heidegger in a dire time, and it is important that they be made available to the public. Yet, to repeat, there nothing here that adds to Heidegger's more considered *Beiträge zur Philosophie* (1936–38) and other already published works. To be sure, I have my own difficulties with the *Beiträge zur Philosophie* as well. But the *Schwarze Hefte* never rise to the level of the *Beiträge.*

Let me begin again, and closer to the beginning—although the earliest *Black Notebook* has only recently turned up and is therefore not yet published. The first volume of the *Gesamtausgabe* publication of the *Schwarze Hefte*, volume 94, which begins with the second *Überlegung* ("Meditation" or "Reflection"), is by far the most worth examining, principally though not only because it stretches from October 1931 to the year 1938. The initial notes are not yet pathological, in my view, even though the tendency to polemic in them is already clearly marked. The polemic is more strident than anything Heidegger's published works or even his lecture courses prepare us for, yet the thoughts are not as disconnected and rambling, the repetitions not as mind-numbing, as in the second and third volumes, *Gesamtausgabe* volumes 95 and 96.

Heidegger's attention to the political events of the day—his total capitulation to *everydayness*—is already evident in volume 94, yet not in as compulsive and reactive a manner as later. Some of the early notes are eerily jubilant. "The world is being renovated," he writes, "a grand faith is moving through the young land" (94:26–27). That, at least, is the ostensibly positive side of things, the "romantic" side of things, which, to be sure, will soon enough manifest its shadow side. A further look at the jubilation, presumably from the year 1931:

> In turn—the world is being restored to itself. We are getting closer to the truth and its essentiality—we are becoming reflective [*gesonnen*], we are of a mind to assume all that is demanded of us and to take our stand in it—to stand our ground [*bodenständig zu werden*].
>
> Only one who stems from the ground can stand his ground and be nourished in it—this is the original thing, this is what often elevates my mood and energizes my body—as though I were trudging across the field behind a plow, or walking along lonely field paths in the midst of ripening grain, through wind and fog, sun and snow, the kinds of things that kept the blood circulating and invigorated in my mother and in her ancestors. . . . (94:38)

Let us pause a moment over the young land and its mother. This is one of the very few references to family—here the mother and her ancestors, as though the soil and the elements were theirs. A second reference to the mother is perhaps more revealing: "*My mother*—my simple memory of this pious woman, who without bitterness beheld in a prescient intimation the path of her son who had *apparently* turned away from God" (94:320). An entire biography hides in these words. A third reference connects the mother and her farm to some of the Swabian heroes of the past, whom Heidegger is careful to exclude from the *Alemannerei* of the Third Reich: "My home-land, the village and the farm of my mother, is blessed by the breezes and nurtured by the streams of *Hölderlin*, possesses the solidity, the power to coin, and the abyssal character of the *Hegelian* concept, and is permeated by that daring, forward-thinking 'speculative' drive of *Schelling . . .*" (94:350).

Yet one does not have to wait long for the negatives. One of the odd complaints that we find repeated among these first notes of the 1930s involves the reception of *Sein und Zeit*. That reception is a success, but it causes Heidegger to grind his teeth: no one is strong enough to refute or even criticize the book, precisely because no one understands the question of being that stands at its center (94:46). That book and all his other writings seem to him therefore to be mere *Schriftstellerei*, mere literary excrescences. Furthermore, no scientist and no philosopher, and especially no theologian, has been able to sustain the crisis into which Nietzsche's writings ought to have thrown them all. Two things are amiss: first, the ancient Greek understanding of being, already distorted by the Christian "worldview," is trivialized throughout the remainder of the history of metaphysics; second, the mathematization of knowledge in modern philosophy since Galileo and Descartes reflects the incorrigible concern with certitude—certitude of salva-tion having become certitude *ordine geometrico* (94:55).

What remains baffling to me is that for Heidegger these concerns with the history of metaphysics are bound up with the political upheavals in the Germany of the 1930s. As Heidegger himself asks, "Who knows where we've gotten stuck?" *"Wer weiß, worin wir hängen?"* (94:60). The struggle should be *der Kampf um die Antike*, the struggle to regain access to early Greek thinking in order to begin to think again; and yet that *Kampf* gets mixed up with a very different struggle, in which thinking plays no role. And so the polemics begin, polemics against church and state, university and research institute, culture, science, and philosophy. One of Heidegger's most counterfactual exclamations is this one: *"No polemic!* But not merely out of consideration or respectability—rather, because fully occupied by and preoccupied with *struggle*—against the nonessence of being" (94:85). For what one sees throughout the *Black Notebooks* is the increasingly violent polemic against everyone and everything, a polemic that suffocates every conceivable effort at thinking. What Heidegger will very soon see is that the Germans, on whom he pins all his hopes, are not up to the task that he, with ostensible help from Hölderlin and Nietzsche, has set them. Whereas this "bunker mentality" comes quite late to Hitler and his cohorts, it comes very early to Heidegger. The result of his bleak disappointment is not overt resistance to National Socialism, however, but internal emigration and end-lessly repeated and bootless polemic.

And yet one does not know which is worse: the persistent polemic or the temporary euphoria of 1931–33, the slough of despond or the "renovated" land: "A splendidly awakening national will is entering into the vast darkness of the world" (94:109). Philosophy must be brought to an end; science must change from top to bottom; the university needs to be reconstituted by a "metapolitics" (94:115). As far as I can see, however, the *Notebooks* offer no details concerning Heidegger's year as rector, his plans to reorganize the sciences, and his hirings and firings on behalf of "syn-chronization," *Gleichschaltung*. No mention of his Jewish colleagues who are forced out, no details of what the university in his view is to become; only the insistence on massive change in every respect—and the almost immedi-ate sense of failure, of regret over a year of wasted effort in the rectorship (94:154–55). At one point Heidegger makes a sarcastic reference to his notorious "rectorate address": " 'The Self-Assertion of the German Univer-sity' or—the minor *entr'acte* of a vast mistake" (94:198; cf. 94:286). Noth-ing in the university is developing as it should, neither the *Studentenschaft* nor the organization of the university faculty and administration, which appear to be led "by soldiers and engineers" (94:157). In the same vein, Heidegger mocks an address by Baldur von Schirach, a National Socialist minister, who transforms the traditional motto of the Germans ("*das Volk der Dichter und Denker*") into "the nation of poets and soldiers" (94:514). Heidegger's own desire soon becomes "the courage to take distance," which, he says, "dare not be botched by the phantasmatic machinations of a noisy 'engagement' " (94:159). Distance from what? From the "machinations" of "the gigantic." *Machenschaft* and *das Riesenhafte* now, by 1934, become the principal polemical words of the *Black Notebooks*. "Machination," "gigan-tism," and the "swamp" or "bog" into which Heidegger sees everything around him sinking: *Versumpfung*.

It is, I believe, impossible to deny that Heidegger's rhetoric in the *Schwarze Hefte* is choleric and confused—unrelievedly repetitive *paraph-rasis* gone to *paranoesis*. This is especially true when Heidegger speaks up for *Seyn*. When Heidegger mocks the *Seinsgeschwätz* or "chit-chat about being" of his confreres, the mockery surely backfires (94:256). Allow me to cite one sentence, not atypical, though longer than most. The context is Heidegger's claim that "catastrophes" such as "world wars," both words in scare quotes, will be withstood and will one day even be declared useful, *brauchbar*, even though they will have decided nothing. Furthermore, the destruction involved in such catastrophes, even at its high point, will no longer be experienced as such, presumably because humankind will have sunk to the nadir of sensibility. If there is a ray of hope, it glimmers in the following sentence. In German:

> Aber immer noch leuchtet in einer unerkennbaren Nacht das Licht der entscheidungshaften Geschichte, in deren von den Göttern durchschrittenem Abgrund das Riesenhafte der Geschichtslosigkeit in den Anschein der "Lebendigkeit" doch nur ein Vordergrund des Unwesens bleibt, dessen die Wesung des Seyns sich nie entschlägt, weil es in sich—als die Notschaft der Götter—alle zu Bedürfnissen umgestellten Nöte des vor- und herstellenden Menschen in ihrem Unwesen schon *entschieden* hat, deshalb aber dem Menschen als dem Seienden, das dem Seyn zugewiesen ist, die Möglichkeit anheimgibt, ein Entscheidender zu sein und *die* Entscheidung zwischen dem Seienden und dem Seyn einmal zu wagen oder immer wieder zu umgehen. (95:133; cf. 164)

But the light of a history that will be ripe for decisions still radiates through a night we cannot descry, a history in whose abyss, traversed by gods, the gigantic shape of a total lack of history remains camouflaged as "vitality," yet only as the foreground of a nonessence that the essential unfolding of beyng can never entirely slough off, inasmuch as the nonessence in itself—as the perduring need for the gods—has already *decided* that all needs be transformed into cravings by the human beings who in their nonessence represent and produce these cravings, and yet an essential unfolding that delivers into the safekeeping of human beings, as the beings that are directed to beyng, the possibility to be the ones who will make decisions and who will dare for once to make *the* decision between beings and beyng, or who, once again, as always, will circumvent it.

In spite of the turbid prose, understatement though this may be, a prose even more turbid in English translation than in the German, despite my efforts, the oppositions seem to be clear: history and lack of history, light and night, abyss and gods, essential unfolding and nonessence, false "vitality" and essence, future decision and everything already decided, hypertrophied representation and production precisely by the beings who are enjoined to the safeguarding of beyng, the possibility of decision and the habitual neglect. Perhaps most difficult to translate, because most difficult to think, is *die Notschaft der Götter*, which could mean either the calamitousness *of* the gods who, like us, are compelled to traverse the abyss, or the wretched need—or craving—of us nonessential ones *for* the gods, which is the way I have read it here. Perhaps only a thorough rereading of what ought to be the final section of the *Beiträge*, "The Last God," would enable me to translate well here. (It *ought* to be the final section, for so it was in the typescript prepared by Heidegger's brother Fritz.) What continues to perplex, however, is Heidegger's insistence that a monstrous *Unwesen* that has shaped human beings (and perhaps the gods themselves) into the miserable creatures they are could be transformed by those miserable creatures themselves through a monstrous *decision*. The word *Entscheidung* appears over and over again in the *Notebooks*, both in terms of what has already been fatefully decided and what we ("we" Germans) are nevertheless called on to decide. One could have translated the phrase *ein Entscheidender zu sein* as "to be the decider," as in the memorable phrase, "I'm the decider here." In Heidegger's case, however, beyng alone can be the decider. "*Die Entscheidung kommt aus dem Seyn selbst*" (96:171). "The decision comes from beyng itself." The decider, even and especially when he wills to be decisive, is the paragon of everydayness, *das Man*, the They.

A further word, then, on the oddness of the perfervid call for "decision." If the history of beyng is itself a sending by and of beyng, a sending in which beyng withdraws and conceals itself, then what decision of mortals can make a difference? At one particularly desperate point in the *Notebooks* Heidegger writes: "*Ist dieses jetzt die einzige Entscheidung: völlige Zerstörung und Unordnung oder Verzwingung eines vollständigen Zwangs?*" (95:70). "Is *this* now the sole *decision*: total destruction and chaos or the compelling of a complete compulsion?" The alternative is unclear, the tautology disarming, the alliteration alarming. Yet what is clear is that Heidegger is talking about some sort of watershed, *Wasserscheide*, not an *Entscheidung* in any usual sense. Which leads us to ask: Why then does Heidegger adopt the tone of a Calvin, Zwingli, or Savonarola? What is Heidegger calling on his fellow mortals to do? Prepare for the coming of the last god, presumably; preserve the capacity for meditative or contemplative thought, presumably, in spite of the wretched example Heidegger is offering us here. Yet how prepare and preserve when the sending of beyng appears as the disastrous alternative of destruction or compulsion?

Above all else, Heidegger's treatment in the *Schwarze Hefte* of the theme of "Jewish civilization," *Judentum*, and in general of people and things Jewish, were the principal cause for scandal when the first three volumes of the *Schwarze Hefte* were published. I cannot say that I have found all the relevant references and allusions in these thousand pages, but the references I have read are dismaying—but also confusing. Sometimes Heidegger seems to be speaking out of the mouth of a National Socialist propagandist, a mouth he clearly despises and wishes to mock; at other times he seems to be speaking out of his own mouth, the mouth of the thinker of beyng. Before I mention at least some of these references, allow me to observe what has caused no scandal. Far more frequent that any reference to Judaism or the Jewish are the scathing references to Christian civilization, Christian faith, and the Christian churches—all of them. Heidegger equates what he calls *Kulturchristentum* with the apparatus of the *Reich* itself, since both church and state are obstacles to what he calls a thinking of beyng, *Seynsdenken* (95:1–6). The critique of National Socialism is thus laced with a similar critique of the politics of the Papacy, as though the Concordat were a recent event instead of one of Hitler's first great diplomatic victories (95:18–19). Religionists of every stamp are conspiring *with* National Socialism in its current form, not against it. All are conspiring to keep beyng at bay.

A second preliminary remark. There are countless references one could cite in order to demonstrate Heidegger's *critique* of National Socialist racism and biologism (see, for example, 95:39–41). Yet Heidegger's critique of racism, while sardonic, is based on his view that racism is a culmination of the calculative thinking of a planning and reckoning "machination" (95:39–41). Oddly, to say the least, Heidegger's stringent critique of biologistic racism does not prevent him from eventually accepting a set of prejudices against "Jewish civilization." I repeat that Heidegger's references are often obscure, the polemic so broad in scope, so all-inclusive and so irate, that it is often difficult to understand the target. Some of the references seem to be harmless, although vague. For example, in a discussion of the prevalence of anthropology and psychology in modern philosophy, Heidegger declares that "all doctrines of human being (for example, the Christian-Jewish) that define it in terms of an immediate relation to a 'God' are anthropological . . ." (94:475). Similarly, in a discussion of the "truth of beyng," Heidegger writes: "This question alone [i.e., that of *die Wahrheit des Seyns*] overcomes the modern *anthropological* definition of the human being and with it all prior Christian, Hellenistic-Jewish and Socratic-Platonic anthropology" (95:322). Elsewhere he refers to the "Hellenistic-Jewish 'world'" (95:339), again without offering any sort of explanation. Because of the massive generalization throughout, one has to wonder what the "Hellenistic-Jewish" anthropology or "world" might be; presumably, Heidegger is referring to the great age of

Alexandria, to which we owe the preservation of so many texts from Greek antiquity, including many fragments of the early Greek thinkers that were so dear to Heidegger himself. Yet we receive no help from Heidegger in this regard, for he nowhere comments on the contributions to the metaphysical tradition by Philo, the Alexandrians, Maimonides, Spinoza, or Moses Mendelssohn (whom he had cited favorably, however, in his 1929 Kant book), to say nothing of more recent writers such as Rosenzweig and Buber. At certain points, Heidegger mocks the National Socialist regime for its persecution of its enemies, as in the following passage:

> Jeder Dogmatismus, er sei kirchlich-politisch oder staatspolitisch, hält notwendig jedes von ihm scheinbar oder wirklich abweichende Denken und Tun für eine Zustimmung zu dem, was ihm, dem Dogmatismus, *der Feind* ist—seien das die Heiden und Gottlosen oder die Juden und Kommunisten. In dieser Denkweise liegt eine eigentümliche Stärke—nicht des Denkens—sondern der Durchsetzung des Verkündeten. (95:325)

> Every dogmatism, whether ecclesiastical-political or state-political, necessarily takes every thought and deed that seems to deviate from it, or that actually does deviate from it, to be in essential agreement with what is *inimical* to the dogmatism—whether it be the pagans and the godless or the Jews and Communists. A peculiar strength lies in this kind of thinking—not a strength of thinking—but the power to make one's own gospel prevail.

Yet a very different tone is struck in the following passage, one that again mocks the regime for its promotion of "culture," but does so in a double-edged way:

> Die "Kultur" als Machmittel [*sic*] sich anzueignen und damit sich behaupten und eine Überlegenheit vorgeben, ist im Grunde ein *jüdisches* Gebahren [*sic*]. Was folgt daraus für die *Kulturpolitik* als solche? (95:326)

> To appropriate "culture" to oneself as a tool and to assert oneself thereby, claiming for oneself a certain superiority, is at bottom a *Jewish* gesture. What consequence follows for the *politics of culture*?

Heidegger's contempt for the "culture industry," whether in music or in the plastic arts, is everywhere present in these *Notebooks*. Here his contempt for the cultural politics practiced by the regime equates the National Socialist propaganda machine with the culture(s) of its principal victim. What remains disturbing is the failure to distinguish between genuine achievements in the arts by that principal victim and the wretched "official" culture of the Third Reich. Not a word is uttered about the 1936 "Degenerate Art" exhibit or the "approved" exhibit that was meant to offer a "healthy" contrast to it. Not a word is uttered about the immense contributions of Jewish musicians, conductors, and composers to German musical life. Yet worse is to come.

In the context of a polemic against the goallessness of his times, which lack a sense for the historic,[2] that is, a sense for *Seynsgeschichte*, Heidegger says that perhaps the real victor in the National Socialist struggle against contemporary "goallessness" will be "the greater groundlessness, which has no ties to anything and which makes use of everything (Jewish civilization) [*die größere Bodenlosigkeit, die an nichts gebunden, alles sich dienstbar macht (das Judentum)*]" (95:97). In case we have any doubts about the sense of who is using and abusing whom, the next entry is more specific:

> Eine der verstecktesten Gestalten des *Riesigen* und vielleicht die älteste ist die zähe Geschicklichkeit des Rechnens und Schiebens und Durcheinandermischens, wodurch die Weltlosigkeit des Judentums gegründet wird. (Ibid.)

> One of the most hidden figures of the *gigantic* and perhaps the oldest one is the tenacious skillfulness in reckoning and manipulating and meddling in which the worldlessness of Jewish civilization is grounded.

---

2. From time to time, but not always, I have tried to render *Geschichte* as "the historic." Heidegger reiterates incessantly his distinction between the discipline of *Historie* and the "historic" as such, *Geschichte* referring always and everywhere to "the history of beyng." Yet the latter phrase is in fact a misnomer, inasmuch as *die Geschichte des Seyns* is all about the *absence* or *default* of beyng: "*Geschichte—das Ausbleiben des Seyns?*" "The historic—the default of beyng?" (95:46). Heidegger's answer to this rhetorical question is always *yes*, so that the expression *Geschichte des Seyns* remains a *lucus a non lucendo*. The resulting complication for our brief discussion (in chapter 4) of Derrida and *epochality* needs to be thought through: the single and singular epoch of beyng, which plays itself out in and as the history of metaphysics, is the epoch in which beyng plays no role at all.

These words, or words like them, could be found in the diaries and tracts of so many nineteenth- and twentieth-century anti-Semites, such as Bernhard Förster or Cosima and Richard Wagner, whom Heidegger otherwise excoriates throughout these notebooks. It is more than disquieting to find such words here, where there seems to be no hope that Heidegger is quoting from, alluding to, or even mocking the beliefs and prejudices of the regime. Even though Heidegger scholars have cited this or that remark from lecture courses of the early 1930s, I know of nothing in Heidegger's published works or even in his lecture courses that equals this kind of disparagement and defamation, this kind of slur. True, Karl Jaspers's account of Heidegger's last visit with him in May 1933 prepares us for the worst; yet there is nothing else from Heidegger's own pen to compare with this.[3] Most disquieting in his account of *Weltjudentum* is the word *Weltlosigkeit*, which Heidegger used in 1929–30 to describe the lifeless stone; in these notebooks, as we will soon see, he is liable to include the *animal* in such deprivation of world. And now the worldless, lapidary animal is joined by a worldless world-Jew.

Other references to Jewishness are more ambiguous, it seems to me. Consider this, on "sociology": "The *völkisch* principle manifests itself in its gigantic modern significance when one grasps that it is a transformation of and a successor to the dominion of a *sociology* of society. Is it an accident that National *Socialism* has obliterated the very *name* of 'sociology'? Why was sociology conducted with particular diligence by Jews and Catholics?" (95:161). The suggestion once again seems to be that National Socialism is secretly and perversely bound up with or even dependent on what it most opposes, and that when viewed in terms of the gigantism of modernity these secret ties and kinships become visible. This tendency toward double-edged criticism manifests itself again when Heidegger tries to distinguish his "attack" on Cartesianism, initiated already in *Sein und Zeit*, from that

---

3. Karl Jaspers, *Philosophische Autobiographie* (Munich: Piper Verlag, 1977), 100–01. Jaspers quotes Heidegger as referring to "a dangerous international Jewish network." Antonia Grunenberg reports on this visit: see the French edition of her fine book, *Hannah Arendt et Martin Heidegger: Histoire d'un amour*, tr. Cédric Cohen Skalli (Paris: Petite Bibliothèque Payot, 2012), 197–98. The German original is Grunenberg, *Hannah Arendt und Martin Heidegger: Geschichte einer Liebe* (Munich: Piper Verlag, 2006). I am grateful to Peg Birmingham, who is cotranslating Grunenberg's informative and thoughtful book into English, for her help with these remarks on the Heidegger-Arendt-Jaspers relationship.

of others; indeed, critiques of Descartes have become so common, writes Heidegger, that *everyone* claims to be "against" Descartes. Heidegger's own "attack" (that is his word) has nothing to do with these popularized criticisms, even though, he adds in parentheses, his attack "has been exploited by both Jews and National Socialists with equal vigor" (95:168). Heidegger does not say which Jews he means, although his own best students may be among them. (I, for one, will not research the question as to who he has in mind.) In all fairness, one must note that Heidegger's most intense vituperation is reserved for the *völkischen* critiques of Descartes, which, although "stupid and arrogant," are "shooting up like weeds" in universities all across the country. The repeated juxtaposition of Jews and National Socialists in Heidegger's text—a juxtaposition we can only find repugnant and twisted—is being used by Heidegger here simply to profile his own profundity and exceptional critical capacity. Repugnant and twisted—after all, the *Kristallnacht* of November 9–10, 1938, may be occurring at the moment Heidegger is writing these words—and perhaps even stupidly arrogant. Yet once again things get worse.

In the later *Notebooks*, those from 1939 to 1941, we find the two following references to German *Emigranten*. The first (96:201) is in the context of a critique of the "lamentation" concerning "the fall of 'culture' after the manner of the *Emigranten*." These lamenting émigrés could of course be Thomas Mann (plus sons, daughter, and brothers) or thousands of others. But the second reference is more specific (96:261–62). Here Heidegger lists ten points concerning the current situation in Germany. Many of these points are quite lucid, such as the fifth, which invokes the mortal danger of a two-front war, which on June 22, 1941, becomes a reality. But then comes number nine:

> Das Weltjudentum, aufgestachelt durch die aus Deutschland hinausgelassenen Emigranten, ist überall unfaßbar und braucht sich bei aller Machtentfaltung nirgends an kriegerischen Handlungen zu beteiligen, wogegen uns nur bleibt, das beste Blut der Besten des eigenen Volkes zu opfern. (96:262)

> The world Jewish order, prodded by the emigrants who were allowed to leave Germany, is everywhere unstoppable, and for all the might it is developing it nowhere has to participate in deeds of war, whereas it is our sole lot to sacrifice the best blood of the best of our own people.

Ausgelassen is doubtless an unintended (and hair-raising) euphemism, and the rest a clear indication that no matter how much Heidegger decries the propaganda machine of the Third Reich, he has clearly "learned" from it. The year is 1941. The passage—even if we succeed in holding in check all retrospective illusion and distortion—defies comment.

Later in these notes from 1941 comes a reference to a Bolshevik by the name of Litwinow (96:242). Heidegger refers to him as "the Jew Litwinow," presumably as an example of Jewish and Bolshevik *Hinterhältigkeit*, "treacherousness." And once again a "world Jewry" enters on the scene, in the context of England as the historic seedbed not only of the industrial revolution but also of modern imperialism and "machination" as such:

> Even the thought of reaching an understanding with England in the sense of a dividing up of "lawful" imperialist conquests does not confront the essence of the historic process that England is playing out to the end, now in the context of Americanism and Bolshevism, and that means at the same time in the context of *world Jewry*. The question of the role of *world Jewry* is not a race-related one, but the metaphysical question of the kind of humanity [*Menschentümlichkeit*] that can take over the uprooting of all beings from being as a world-historical "task," and to do so in a way that is *altogether unbounded* [schlechthin ungebunden]. (96:243)

Not racially but metaphysically, the uprooted Jew of the Diaspora is suited to the eradication of all possible well-rooted *Seynsdenken*—that would be his or her "metaphysical" *Menschentümlichkeit*. This German word is itself belittling in a troubling way: ostensibly not a racial slur, it nevertheless evokes the squalid contribution to "humankind" by the rootless and calculating Jew. One is reminded of Derrida's challenging question as to whether Heidegger's "metaphysical" racism, as opposed to the "biological" sort, can grant anyone any sort of comfort. No doubt, Heidegger is mindful here of the importance of imperial conquest in the background of both world wars. Yet the attribution of such a scheme to England, which at the moment is worried about its survival, seems phantasmatic—even before we get to *Weltjudentum*. Apparently, in addition to the powerful nation-states of England, Soviet Russia, and the United States, there is another world power—stateless yet mighty—that can be identified as the international Jewish conspiracy. That, at least, would be the U.S.-American translation of *Weltjudentum*. The "idea" is an old one. It is based on the importance traditionally attributed to "outsiders" in banking and finance, those who are permitted to be "usurers," principally the Huguenot and the Jew. Heidegger is not worried about the Huguenots. He is worried about the Rothschilds. The "unbounded" or, better, the "uncommitted" character of the Jew has to do with his or her rootlessness and statelessness; or, more likely to be disturbing to Heidegger, his or her lack of attachment to the land, to the farm and the village. That would be the secret of the Jew's endless calculations and possible treachery. The Jew lacks world and earth.

As I read these pages of the *Notebooks* I could not help thinking of my undergraduate and early postgraduate years as a history major, studying principally medieval and early modern Europe. The most powerful banking family in Austria, Germany, and Italy was that of Jacob Fugger of Augsburg. For generations the Fuggers funded the Papacy, the Holy Roman Empire (which, as we learned, was neither an empire, nor Roman, nor holy), and the German principates, gradually making each of these powers dependent on their house. Even Montaigne marveled at the palatial residences of the Fuggers as he passed through Augsburg. When I read the *Schwarze Hefte*, I felt the sudden need to remind myself whether the Fuggers of Augsburg were Jewish. Imagine my surprise when I learned that they were loyal Catholics and that their homeland was *Swabia*, Heidegger's own Swabia, the eastern part of the Schwarzwald. Perhaps Heidegger should have been worried about the international *Swabian* conspiracy? Yet criticism of his own and of himself was not Heidegger's strength.

Now that I have lowered the level of the conversation, if that is possible, my readers will allow me to mention a minor yet irritating point. The Klostermann edition of the first three volumes of the *Schwarze Hefte* includes a subject index of the principal themes for each of the dozen *Überlegungen*. The editor tells us that Heidegger himself added them (96:283); *when*, he does not say. Yet why does Heidegger index these volumes when no other *Gesamtausgabe* volumes contain indexes, ostensibly in conformity with Heidegger's own wishes? A more major and more disquieting point is this: even though Heidegger's attacks on *Christentum* are indexed, his mentions of *Judentum* are not. True, the references to Catholicism, Protestantism, and Christianity in general far outweigh those to *Judentum*, as I have mentioned. Yet if the latter is a treacherous *world* power, one would think it worth indexing.

Since I mentioned Wagner a moment ago, it may be worth recording one or two of Heidegger's remarks, if only as a weak attempt at comic relief. None of Heidegger's remarks achieves the complexity or the wit of

Nietzsche's writings on Wagner, however, if only because Heidegger had no musical education to speak of and little musical talent. At any rate, here are three samples we might allow ourselves to relish. Wagner, writes Heidegger, is a "cardinal in the new Christian-Pagan cathedral" (95:108–09; cf. 52). In one of the earliest references, Heidegger names Wagner in the same breath with Wagner's son-in-law, Houston Stewart Chamberlain, and he does so with obvious contempt (94:446). And then this: "*Lohengrin*, always and everywhere *Lohengrin, Lohengrin* and armored cars and airplane squadrons—these things belong together and are the selfsame" (95:132–33). This is long before Francis Ford Coppola's use of "The Ride of the Valkyries" in *Apocalypse Now*, which, admittedly, is a film about Vietnam rather than the Third Reich. Yet Heidegger's *Black Notebooks* are all about apocalypse, now as then, and there is no comfort or relief in reading them. No comfort for anyone.

As far as I can see, the word *Aryan* falls but once in the *Notebooks*, but it is used as a sarcastic critique of National Socialist psychologists who are trying to cleanse psychoanalysis of its Jewish origins: Heidegger mockingly refers to "the Aryan transformations of the basic doctrines of psychoanalysis" (95:62). However, it is psychoanalysis of any and every stripe that Heidegger despises. "Depth psychology" is for him the nadir of modern subjectivity, precisely because it emphasizes the first term of the traditional definition of the human being as *animal rationale*. All that talk of drives and instincts! Observe the sordid inquisitiveness of the therapist, who goes snooping into everything! Heidegger recoils in horror from the way depth psychology, as he says, "creeps along" and "sniffs everything" (95:107: *entlangkriecht, beschnuppert*), like a dog on a leash. The leash would be held firmly in the hand of Descartes. Psychoanalysis is perhaps itself the bottomless bottom of depth psychology, and as one reads the *Black Notebooks* one waits—in vain as it turns out—for a diatribe that will have to include Freud's own Jewishness, a Jewishness endlessly contested by Freud himself when it comes to psychoanalytic theory but embraced when Jews were under threat, and that was often enough.

For Heidegger, psychoanalysis is an especially powerful enemy. More than any other cultural "event" of the twentieth century, psychoanalysis boldly enters where ontology of Dasein fears to tread and where a thinking of beyng is made to look like a screen memory. Psychoanalysis distracts everyone from the need for beyng because it reduces *Seynsnot* to petty *Bedürfnisse*, "needs" or "cravings" of a baser sort. It views the human being as one living entity among others, well-nigh an animal, leaving the *rationale* to fend for itself. And see what it does to the innocence of childhood, which

Heidegger will many years later celebrate as "the gentleness of a simple twofold," in which boy and girl are indistinguishable, and in which their blood, as Hegel says, is never agitated by desire.[4] The emphasis on drives, *Triebe*, in psychoanalysis transforms the human subject (for it is still all about subjectivity, even if "consciousness" is abashed and the "unconscious" is elevated to central importance) into an object for biology. To be sure, in these diatribes Sigmund Freud is mentioned by name only once, even if he is the principal malefactor. And yet, if I read the *Notebooks* correctly here, Heidegger's polemic suddenly shifts, taking a direction that might surprise us. Heidegger laments that the *form* of psychoanalysis, which carves up the subject into sundry "lived experiences," *Erlebnisse*, and exposes their "hidden grounds," *Erlebnishintergründe*, remains at work in our culture "even after Jewish 'psychoanalysis' has been done away with [*vorgeschoben*]" (95:258). Done away with, shut down, locked up, put a stop to, scotched, precisely by the National Socialist arbiters of culture and science. Heidegger *seems* to be saying that National Socialist propaganda has thrust the Jewish character of psychoanalysis to the fore in order to cast opprobrium on it—whereas its flaw is that like all *Lebensphilosophie* it distracts us from facing up to our wretched incapacity for *Besinnung*, the meditative thinking of beyng. Two years later, a harsher passage appears, but, as I believe, to the same effect:

> Man sollte nicht allzulaut über die Psychoanalyse des Juden "Freud" empören, wenn man und solange man *überhaupt* nicht anders über Alles und Jedes "denken" kann als so, daß Alles als "Ausdruck" "des Lebens" einmal und auf "Instinkte" und "Instinkt-schwund" "zurückführt." Diese "Denk"-weise, die überhaupt im voraus kein "Sein" zuläßt, is der reine Nihilismus. (96:218)

> One should not too vociferously express one's horror concerning the psychoanalysis of the Jew "Freud," if one—and as long as one—*in general* cannot "think" otherwise about anything and everything than as though it were all an "expression" of "life" in the first instance, to be "traced back" to "instincts" and "the diminution of instinct." This way of "thinking," which in general allows no place for "being," is pure nihilism.

---

4. For a full discussion of Heidegger on *die Sanftmut einer einfältigen Zwiefalt*, see my *Phantoms of the Other*, especially chapters 5–7.

The passage is garbled, if only because it is overloaded with unspecified citations and allusions. Yet the sardonic quotations seem to refer to those "Aryan" reformers of psychology mentioned a moment ago. Heidegger is aiming less at the Jewishness of Freud than at the ontological bankruptcy of psychoanalysis—the nihilism that, according to Heidegger, advenes when one sniffs for instincts instead of hearkening to beyng.

To be sure, none of this turns Heidegger into a philo-Semite or into some sort of hero of the Resistance. It is his crass indifference to persecution and violence—and after November 1938, when the synagogue adjacent to the University of Freiburg too was destroyed, no one could have been unaware of these things—along with his blindness to the difference between perpetrators and victims that remains so shocking. Why does *Besinnung* produce such hardness of heart? True, one is surprised to find, amid all the razor blades, aphorisms like the following: "*Das jetzige Geschlecht ist und wird nicht, wie man vorgeben möchte, hart, sondern nur stumpf.*" "Our contemporary generation is not and will not become hard, as one would like to pretend, but only dull" (95:376). And: "*Milde kann große Stärke in sich bergen, und Härte ist oft nur die Vorderfläche einer Schwäche.*" "Gentleness can conceal in itself great strength, and harshness is often only the protective cover of a weakness" (95:288). Yet *Milde* does not show her face very often in these pages, even if Heidegger on occasion asks what the Greeks mean by χάρις. Beyng is obviously no gentle taskmaster: it demands "sacrifice" and it thrives on eschatology, apocalypse, ἐκπύρωσις, conflagration, pyrification. "Every philosophy is in-humane [*un-menschlich*] and an all-consuming fire" (94:481). *Geist* is flame, says Heidegger in his second Trakl essay (US 59–60), and Derrida confirms this in his *De l'esprit*. Yet why does it not occur to Heidegger, who had so many brilliant Jewish students, that among the persons who were facing violent death there might be one or other thinker of beyng, one or other who might be eminently capable of *Besinnung*? Nietzsche's Zarathustra dreams of those students who will surpass their teacher. Why is Heidegger, at least in these private notes where he would have been most likely to confess it, so indifferent to the fates of his very best students? Why does it mean nothing to him that a Marburg colleague, Paul Friedländer, who was so important to him as a reader of Plato, will be lucky enough to end his days in California? Why does it mean just as little that so many gifted colleagues will not escape in time? Is beyng so recalcitrant, so self-absorbed, so cruel? Is the last god, as Mephistopheles says of himself, *der Geist, der stets verneint*? At the end of a diatribe concerning "the ruination of humankind" in modernity, Heidegger lets something of the humor of his gods be revealed: "*Und fernste Götter lächeln über diesen Taumel*" (95:393). "And the most remote gods smile upon this mayhem." The smile, of course, is here a contemptuous grin, a grimace, and one must be happy that deity is so remote.

Which leads me to a further remark concerning what is missing from Heidegger's *Notebooks*. Can we not, at least on occasion, afford to be candid in our journals, diaries, and *Tagebücher*? Can we not allow ourselves, if only on the rarest occasions, to be self-critical in our "notes to self"? What we *never* find in Heidegger's *Schwarze Hefte* are statements even remotely like the following: *Has beyng really abandoned us? Are we the jilted lovers of beyng? Is the beyng that is so dear to us—a gigolo? What sort of nonsense is this?* Or: *Is Nietzsche really trapped in the structures of Platonism? And I, who am always on about* τὸ ὄv*? Is my own case clear?* Or: *The German university is in such a sorry state now—but did I help it much back in '33–'34?* Or: *Mon Dieu! Did I screw up or what?* In short, one yearns for a bit of common, run-of-the-mill self-remonstrance, a touch of abashed humor—dare one say it, a touch of Jewish humor?—an instant of candor. Any one of these things, anything to relieve the endless vituperative drone. Which I fear I am beginning to imitate. . . .

⁂

In a text from the year 1939, Heidegger explains when and why he believed in the "inner truth and greatness of the National Socialist 'movement.'" That is the way his 1935 *Introduction to Metaphysics* puts it, a text whose editing caused such a scandal in the 1950s and even later when the *Gesamtausgabe* edition of the *Introduction to Metaphysics* was published. Here, presumably in 1938, Heidegger admits to an even stronger affirmation of the "movement," however distant he feels from its current form:

> Rein "metaphysisch" (d. h. seynsgeschichtlich) denkend habe ich in den Jahren 1930–1934 den Nationalsozialismus für die Möglichkeit eines Übergangs in einen anderen Anfang gehalten und ihm diese Deutung gegeben. Damit wurde diese "Bewegung" in ihren eigentlichen Kräften und inneren Notwendigkeiten sowohl als auch in der ihr eigenen Größengebung und Größenart verkannt und unterschätzt. Hier beginnt vielmehr und zwar in einer viel tieferen—d. h. umgreifenden und eingreifenden Weise als im Faschismus die Vollendung der Neuzeit—; diese hat zwar im "Romantischen" überhaupt begonnen—hinsichtlich der Vermenschung des Menschen in der selbstgewissen Vernünftigkeit, aber für die Vollendung bedarf es der Entschiedenheit des Historisch-Technischen im Sinne der Vollständigen "Mobilisier-

ung" aller Vermögen des auf sich gestellten Menschentums. Eines
Tages muß auch die Absetzung gegen die christlichen Kirchen
vollzogen werden in einem christentumslosen "Protestantismus",
den der Faschismus von sich aus nicht zu vollziehen mag.

Aus der vollen Einsicht in die frühere Täuschung über das
Wesen und die geschichtliche Wesenskraft des Nationalsozial-
ismus ergibt sich erst die Notwendigkeit seiner Bejahung und
zwar aus *denkerischen* Gründen. Damit ist zugleich gesagt, daß
diese "Bewegung" unabhängig bleibt von der je zeitgenössischen
Gestalt und der Dauer dieser gerade sichtbaren Formen. Wie
kommt es aber, daß eine solche wesentliche Bejahung weni-
ger oder gar nicht geschätzt wird im Unterschied zur bloßen,
meist vordergründlichen und alsbald ratlosen oder nur blinden
Zustimmung? Die Schuld trägt zum Teil die leere Anmaßung
der *"Intellektuellen"*. . . . (95:408–09)

Thinking purely "metaphysically" (i.e., in terms of the history of
beyng) in the years 1930 to 1934, I took National Socialism to
be the possibility of a transition to another beginning, and that is
the meaning I gave to it. In that way I misjudged the "movement"
in terms of its proper forces and inner necessities; I also underes-
timated the greatness of its dimensions and the kind of greatness
it possesses. Rather, what is beginning here is the completion of
modernity, and in a much deeper—that is, more comprehensive
and pervasive—way than in fascism—; this completion began in
the "Romantic" period generally, to be sure—with a view to the
humanization of the human being in its self-certain rationality.
But for the completion what is needed is the decisiveness of the
historic-technological in the sense of the Total "Mobilization" of
all the capabilities of a humanity that is now standing on its own.
One day the disempowerment of the Christian churches has to be
consummated in a "Protestantism" without Christianity, something
that fascism in and of itself cannot accomplish.

Only on the basis of a clear insight into my earlier having
been deceived about the essence and the essential historic force
of National Socialism has the result been the necessity of an
affirmation, and indeed for reasons that have to do with *thinking*. To say that is also to say immediately that this "movement"
remains independent from any given contemporary configuration
and from any duration of the forms that are visible just now.
Yet how does it happen that such an essential affirmation is less

appreciated, or perhaps not at all appreciated, as distinct from mere agreement, which is usually superficial and soon enough without an inkling, if not completely blind? The guilt falls at least in part on the inane presumption of the *"intellectuals"*. . . .

This passage, quite similar in its tone and rhetoric to Heidegger's postwar statements, except for its admission of a second "affirmation," goes on to criticize the role of the intellectuals in the university for their mindless adoption of science and their refusal of meditative thought. What is most astonishing about the passage—the second "affirmation," while crushing, is not unexpected—is Heidegger's disappointment that his reservations concerning the "movement" remain unappreciated by the regime. That, along with the clear indication that in Heidegger's own estimation a thinker of beyng bears no relation to mere "intellectuals," who are so "presumptuous."

Heidegger's growing opposition to the Third Reich stems principally from his realization—with the aid of Ernst Jünger—that National Socialism, which is all about technology and *totale Mobilmachung*, is precisely in this respect mere gigantism and machination (*das Riesenhafte, die Machenschaft*). In this respect National Socialism is complicit with Bolshevism and American pragmatism. Heidegger's insights into "the essence of technology," especially as developed in his essay of the 1950s, remain one of his enduring contributions to philosophy. Yet in these *Notebooks* his critique of technology often appears to be Luddite. He despises the slogan *Blut und Boden* primarily because it goes hand-in-hand with urbanization (*Verstädterung*) and the destruction of village and farm life (95:361: *Zerstörung des Dorfes und des Hofes*). That is perhaps one of the reasons for his inability to identify with or even acknowledge the suffering of the German Jews, at least as of 1938–41. There are none, or precious few of them, down on the farm, at least in Todtnauberg. Their fate is that of a city people—*all* of whom, in Heidegger's view, are already lost. In this respect Heidegger is correctly characterized at least in part by Schelling's description, in a late lecture course, of members of the ancient Alemannic tribes: "Testimony to the resolute repugnance of the Alemannic tribes to a national existence [*gegen volksartige Existenz*] is later delivered by the visible and deeply rooted preference of the Alemannics for a life as free and solitary individuals [*zum freien Einzelleben*], by their hatred of cities, which they view as tombs in which the living are interred, and by their passion to destroy the Roman settlements."[5]

5. F. W. J. Schelling, *Ausgewählte Schriften*, 6 vols., ed. Manfred Frank (Frankfurt am Main: Suhrkamp, 1985), 5:169.

Perhaps a word has to be added on the "disempowerment of the Christian churches" and the bizarre "Protestantism" without Christianity invoked by Heidegger a moment ago. One of the most surprising aspects of the *Schwarze Hefte* from the late 1930s is the virulent anti-Catholicism. True, Heidegger fights a battle with the Church—and thereby with his own youth and education up to and including his university years—from beginning to end. Yet the attention he pays to ecclesiastical politics is surprising in view of his hatred of the Church. In one detailed remark, Heidegger expresses his contempt for a Catholicism that is still dominated by the Counter-Reformation and by the Jesuit emphasis on military organization ("soldiers of Christ") and propaganda, which is the falsifying or at best the "managing" of historical records. The militant Church's heroism of the will, says Heidegger, is more Spanish than Roman; in any case it is "non-Nordic and entirely *undeutsch*" (95:326). His disdain for Christianity in general runs both deep and wide, and it includes both the churches that cooperate with the regime and those that oppose it. At one point Heidegger fulminates against Karl Barth, precisely for his role in the Resistance: "The Phariseeism of Karl Barth and his comrades exceeds even that of the ancient Jews [*das Altjüdische*]" (95:395). Shall we derive any satisfaction from Heidegger's allusion to the Bible? Surely not. Yet this opposition to the Christian churches, especially the Catholic Church, complicates the argument made by many—an argument otherwise not without weight—that Heidegger's anti-Semitism arises principally from his conservative Catholic background.

A particularly disturbing passage on "racism" and *Judentum* lays the charge of racism against the Jews themselves. It is particularly disquieting inasmuch as racial and religious laws often do seem to be intertwined in many world religions, so that judgment is difficult. Be that as it may, and I am not competent to say, here is the passage, which closes with an especially shocking twist of "logic":

Daß im Zeitalter der Machenschaft die Rasse zum ausgesprochenen und eigens eingerichteten "Prinzip" der Geschichte (oder nur der Historie) erhoben wird, ist nicht die willkürliche Erfindung von "Doktrinären." sondern eine *Folge* der Macht der Machenschaft, die das Seiende nach allen seinen Bereichen in die planhafte Berechnung niederzwingen muß. Durch den Rassegedanken wird "das Leben" in die Form der Züchtbarkeit gebracht, die eine Art der Berechnung darstellt. Die Juden "leben" *bei ihrer betont rechnerischen Begabung* am längsten schon nach dem Rasseprinzip, weshalb sie sich auch am heftigsten gegen die uneingeschränkte Anwendung zur Wehr setzen. (96:56)

The fact that in the age of machination race is elevated to the position of being the exceptional and expressly instituted "principle" of the historic (or of mere history) is not an arbitrary invention of those who are "doctrinaire." Rather, it is a *consequence* of the might of machination, which has to subject every single region of beings to a planned reckoning. By means of the thought of race, "life" is subsumed under the form of breeding, which itself represents a kind of reckoning. The Jews, *for all their emphatic gift for reckoning*, have for the longest time "lived" in accord with the principle of race, which is why they are erecting the most vigorous defense against its unrestricted application.

Let me repeat a point made earlier. Many years ago, in *De l'esprit* and elsewhere, Derrida asked whether Heidegger's putative "metaphysical" notion of race and racism was better or worse than the "biological" racism that Heidegger clearly despised. It is that sort of insecurity that rattles us when we read this last passage, for, as Derrida was also fond of saying, there are traps on all sides. What is clearly nonsensical and horrific in what I have just cited is the claim that the Jews, who have "for the longest time 'lived' in accord with the principle of race," base their intense resistance to National Socialism solely on the happenstance that the Nazis are applying that principle relentlessly. Surely even the strictest religious or racial laws and customs, say, those surrounding marriage, do not normally kill those who fail to pass the test. Furthermore, to associate the *ancient* principle of race in Judaism, if there is or ever was such a thing, with the *modernity* of reckoning and machination is—on Heidegger's own terms—either a half-baked thought or nonsense, soon to be or already become murderous nonsense. All that one can or might salvage from these disturbing remarks, it seems to me, are the worrisome thoughts that (1) no matter how visceral racial hatreds may be, it could well be that the planning and calculating machination of our highly technologized societies fosters them, that (2) racism did not first arise during the 1930s in Germany, and that (3) its carcinogens are found in so many peoples, in so many places, at so many times. Perhaps it is especially difficult for a white U.S.-American to discuss issues surrounding racism without a sense of paranoia—a paranoia that for once is thoroughly justified. This is said not to soften anyone's judgment of Heidegger but to deny all pleasure, satisfaction, and false sense of righteousness to the judges, all of them, and me in the first place. Traps on all sides, indeed.

Even though these passages on racism, whether "biological" or "metaphysical," are wretchedly difficult to unravel, there is something that is much more transparent, and that is Heidegger's well-nigh Wilhelmine Germanism. A long passage called *Die verborgene Deutschheit*, "Concealed Germanness," begins with this: "—*unantastbar sei das Opfer der Gefallenen* . . ." (96:29). "The sacrifice of those who have fallen shall be irreproachable." Soon enough, however, comes the word, *Gleichwohl*, "All the same . . ." The warriors have a very high status for Heidegger, as they must for any young man (Jaspers and Heidegger, for example) declared unfit for service during World War I, and only at the end (this is Heidegger's case) sent to serve at a meteorological station near Verdun. Yet the warriors must yield pride of place to the thinker of beyng, who, while in safe hiding, himself prepares the future of "another beginning." As for the warrior, "*Der Krieger . . . ist gerade nicht die prägsame Gestalt des endgültigen Typus*" (ibid.; cf. 94:299). "The warrior . . . is precisely not the figure that sets its stamp on the ultimate type." Even if Heidegger is here derisorily quoting the "type" of the Nazi propagandists, he does not shy from the claim to ultimacy for his own *Seynsdenken* and for the solitary *Seynsdenker* he takes himself to be. And even if he berates his contemporaries for failing to think beyng, he is secretly proud to be able to claim it as his own: "How good that only the very few, and even they only rarely, intimate something of the truth of beyng" (94:277).

Concerning "the fallen," one must note this: they are obviously *German* fallen. The other victims of the War are at best collateral damage. Yet this is both monstrous and incomprehensible. For the dead, whether on the battlefield or in the camps, are radically individualized in their death, no matter what their unimaginable number or their collective destiny. How could the thinker of *Vereinzelung* and *Vereinsamung*, individuation and solitude, of *Sein zum Tode* and *Selbstsein*, being toward death and being a self, be so unmoved by mortal annihilation? If only *German* deaths count, what happens to the existential-ontological claim of *Sein und Zeit* that fundamental ontology investigates Dasein as such and as a whole? If death is the possibility that is ownmost, nonrelational, unsurpassable, certain, and as certain indeterminate as to its *when?* how can that possibility be restricted to the Germans? And how can the clearing of being, no matter how it is spelled, be restricted to the Germans? Was it not enough to restrict it to the human animals?

"The Germans." What does Heidegger expect of them? The opening aphorism of *Überlegungen VII* (95:1), on "*The essence of the Germans,*"
reads: "That they may be fettered to the *struggle* for their essence; only in
this struggle are they the people they alone can be." We gasp at such great,
and greatly violent, expectations. Yet even Karl Jaspers, in his *Philosophical
Autobiography,* is preoccupied with *das deutsche Werden,* "German Becoming," and, responding to his readers' queries as to why, he simply says, "We
have to be."[6] Heidegger, for his part, is aware that the charge of "barbarism"
against the Germans, a charge made a century earlier by Hölderlin in the
second volume of *Hyperion,* has a special relevance for his own time. "Barbarity," he remarks at one point, "is a primary trait of civilized peoples"
(95:280; cf. 95:12 and 96:114). The *Schwarze Hefte* are laced with bitter
remarks on "the drives to violence and destruction that are running amok,"
die Losgelassenheit der Gewalt- und Zerstörungstriebe (95:26). By contrast,
when Heidegger says, "National Socialism is a *barbaric principle,*" he is
referring to Schelling's use of that phrase, a usage that Maurice Merleau-
Ponty repeats in his lectures on nature. For all three, the "barbarism" in
question is the force of *natura naturans,* that is, the creative and nurturing
energies of nature, not a destructive force. Yet to identify National Socialism as such a creative force, and to add, "That is what is essential about
it and that is its possible greatness," is to abuse Schelling's intention and
to miss the thrust of Hölderlin's dire portrait (94:194 and 329–30). For
what Hyperion bemoans is that he finds only *fragments* of human beings
in Germany, but no complete human beings as such; among such inhuman
shards, he says, are the "thinkers," *Denker,* but again, "no human beings,"
aber keine Menschen (CHV 1:754). As far as I am aware, Heidegger, the
self-styled thinker par excellence, never faces up to Hölderlin's accusation.

The truth is that after Schelling, Hölderlin, and Nietzsche, Germany
is in Heidegger's judgment no longer Germany, no longer the land of poets
and thinkers (95:30). Yet precisely this makes Heidegger's devotion to "Germanness" so odd. The adulation of *Deutschheit* on the exclusive basis of
Nietzsche and Hölderlin, as though their heritage were enough to enable
him to forgive and forget all the rest, would be like saying that the very
worst deeds and omissions of our own "U.S. and A." count for nothing
because of Twain's late essays and Melville's *Moby-Dick.* The parochialism
of such adulation of the fatherland (and motherland?) is astonishing, the

---

6. On the Heidegger-Jaspers relationship, and for the sources cited here, see the *Journal
of the British Society for Phenomenology,* 12:2 (May 1978), 126–29.

Borniertheit depressing. Above all, to repeat, it reflects a certain hardness of heart and mind. In more than one place Heidegger chides the weak of heart who fear that we are entering an age of "barbarism." It is "childish" to worry about barbarity, he says, inasmuch as *Seynsverlassenheit* is the real problem. As for Heidegger's absolute identification with *Seynsdenken* and with "the last god," it seems he has forgotten the meaning of his own name. With disbelief and astonishment one reads the following note from the years 1934–35 (94:273): "Why do I have two *g*'s in my name? Why else than that I recognize what always counts: *Güte* (not pity) and *Geduld*, that is, supreme will." *Güte* is benevolence, kindness, generosity; *Geduld* is patience, which Heidegger here equates with "supreme will." Benevolence is hard to find in the *Schwarze Hefte*, and patience is nowhere, although willfulness abounds. Heidegütiger? Heidegeduldiger? Oh, my.

Apropos of barbarism and brutality. While discussing the National Socialist struggle against Bolshevism Heidegger writes that "the fact that executions by a shot in the back of the neck [*Genickschuss*] have come into existence is but a coarse, superficial, and impotent sign of 'terror'" (96:139). The genuine terror, he continues, is reserved for something beyond "beings," something doubtless like the abandonment of beings by beyng. As for the current war, it will have no victors, not because of the mutual destruction but because "all are becoming slaves to the history of beyng, for which they have all been found to be too petty from the outset and therefore were impelled into war" (96:141–42). Heidegger has no interest in the number of the dead. Whether the Bolsheviks kill one person or hundreds of thousands of those they consider "*Untermenschentum*" is a question only for those who are obsessed with quantity. The danger, says Heidegger, is that one may come to think that killing just a few persons "is not so bad" (96:234; cf. 241). One is grateful for Heidegger's humanity in this instance, but it is startling to see the atrocities committed against *Untermenschentum*, including the *Genickschuss*, attributed to the Bolsheviks and to them alone. The language alone, the *German* words *Untermenschentum* and *Genickschuss*, should have spoken to him. It did not.

Heidegger often in these pages confesses his interest in Russia—not in the Soviet Union, whose Bolshevism is a Western invention, but in the Russia that melts into Asia. This fascination began in his high school days, when he tried to learn Russian (96:148), perhaps in order to be able to read Dostoyevsky. It is the "darkness" of the Slavic and Russian that promises most for Germany, provided the Germans one day confront beyng. Whereas the French only want revenge and the British only want to make money, the Russians remain deeply mysterious. Even Lenin is treated with greater seriousness in Heidegger's *Notebooks* than any other political leader; none of the others are in fact ever named. The "mixture" of these two great and greatly opposed civilizations, the German and the Russian, is both the gravest danger and a source of speculative delectation for Heidegger, as the creatures of daylight go to confront the creatures of the night. Yet, to repeat, as Heidegger does ceaselessly, there will be creatures of daylight only if the Germans learn to think *Seyn*.

The confusion of levels throughout the *Schwarze Hefte* is quite striking—here, the mystique of Mother Russia and the history of beyng appear in the same breath. Or, again in the same breath or with the same stroke of the pen, we find the universal uprootedness of beings in modernity and an international conspiracy of uprooted Jews. It is as though one were to imagine Kant making his scurrilous remarks on Africa and Africans the basis of a fourth synthesis in the transcendental deduction. Perhaps this confusion of levels is the thinker's form of vulgarity? In any case, the confusion of levels appears to be Heidegger's own form of everydayness. The catastrophe of the *Black Notebooks* may be best described, to repeat, as Heidegger's surrender to the *Alltäglichkeit* that he excelled in portraying.

In the *Notebooks* of 1939–41, Heidegger makes even his positive views, for example, his allegiance to early Greek thought and culture, seem grotesque. He writes:

> Der Anfang unseres abendländlischen geschichtlichen "Da-seins" ist das Dichten und Denken des frühen und hohen Griechentums—und nichts anderes; gesetzt, daß wir nicht "Geschichte" mit dem tierhaften Erbgang der Geschlechterfolgen von auftauchenden und verschwindenden Gruppen von Lebewesen zusammenwerfen, die eine "Kultur" "machen" wie die Biber ihre "Bauten." (96:85)

> The beginning of our Western historic "Da-sein" is the poetizing and thinking of early, elevated Greek civilization—and nothing else; provided that we do not absurdly conflate "the historic" with the animal-like genetic sequence of groups of living creatures that arise and disappear, "constructing" their "culture" in the way beavers "build" their "dams."

Leave it to the beavers to serve as a lowly vehicle for the tenor of mere animal inheritance, which enables both animal species and inferior human cultures to flourish and falter, prevail and fail, whereas the ancient Greeks last. No, the beavers do not perdure, do not withstand the test of time, are not *selbst-ständig*. Likewise, the "historic" should never be tossed into the mix of categories that pertain to mere "culture." No, where historic being-there is concerned, it must be all Greek, all the time. And not the Greece of Plato, or even of Aristotle, but only Greece prior to Socrates. Anaximander, Heraclitus, Parmenides—theirs is the *Dichten und Denken* that, if one were not careful, one might hear as German words.

I hear my readers ask in desperation, "So, what's wrong with the beavers?" and again I cite Heidegger, who hastens to make reply. "*Das Lebendige*—(im Unterschied zum Da-sein) ist der vorzeitig abgefangene, sich genügende und verdumpfte Anlauf zur grundlosen Gründung eines Offenen Grundes—zur *Freiheit*" (96:91). "*The living*—(as distinct from Da-sein) is a head-start for the groundless grounding of the ground for something open— a head-start for *freedom*, but one that is cut short ahead of time, self-satisfied and evanescent." Schelling could almost have written these words, but he would—and did—think the better of it. Likewise Novalis, and likewise Goethe. Perhaps only Hegel, the most imperious and unforgiving of all metaphysicians, could have written this way. As one reads the *Schwarze Hefte*, it becomes clear that Heidegger has not achieved the radical think-ing of nature and of other life forms that Goethe, Novalis, Schelling—and, yes, Hölderlin—accomplished; none of these four fall prey to the classic metaphysical *exceptionalism* that Heidegger claims for human being-there. Heidegger's polemics against ontotheology and metaphysics pale in the face of his polemics against biology and the living. His polemics against the living, against the wretched animal and the squalid organism, once again deafen his ability to hear his own language. He wants his rhetoric of *Seyn* to be a litany or a Pindaric ode. It is instead the repetitive and uninspired *No! No! No!* to what he once called "our abysmal bodily kinship with the beast" (W 157; BW 206). Heidegger's anti-Semitism, if that is the right word, may ultimately be bound up with his inability to mutter, much less to shout, *l'chaim*, "to life!"

If that seems too low a reference to popular culture on my part—and how must Heidegger have despised the American musical theater, one of its greatest and most pragmatic contributions to world culture—then consider this emendation by Heidegger of his 1929–30 lecture course on organism and animality, an emendation I wish I had seen before writing *Daimon Life* and *Derrida and Our Animal Others*:

> The designation of stone, animal, and man by means of their relation to the world (see the lecture course of 1929–30) is to be maintained in the orientation of its question—and yet it is

inadequate. The difficulty lies in the definition of the animal as "poor in world," in spite of the reservations and qualifications made there concerning the concept of "poverty." It should not be a matter of being worldless, poor in world, or world-shaping. Rather, *without field and world,* / *benumbed by the field and without world,* / and *shaping the world-disclosing earth* / are the more suitable versions of the question's scope. Therewith the designation of the "stone" as without field and world, at the same time and even ahead of time, needs its own "positive" definition. But how is this to be articulated? Surely, in terms of the "earth"—but then indeed entirely out of "world." (95:282)

The stone is without field and without world.

The animal is benumbed (*benommen*) by the field and is without world.

The human being shapes the world-disclosing earth.

What *field* means in the first two statements is difficult to say. If it means the "force field" of physics, then the stone would be impossible to exclude, especially the magnetic stones that were identified in antiquity with Samothrace. If it means the farmer's field, then the farmer would have to attest that even if the stone is without field the field is never without stones. If "field" is here trying to translate *die Gegend,* the "region" in which being (*Sein*) is disclosed, then we may have to agree that *der Mensch* is never entirely lapidary. The final phrase of the quoted passage, *aus "Welt,"* is difficult to understand: *"dann aber vollends gar aus 'Welt.'"* Is the sense that the stone is to be interpreted "positively" in terms of "earth," which is disclosed to human beings alone, but then "entirely" *excluded from* the concept of world—or, quite the contrary, "entirely" *on the basis of,* or *in terms of* world? The latter would not make a nonsense of the claim that the stone is *weltlos,* although it may seem to; but it would require us to consider once again the final chapters of *Sein und Zeit,* especially section 80, where "nature" plays a more positive role in the analysis of Dasein than hitherto suspected. Be that as it may, it is clear that Heidegger is now even less generous to the animal than he was in the 1929–30 lecture course. There the animal is "poor in world," or "has a world in not having it," whereas now the animal is stony broke—benumbed by its "field" and deprived altogether of world, whatever the research of biologists Uexküll and Buytendijk may have revealed. Whereas one would like to believe that Heidegger softens his attitude toward the beast, every indication defeats such optimism. The exceptionalism of Dasein and the exclusion of all other life forms from the realm of disclosure become all the stronger after 1929–30.

※

My own dismal discussion of the *Black Notebooks* will continue in the following chapter. Yet at this point I wonder whether the proper accusation against Heidegger is not anti-Semitism—the virulence of visceral hatred is arguably lacking there—but, ironically, terribly, something that Hegel in his early writings, apparently following the judgment of Moses himself, attributed to "the spirit of Judaism" itself, namely, σκληροῖς καρδίᾳ (HW 1:329), a certain "hardness of heart." Especially in Heidegger's case, though perhaps also in Hegel's, the sclerosis seems to have affected the brain as well as the heart. In all the notes Heidegger writes at the outset of World War II, one does not find a single "reflection" on the danger to his loved ones—for example, the sons who may be serving—or the danger to the young people he has taught, to say nothing of those human beings who belong to what Heidegger clearly takes to be the enemy. Nor does one find a trace of what Alexander Mitscherlich vainly searched for in Germany after the war, namely, anything like a capacity to mourn. Granted such hardness of heart toward all and sundry, the venomous outpourings against Christianity and *Judentum* are not surprising. Shocking, but not surprising.

As I searched for words to describe Heidegger's diatribes, or to portray the person behind the polemics, all I could think of was every possible antonym of the words *urbanity* and *thoughtfulness*, the latter word in Hannah Arendt's sense. I repeat my own judgment, which is also that of a well-informed and reflective philosopher and critic, Ludger Lütkehaus, that Heidegger's anti-Semitism does not exhibit the visceral hatred that marks the racism of, say, a white supremacist who aims his hatred at persons of color.[7] Nevertheless it does seem to stem from one or more of those *ressentiments* that never surface so that one can see them for what they are—*eine*

---

7. The comparison between Heidegger's anti-Semitism and white supremacist hatred is mine, not that of Ludger Lütkehaus. See Lütkehaus, " 'Dankbarer Sohn' des Katholizismus," in the *Badische Zeitung* for April 12, 2014, section IV, "Literatur." Lütkehaus, whose judgments of Heidegger are never mild or merciful, and whose opinion regarding Heidegger's anti-Semitism I therefore value all the more, is reviewing not the *Schwarze Hefte* but Martin Heidegger, *Briefwechsel mit seinen Eltern und Briefe an seine Schwester*, ed. Jörg Heidegger and Alfred Denker (Freiburg and München: Karl Alber Verlag, 2013).

Dummheit and *ein Makel* in one's own character, a stupidity and a stain, a *human* stain, as Philip Roth says, a weakness and a flaw in mind and heart, a festering wound in the *Gemüt*. Again I am reminded of Slavoj Žižek's application of Lacanian theory to ethnic hatreds: "they," the foreigners, the enemy, especially the "enemy within," have stolen my pleasure, the pleasure I take in my nation; they are responsible for that gaping hole in my midriff, that otherwise inexplicable zero at my core; and they will have to be punished.[8] In the present instance, it is the "uncommitted" and "rootless" nature of the Jew, his or her lack of "ties" or "commitment" to earth and world and nation, that lies at the core of Heidegger's enmity—that and the Jew's ostensible nature as treacherously calculating, his or her profiteering on the sufferings of others, especially on the Germans at war. We generally count on a person's intelligence, if not to understand the weakness and the wound within, at least to have a sense of the ineptitude of the targeting, a sense that one is lashing out aimlessly and that the problem lies elsewhere and closer to home. Such intelligence fails Heidegger at critical moments, especially in those—admittedly rare, and oddly quite late—moments when he writes the word *Judentum*. These are moments when Heidegger attaches himself to the most vulgar form of machination that is available to him, and no thought of beyng comes to rescue him. Does rescue always grow? No, sometimes the heart and mind are barren, swept by an ill wind, although the wind alone does not cause the barrenness.

For me, however, it will never be a matter of joining the Heidegger Scandal industry. True, journalists will flock to industry events ("conferences"), even though philosophy means less than nothing to them. Heidegger Scandal books will be hastily keyboarded and university presses will make more money on them than they ever do on philosophy books. Certain academics will demonstrate once again that they belong to the Good and the Just, if only when they face backward. For me it will be a matter of adding Heidegger's vulgar and stupid talk about the international Jewish conspiracy to all the other things that weigh on his thought, distorting and diminishing it, marring it in ways one never can and never should forget. Here is a list, my own private list, of those oppressive aspects, to which the anti-Semitic and anti-Everyone remarks now have to be added:

---

8. This is my own compressed version of Žižek's insightful argument in "Eastern Europe's Republics of Gilead," *New Left Review* 183 (September–October 1990), 50–62. I discuss Žižek at some length in "National Erotism (Derdiedas Responsibilities)," in *Ethics and Responsibility in the Phenomenological Tradition*, ed. Richard Rojcewicz (Pittsburgh: Duquesne University Press, 1992), 33–56.

1. Heidegger's fervent *Deutschtümelei,* the *Deutschtum* that he would oppose to *Judentum* and to every other *-tum* except *Griechentum,* is unworthy of a thinker; it mars his work on Hölderlin and Nietzsche in particular.

2. Heidegger's militant "decisionism" runs counter to his thought of the sending of being; it therefore seems to have symptomatic value only, and the symptom betrays a pathology.

3. Heidegger's fervor to reform all science and philosophy and his ambition to assume *geistige Führung* ("spiritual leadership") of the university cast a shadow over his thinking. Hubris is unlikely to have left the thinking untouched, especially when that thinking descends to polemic. And yet Heidegger *is* a thinker.

4. Heidegger's silences concerning the suffering and death of others—above all, the victims of National Socialist crimes—are worse than unforgivable. They are *unforgiving.* None of Heidegger's own heroes, from Sophocles through Nietzsche, was so hard—or so weak—of heart.

The list could go on, but in any case it is not only a list of charges against Heidegger but also a series of warnings to me. I will continue to read Heidegger and I will urge others to read him. Yet the burden placed on the reading—placed there by Heidegger himself—gets more and more difficult to bear. Perhaps it is not overweening to say that the *Black Notebooks* represent a *tragedy.* Especially if thinking demands that one magnify what is great in past efforts at thinking.

6

The Tragedy of the *Black Notebooks*

The following two statements on "tragedy" and "the tragic" in the *Schwarze Hefte* of the late 1930s, when apparently many of the *Notebooks* were written, offer the most promising explanation of their somber and even desperate tone:

> *Das Seyn* selbst ist "tragisch"—d. h. es fängt aus dem Untergang als Ab-grund an und duldet nur solche Anfänge als Jenes, was seiner Wahrheit gerecht bleibt—das Wissen vom Seyn ist deshalb je nur der Einzigen, und zwar Jener aus ihnen, die *notwendig* bei aller historischen Bekanntheit die Unerkennbaren bleiben müssen. Die Grenze auch der echten geschichtlichen Besinnung liegt daher nicht im Vermögen der Aus-einander-setzung—sondern in der wesenhaften Verkennbarkeit, die sich, von einem bestimmten Ring der Einsamkeit an, um jene Einzigen lagert. (95:417)

> *Beyng* itself is "tragic"—i.e., it begins with downfall, as an abyssal departure from all grounds. It makes its peace only with such beginnings, those that remain faithful to its truth—knowing beyng therefore pertains only to individuals, indeed, to those who *necessarily* have to remain the unrecognizable ones, in spite of every historical familiarity they might yield. The limit of genuinely historical meditation too therefore lies not in the capacity to confront—but rather in the essential misrecognition that encloses those individuals within a determinate ring of solitude.

And this, again on the "tragic":

> "Tragisch" ist, was aus dem Untergang seinen Anfang nimmt, weil es im Ab-grund eine Gründerschaft übernommen. Die "Auf-

fassung" des Tragischen, d. h. zuvor die Durchmessung seiner jeweiligen Wesenstiefe, bestimmt sich aus der je in ihm selbst erreichten Wahrheit des Seyns. Die Ent-schlossenheit in das Fragwürdige gehört zum Wesensbestand einer "Tragik". Warum in der Zeit des Mittelalters "Tragödie" (nicht als Dichtungsform genommen) unmöglich war? Weshalb sie in der Neuzeit immer seltener wird und nur das Geschenk an die jeweils Zukünftigen sein kann? Inwiefern zum "Tragischen" die Verschweigung gehört? Warum die bloße Freiheit zum Seienden das Tragische ausschließt; woraus die Freiheit zum Seyn entspringt in einem Zeitalter der Seinsverlassenheit? (95:418)

That is "tragic" which arises out of downfall, because it has assumed the task of grounding in the absence of all grounds. The "conception" of the tragic, i.e., above all, surveying in any given case its essential depths, is determined in each case by the truth of beyng that it achieves in itself. The tragic is an exceptional directedness to the essential unfolding of beyng in any given human being who is open to that essence. Resolute openedness to what is worthy of questioning pertains to the essential core of anything "tragic." Why was "tragedy" (not merely as a form of poetry) impossible during the Middle Ages? For what reason is it becoming ever more rare in modernity, so that it can be a gift only to those who may be in some way futural? To what extent does taciturnity belong to the "tragic"? Why does mere freedom toward beings exclude the tragic; and whence may freedom to beyng spring in an age abandoned by being?

What, then, is the nature of *this* tragedy, the tragedy of the *Black Notebooks*? If some years ago, in *Daimon Life*, I devised an ontological application of *paranoia* for Heidegger's thinking of beyng, a thinking of beyng in the utter absence of all beings, I feel now, after reading the *Schwarze Hefte*, that an additional diagnosis is needed.[1] Heidegger's *Black Notebooks* may well be paranoetic, as I argued the *Beiträge* were, but they are also and above all an expression of the repetition compulsion. In fact, the repetitiveness throughout the thousand or more printed pages of the *Notebooks* makes us

---

1. For two earlier discussions of "paranoetic thinking," see chapter 6 of *Daimon Life* and chapter 4 of *Phantoms of the Other.*

imagine that a special kind of amnesia has intervened between each entry. The repetitiousness takes on a comic aspect when at the end of a given entry Heidegger adds a parenthetical reference, inviting the reader (himself? us?) to "compare" some other page. One presumes that it is Heidegger himself who makes the addition—with an *Ausgabe letzter Hand* one never knows to whom the last hand belongs. In any case, the comic aspect is that one could add literally dozens of page references to the one given, dozens upon dozens, inasmuch as it is all a ring dance of all-too-familiar condemnations. Pierre Klossowski once speculated that the affirmative thought of eternal return of the same, because it is each time greeted with elation, requires the periodicity of amnesia and anamnesis; he even felt that a series of different *selves* would be needed to think the thought with sufficient astonishment each time it recurs. Likewise, the vituperation that Heidegger is able to exercise *each time* it is a question of the Christian churches, culture, aesthetics, Jewish reckoning, National Socialist propaganda, Bolshevism, pragmatism, biologism, the radio, movies, brutality, Descartes, subjectivity, humanization, and the swamping effect of modernity in general suggests that Heidegger has in the meantime, from day to day and day after day, entirely forgotten that he has written the same things over and over again with the identical amount of dudgeon. One almost pictures Jack at the typewriter—even though Heidegger hated and feared the typewriter too—working day after day high in the wintry Colorado mountains on a typescript that consists solely of the words, "All work and no play makes Jack a very angry boy." Some may take this to be an unfair comparison. But I suspect it will seem unfair only to those who have not yet had the dire experience of reading the *Black Notebooks*. If only the *Schwarze Hefte* had been slightly varied in color, with an occasional pastel.

In *Of Spirit* and in his *Geschlecht* series, Derrida complains that Heidegger never dreams of *Geist* as ghost or revenant—which is always the first thing that haunts Derrida about the word. A text Derrida was unable to see, and one that might have perturbed him more than any other by Heidegger, is in *Überlegungen XIII* of the *Schwarze Hefte*. Here Heidegger identifies his nightmare about modernity, namely, "machination," as something ghostly. Moreover, its spectral character has something to do with the *suddenness* we attribute to the ecstatic:

> Die letzte Form der Machenschaft kommt dann ins Spiel, wenn das "Wirkliche" und "Seiende" einen *gespenstischen* Charakter annimmt—das Gespenst erschreckt, spukt im Plötzlichen, gebärdet sich aufdringlich, ist ohne Hintergrund und Gehalt und die

Grund-losigkeit selbst—sie läßt jede Art von Maßnahmen in jeder Hinsicht zu und verbreitet eine unwiderstehliche Verzauberung—setzt sich als das Unbedingte. — (96:108)

The final form of machination comes into play when the "actual," that which is "in being," takes on a *spectral* character—the specter affrights and haunts us in its suddenness; its gestures are intense; all is without background and content; it is groundlessness itself—it is open to every kind of measure in every respect, and it spreads abroad an irresistible entrancement—positing itself as the unconditioned. —

Heidegger is here speaking about his *times*, and yet his words apply equally to his own *writing*. That writing is often confused, mixing cultural critique with slogans of its own devising, conjuring *Seyn* out of newspaper headlines that report approaching or recently past catastrophes. The insistent gesture of unconditioned positing, the ghost of Hegel at his polemical worst, is everywhere in these pages. A specter is haunting Heidegger—the specter of the They.

A good example of this confusion appears a few pages later. Heidegger is arguing that in a time of political *Machenschaft* no real (that is, no *seynsgeschichtliche*) decisions can be made. The worst are full of passionate intensity while the best prepare for the unlikely arrival of the other beginning. Thus Heidegger declares the essential identity of both militaristic imperialism, represented equally by National Socialism and Bolshevism, and humanistic pacifism, represented by persons he does not identify. But then this: "Therefore, 'international Jewry' can make use of both [*sich auch beider das "internationale Judentum" bedienen*], soliciting the one and manipulating it as a means for the other [*die eine als Mittel für die andere ausrufen und bewerkstelligen*]" (96:133; cf. 95:97). The many possible meanings of *ausrufen* and *bewerkstelligen* defeat me here, as I believe they may have defeated Heidegger. And who would not be defeated by the phantasm of an international Jewish conspiracy manipulating both Bolshevik Russia and National Socialist Germany? For his text continues: "*—diese machenschaftliche 'Geschichts'-mache verstrickt alle Mitspieler gleichermaßen in ihre Netze—; im Umkreis der Machenschaft gibt es 'lächerliche Staaten,' aber auch lächerliche Kulturmache.*" "—Such 'history'-making in a time of machination entangles all the players to the same degree in its net—; in the scope of machination there are 'risible states,' but also risible flourishes of culture." The only thing that is clear about such polemics, or that I take to be clear, is that Heidegger is doing everything he can to resist the realization that a terrifying criminality has overtaken his beloved Germany; by equating victims and victimizers he hopes to lay everything that is happening in Germany at the feet of the machinations of modernity. The problem is not Germany but Occidental history since the occlusion of beyng. That leaves him with nothing to do but rage against the machination and whine for *Seyn*.

It is disquieting to read Heidegger's remarks on "language" in the *Notebooks*, inasmuch as his own language throughout the *Schwarze Hefte* is so strained, so strident, so full of cliché and slogan, at times simply insulting and vulgar. The two most succinct of all the aphorisms in the *Notebooks* are the following. First, " *'Realpolitik'* as total prostitution" (96:138). The second, by far the most succinct aphorism (96:229) is this: "*Ihr Ahnungslosen!*" I first translated this as "Oh, you who haven't a clue!" While I resonated with the rhyme, I decided I had to abbreviate: "You dolts!" And that about says it all.

It is cruelly ironic to read Heidegger contrasting the German language, presumably his own, to *römisch-italische Phrasenhaftigkeit*, "Roman-Italic cliché" (95:104). All things Italian or Mediterranean arouse his contempt: Nietzsche's is *eine verrömerte Antike*, a Greek antiquity viewed from the base perspective of Rome (95:110); the Italians have always been jealous of the Greeks, says Heidegger, and that is why the Italian army will devastate Greece. Heidegger's German-Greek axis (a "spiritual" axis, to be sure) presumably means that the German army will be gentle with Greece and Crete. . . . Elsewhere, in a passage that Derrida would have found particularly enlightening, Heidegger says that it is no accident that the words *sensation*—in the sense of journalistic *sensationalism*—and *propaganda* "are Latin-Roman designations"; why, he laments, "are we making such counter-German things into the essence of *Deutschheit*?" (95:362). Later he goes so far as to say that the *brutalitas* of the times is "not by accident Latin" (95:394). He is clearly thinking of the definition of man as *animal rationale*, and blaming the brutality he sees all around him on the counter-German Latin. Nietzsche would have responded in his own highly developed Classical Latin, remarking how at the most absurd moments in New Comedy a donkey would be led out onto the stage: *Adventavit asinus, pulcher et fortissimus.* "And then the ass would join the crowd, so beautiful and O so loud!"

Perhaps the most disconcerting aspect of Heidegger's writing is the way in which the violent polemic of his texts—and the *Schwarze Hefte* represent the extreme in this respect—often bathes itself in a viscous and saccharine piety. Every bit as often the unctuous rhetoric achieves the very opposite of what it intends: it becomes laughable. *Überlegungen V* (94:111) begins with an entire page devoted to this:

Winke,

die Zugewunkenes
weiterwinken.

Signals

that signal further
what has been signaled.

What is comic is the image (for me unavoidable) of children at the
train station waving their white handkerchiefs as grandma's train pulls out.
The Germans call this scene *Winke-Winke*. Heidegger plays winky-winky
with beyng and the last god. Yet for him it is no play. "How should the
god's signal [*der Wink des Gottes*] reach us waiting ones when we idolize
the anti-godly? But how should we leave off from such doings unless a
god appears?" (94:341). Although it will strike many of my readers as a
blasphemy of the worst sort, blasphemy rather than comedy, I cannot help
but think of Jeremiah as I read the *Black Notebooks*. Luther prefaces the
Book of Jeremiah by noting that "the land was full of vice and idolatry"
and that "they strangled their prophets with impunity." And who can resist
the word *jeremiad*, or who can dispel altogether the image of Isaiah, when
reading that the "stillness" of the futural ones will "swallow the thunder of
the god's passing" (94:412)? Heidegger doubtless hopes that the last god will
be Zeus-like, the Cloud-gatherer on the plane of power rather than on the
plane of weakness, the latter being the newborn Zeus who needs his mother's
protection; even though it may be blasphemy to say so, blasphemy and an
insult to millions of the victims of Nazism, the rhetoric of the last god is
actually reminiscent of a certain Yahweh—a wrathful Yahweh, a Yahweh,
as Kafka once said, on one of his bad days.

The theme of "the last god," to be sure, disappears from Heidegger's
thinking after World War II. It is "replaced," if one can say so, by the
thinking of the fourfold of gods, mortals, sky, and earth. One must wonder whether "the last god" could have passed the test of Heidegger's 1957
"Onto-theo-logical Constitution of Metaphysics." Presumably not. For the
very juxtaposition of the truth of *Seyn* and the supernal *Seiendes* that any
and every god must be is, in the light of Heidegger's critique of onto-theo-
logy, simply jarring: "*Beyng*—refusal, as the trembling of the becoming-god
of the last god [*Das Seyn—die Verweigerung als die Erzitterung des Götterns
des letzten Gottes*]" (94:429). Perhaps the only thing that is clear about the

coming of "the last god" is that it has nothing to do with salvation or rescue: "How steep the cascade to death is may be measured in terms of the nearness to beyng achieved. The time-space of this measure is Da-sein" (94:515).

In the late 1930s, however, Heidegger is still gripped by the theme of "the last god." It is perhaps the most uncanny of his obsessions during these years, uncanny if only because he is endeavoring to leave metaphysics and ontotheology behind. Although Hölderlin is the source for much of Heidegger's nostalgia concerning the gods who have "flown," I believe that Schelling and Nietzsche are the principal sources for this theme. In the first draft of his *Ages of the World* (DW 40–41), Schelling stresses the "terrors" and "monstrous births" suffered by the deity in its primal state; deity "trembles," *zittert*, in the face of its own nascent being. Heidegger's cryptic gerunds, *die Erzitterung des Götterns* (65:239) likewise emphasize the *birth* of the last god, as though that birth were his death. Nietzsche's *Birth of Tragedy from the Spirit of Music* (KSA 1:63) describes tragic drama as the "shivering" or "trembling [*zitternden*] image" of Dionysos in the soul of the spectator. Later, as we shall see, Nietzsche's Zarathustra invokes "the last god." To these sources one may add the Kierkegaard of *Fear and Trembling*, provided one thinks of deity itself as shivering with anxiety. At all events, it is clear that the *Beiträge zur Philosophie* would serve as the text for a more detailed discussion of this theme, and not the *Schwarze Hefte*.[2]

With regard to the lugubrious piety of Heidegger's rhetoric, one might well contrast Nietzsche, who in *The Gay Science* and in *Ecce Homo* asks himself to what extent he is still pious; there a crisp and cool rhetoric enables one of Nietzsche's most radically recoiling questions and self-critiques. There is nothing syrupy or saccharine about Nietzsche's rhetoric. The piety of the later Heidegger, his "questioning" that takes itself to be "the piety of thinking," and even the piety of the language of *Gelassenheit*—all of these are troubling inasmuch as the incense once curled about a hoisted flag, the liturgy was a mummery of militarism and crusade. The holier-than-thou attitude of the thinker reflects as it always does the repetition-compulsion of chiliastic decision, decision to the point of a secular Last Judgment. The only possible response to such pious prattle and decisionism is the horror reflected in the faces painted by the wily Michelangelo on the Sistine Chapel altar wall. Far better the horror and dismay of Peter and Paul, far better

---

2. For further discussion of this theme see *The Tragic Absolute* (TA 130–32). I remain grateful to Professor Iris Därmann for the reference to the "shivering image" of Dionysos in Nietzsche's *Birth of Tragedy.*

even the conniving of Bartholomew, who tries to fob off the flayed skin
of the artist as evidence of his own martyrdom, than this from Heidegger:

> Uns fügend in die Fuge des Seyns
> stehen wir zur Verfügung den Göttern.

> Die Besinnung auf die Wahrheit
> des Seyns ist das erste Beziehen
> des Postens der Wächterschaft
> für die Stille des Vorbeigangs
> des letzten Gottes. (94:113)

> Adjoining ourselves to the jointure of beyng
> we stand at the disposal of the gods.

> Meditation on the truth
> of beyng is the initial taking up
> of our post on the lookout
> for the stillness of the passing
> of the last god.

Related to such pious and self-aggrandizing prattle is Heidegger's tendency—unbearable in these *Notebooks*—to stylize his own childhood, seeing
in it the heroic-bucolic origins of the future thinker of beyng (95:290).
Childe Heidegger becomes the youthful Achilles on the slopes of Mount
Pelion, flourishing under the vigilant care of the centaur Chiron. A bizarre
example of this self-stylization appears at the end of *Überlegungen VI*
(94:523), where Heidegger "plays" with some dates in German history in
an admittedly "uncanny" way: 1806, Hölderlin is interned in the Autenrieth
Clinic; 1813, Wagner is born at the peak of German power and influence;
1843, Hölderlin quits the world and, one year later, Nietzsche joins it;
1870–1876, the German *Gründerjahre*, that is, Germany's "Gilded Age," also
sees the publication of Nietzsche's *Untimely Meditations*; 1883, the first part
of *Thus Spoke Zarathustra* is published, and Wagner dies; 1888, at the end
of December, Nietzsche's "euphoria" in Turin leads to his collapse in early
January 1889. Heidegger now enters two dashes into his notebook and,
in the lower-right-hand corner of the page he enters the date September
26, 1889, *the date of his own birth*. Such self-lionizing, reminiscent of the
pompous "Why We Are Staying in the Provinces," eventually leads him
to make the most absurd of gestures: "For the spirited, active man [*den*

geistigen, handelnden Mann], there are today only two possibilities: either to stand out there on the command-bridge of a minesweeper or to steer the ship of uttermost questioning out into the storm of beyng" (96:160).

In all this self-stylization of the thinker of beyng, the precursory openness of open resoluteness, *Entschlossenheit*, seems to have shut down altogether. It is buried under the debris of Heidegger's own special form of everydayness. And even if he should condemn above all else the alternating current of optimism and pessimism in his own times, his texts of the 1930s do not give optimism much of a chance. What frightens one, of course, is that the 1930s themselves do not seem to be giving optimism a chance, so that this troubling rhetoric of Heidegger's may be taken as symptomatic. When that rhetoric is most effective, it is indeed frightening. Consider this, from 1941: "*Ein Totentanz durchwirbelt das im Unwesen angelangte* animal rationale" (96:255). "Now that the *animal rationale* has achieved its monstrous nonessence, a *danse macabre* has sent it spinning." Sometimes the rhetoric of the *Totentanz* spins out of control: the War, which in terms of the history of beyng is utterly without effect, will nonetheless bring about the full accomplishment of technology, "the final act of which will be that the earth detonates itself and humanity as we now know it will disappear" (96:238). By way of consolation, Heidegger adds, "Yet this is no misfortune, but rather the first purification *of being* of its most profound disfigurement due to the dominance of beings" (ibid.). Earth and mortals trashed—for the sake of being's purification. But what if being "needs and uses" human beings? And where would human beings dwell in being, if not on the earth?

What is perhaps most disquieting to the reader (to *this* reader) of the *Black Notebooks* is the fact that the "darkening," *Erdunkelung*, of both world and earth that comes to obsess Heidegger in the 1930s is a common experience in our own time and place. At least part of the allure of the ongoing Heidegger Scandal is that it distracts us from our own appalling national stupidities and our galling national avarice and aggression—our own little darkenings, if you will. It is so much easier to fight battles that have already been decided and so reassuring to feel oneself securely moored in the harbor of god's own country. Not the nation of last god, but that of the good old reliable god, who blesses every stupidity and earns interest on every act of avarice. Perhaps the joy with which the *Schwarze Hefte* were greeted in some quarters has to do with this need to look backward rather than forward? The irony is that Heidegger's *Notebooks* themselves radiate this dire mood. Perhaps by condemning them and by prosecuting Heidegger generally we hope to gain a bit of space for ourselves, some impossible space for ourselves? That would be the *Notebooks'* most terrible victory: it is not that the last laugh laughs best, for there is no joy and no laughter in the *Notebooks*, but that their helpless rage recurs in those who rail against them.

Even so, after having been warned, allow me to continue with this dark retrospect. As I mentioned earlier, Heidegger's situation as a thinker is worse than that of paranoia. The paranoid person can fix on this or that being that hates me and persecutes me even though I love him. I must, there-fore, through reversal of affect, hate him in return, even as he pursues and plagues me. In Lacanian terms, as we heard in the foregoing chapter, some being or group of beings has stolen my pleasure and left me with a gigantic zero at the heart of my being. That alien being or group of beings must be made to suffer, even as I suffer. Yet Heidegger's situation is more desper-ate. As he reiterates over and over again, it is not we who have abandoned being, but being that has abandoned us, abandoned *all* beings, and long ago. Furthermore, being, *Sein*, to say nothing of *Seyn*, is not any particular *Seiendes*. Thus there is no one and no thing to blame for the situation that elicits paranoetic thinking, no noematic correlate or objective correlative that pursues and plagues us, no recognizable mechanism of reversal of affect that could explain our malaise. This, of course, would make it impossible for Heidegger to blame this or that group of human beings for contributing to the oblivion of being. Oblivion belongs to beyng, not to us. *Vergessenheit des Seyns* and *Verlassenheit des Seyns* are both preeminently *subjective* genitives. *Beyng* has forgotten us. *Beyng* has abandoned us. And so we are bedazzled by beings, material items, money, flags, gods—and shibboleths. This is Hei-degger's central teaching early and late. The result, to repeat, is not paranoia but paranoetic thinking. And if Heidegger should ever polemicize against his contemporaries, or against any subset of his contemporaries, it must be that he has forgotten to *think*, forgotten to *remember*. For you and me, this lapse in thinking would be risible, and we would laugh at ourselves for it, were we alert enough for self-critique. For Heidegger, by contrast, this lapse in himself is unforgivable, unpardonable; he would collapse on account of it. This lapse and collapse, this failure of *thinking*, is not the sort of condem-nation or death-sentence that the self-appointed tribunals of our own time might wish for him. Yet for anyone who *reads* him, *and precisely for those who will continue to read him*, he being one of the most strikingly original thinkers of the twentieth century, this lapse and collapse will be worse than unforgivable—they will remain *unforgiving*. To that extent, Heidegger's situ-ation, mired in the quicksand of an everydayness that is bestowed by beyng and by nothing else, is truly tragic, truly catastrophic.

It may well be that Heidegger's thinking immediately after World War II confronts the tragedy of his own situation. It is, to repeat, the situation that makes paranoetic thinking inevitable. It is the situation in which, on the one hand, the thinking of being must get along without beings, but also the situation in which, on the other hand, being itself withdraws and abandons the thinker. Such abandonment creates a remarkable situation for Heidegger's language. At the end of "Anaximander's Saying," Heidegger observes that his thinking is *bildarm*, "poor in images," anything but picturesque. (*Bildarm* reflects both morphologically and semantically the *weltarm* quality attributed to the animal in the 1929–30 seminar: not only does an anxious Dasein share its *Benommenheit* with animals, such that anxiety has to be thought as *animal* anxiety, but the poverty of the animal with respect to both "world" (or "field") and language is shared by the thinker of being, whose penurious "word" is anything but picturesque. Needless to relate, Heidegger is reluctant to reflect on such shared poverty.) Recall those two underscored words in Derrida's seminar on being and history: *métaphore ontique*. There is no language of beyng apart from the language borrowed from beings and reverting back to beings. The effort to dry-clean language until there is nothing left but the pure concept, the "patience" and the "labor" of the concept, has to be left to Hegel. No "uninhibited word mysticism," against which Heidegger himself warns his students in 1935, will help the thinker of beyng. The repetitive, self-referential litanies of *Seyn* and *Ereignis* will not circumvent the difficulty. By the late 1940s and throughout the 1950s, Heidegger's own language will meekly submit to the yoke of ontic metaphor, and such meekness will be Heidegger's strength, the strength that failed him in the 1930s. "The house of being" and "the clouds of the sky" will make him an easy target for tough-minded analysts of language, but these metaphors, no matter how bucolic and "Romantic," will still reflect Heidegger at his best. For the tough-minded, the late Heidegger's language will seem to be white noise, whereas it is in effect white mythology.

⁂

There are some meager lights in the *Notebooks*, and one wants to acknowledge them, if only to resist the general obscurity. The vast majority of these luminous moments occur in volume 94, which reproduces the notebooks of 1931 to 1938. The volumes that cover 1938 to 1941 are increasingly negative, drearily polemical, and endlessly repetitive. It is also very odd that the anti-Semitic remarks ("*Weltjudentum*") occur only in these two final volumes and are absent from the much larger first volume. Why odd? Precisely because Heidegger's critique of National Socialist propaganda becomes increasingly strident as the *Notebooks* proceed. Already in the mid-1930s

Heidegger writes, "Propaganda is the reverse side of a 'defamation' that is unsure of itself" (94:508). Why and how, then, could he have sunk to the lowest level of such defamatory propaganda so late, precisely at the point of his greatest allergy to the current form of the National Socialist "movement"? Certainly no one who is busily engaged in the Heidegger Scandal industry will be able to respond to this question—one of the most serious and difficult questions posed by the *Black Notebooks*.

But to acknowledge some of these lights, as I am calling them. In the mid-1930s Heidegger evaluates Nietzsche's *Thus Spoke Zarathustra* in this way: "Is Nietzsche's *Thus Spoke Zarathustra* a crying out, perhaps *the* cry, for the stillness of beyng? And this, because here a transition is in progress—a single-span bridge whose pillars remain unseen, which is why the bridge span goes its way with such *élan*" (94:349). This remark conforms to Heidegger's best writing and thinking on Nietzsche, namely, the 1936–37 lecture courses on "Will to Power as Art" and "The Eternal Recurrence of the Same," where Nietzsche's magnum opus plays a central role. A second light involves a refutation of the usual view of Heidegger's own reading of Nietzsche, namely, the view that Heidegger prefers the unpublished *Nachlass* to Nietzsche's own published writings. Here Heidegger insists that Nietzsche's essential insights, the ones that would have gone toward a more systematic treatment of his thought, are found equally in the published and the unpublished work. Indeed, the two places he cites positively are from the (published) *Beyond Good and Evil*, namely, the sections on "the prejudices of the philosophers" and on "the religious essence" (94:376). More comprehensively, in the mid-1930s Heidegger offers a brief syllabus for a philosophy worthy of the name: "The saying of Anaximander, the sayings of Heraclitus, the 'doctrine' of Parmenides, Plato's *Phaedrus*, Aristotle's *Metaphysics*, Books Z–Θ; Descartes's *Meditationes*, Leibniz's "Monadology," Kant's *Critiques* (all three); Hegel's *Phenomenology of Spirit*, Schelling's treatise on freedom, Nietzsche's literary corpus in the direction of a 'major work'" (94:493). Never mind that the syllabus ends without specific mention of Nietzsche's *Beyond Good and Evil* and *Zarathustra*.

As for what Heidegger is *reading* during this decade, there is very little evidence of it in the *Schwarze Hefte*. There are endless diatribes against daily newspaper and radio reports, but very little record here of what Heidegger may be reading outside of the works required for his courses. Whereas Ernst Jünger, the "sole *homo literatus*" of the times, begins to undergo critique in spite of Heidegger's general appreciation (see 96:202–03, 219, 234–35, and 275), it is Colonel T. E. Lawrence's *Seven Pillars of Wisdom*, read in translation, that receives Heidegger's full approbation and even enthusiasm (95:423). The brightest light, however, shines in what are called *Beilagen*,

"Supplements," in the second of the three *Gesamtausgabe* volumes in question (95:260–67). Oddly, although no detailed editorial note accompanies them, these "Supplements" are in my view clearly from the 1950s. How they wound up in the *Notebook* of the late 1930s neither I nor the editor can say. The dour tone of the 1938–39 notes suddenly evanesces and Heidegger begins to do again what he always did best: *read.* Here, in numbers 4, 5, and 7 (95:261–62), along with number 14 (95:265), he reads Parmenides, Sophocles, Hölderlin, and Hannah Arendt. Number four is a fragment (or possibly two fragments) from Hölderlin's Homburger *Folioheft:*

> Und mitzufühlen das . . .
> . . . sondern Leben, summendheißes auch von
>   Schatten Echo
> Als in einem Brennpunct
> Versammelt. Goldne Wüste. II, 249
>   und verlorne Liebe[3]

> And to feel with others . . .
> . . . rather, life, buzzing hot even in
>   echoes of shade
> As in burning focus
> Gathered. Golden desert. 2:249
>   and lost love

Here "life," which is the word replaced by the first set of ellipsis points, then repeated by Hölderlin in the following line of the fragment, does not receive the usual bashing from the Heidegger of the 1930s; it is not denigrated as the swampland of post-Nietzschean *Lebensphilosophie* or of "lived experience" in, say, Karl Jaspers's *Existenzphilosophie* (94:398–400). (*Versumpfung*, as I noted earlier, is one of Heidegger's constant gripes during the 1930s: virtually everything in his time is swampland and morass—hence, the surprising appearance in the *Notebooks* of "life" as light and heat.) It is that scorching, singeing light and heat of the sun felt even in the shade, as in a desert of gold, which is related in some way perhaps to a love one has lost.

---

3. The editor cites Heidegger's source as Friedrich Hölderlin, *Gedichte nach 1800*, ed. Friedrich Beißner, Stuttgarter Ausgabe, vol. 2.1 (Stuttgart: W. Kohlhammer Verlag, 1951), Heidegger himself noting "2:249." This is perhaps the most convincing internal evidence for the 1950s as the time of the *Beilagen*—that and the reference to Arendt. See now DKV 1:415 and 1082, along with CHV 1:415, for two different versions of the fragment or fragments.

Hölderlin, in his notes on Sophocles, writes of the life-giving sun scorching the land as well as evoking life from the impervious night of the soil.

The next fragment too focuses on love, night, and light. Heidegger cites Parmenides's fragments B13–15a:

πρώτιστον μὲν Ἔρωτα θεῶν μητίσατο πάντων

(σελήνη)
νυκτιφαὲς περὶ γαῖαν ἀλώμενον ἀλλότριον φῶς . . .
αἰεὶ παπταίνουσα πρὸς αὐγὰς ἠελίοιο   14. 15
γαῖα   ὑδατόριζον 15a[4]

Among all the gods she thought of Eros as the very first

(Selene, the moon)
Illuminating the night, strangely, wandering the earth . . .
Forever gazing at the beams of the sun   14. 15
Gaia, the earth   rooted in water. . . .   15a

If I am not mistaken, this attention to Selene (the Moon), related to Semele (the mother of Dionysos), is an important part of the change that takes place in Heidegger during the early 1950s, a change in the direction of *Gelassenheit* or letting-be and of what Heidegger calls "poetizing thought." Heidegger's attention here to Selene, the Moon, is highly reminiscent of his second essay on Georg Trakl, written in 1953, which makes explicit reference to σελάννα (US 48–49). Yet the light of the moon is reminiscent of another goddess who is important for both Sophocles and Hölderlin. "Supplement" 7 cites an article by Wilhelm Michel on Hölderlin's translation of the name *Persephone* as Light, or, more completely, as "Furiously compassionate . . . a Light"; *Zornigmitleidig . . . ein Licht.*[5] The dead, says Antigone (at line 926)

---

4. The editor cites the first volume of *Die Fragmente der Vorsokratiker. Griechisch und deutsch*, 4th ed., Hermann Diels (Berlin: Weidmann'sche Buchhandlung, 1922), 1:97.

5. Wilhelm Michel, "Hölderlins Übersetzung eines Götternamens," in *Der Kunstwart: Deutscher Dienst am Geiste*, 41:7 (April 1928), 59–61. The date of the article conflicts with the internal evidence cited a moment ago, but it is not decisive. And yet, because Heidegger is teaching Sophocles's *Antigone* during these years in his course on *"Der Ister,"* and because *Antigone* plays an important role in EM, these *Beilagen* could indeed be from the 1930s. If that is the case, they stand out as absolutely remarkable and exceptional in the *Notebooks*. The question of dating aside, it is interesting to note that Michel's

are "greeted there by a furiously compassionate light." Heidegger jots down a reference to the Eleusinian mysteries and then enters two long explanatory notes on the rites from the Michel article. When the purified soul enters the underworld it confronts a bed that symbolizes a mystic marriage with Persephone. A bright lunar light shines in order to show the initiate the way, a "counter sun" that banishes the gloom of a world lost in night. Hölderlin makes the myth and rite "more evident," "more convincing," *beweisbarer*, for us Hesperians by means of this translation of the name *Persephone*.

Heidegger does not comment on the oxymoron *zornigmitleidig. Zorn*, from which we have the English word *torn*, is fury, but also orgiastic ecstasy. *Mitleid* is com-passion. One can hardly withhold the comment that such compassion is missing altogether from the *Schwarze Hefte* of the 1930s, and that whatever *Zorn* we find there is eminently unerotic. Even the earlier analyses of 1928–29 on the *Miteinander* of Dasein are contemptuous of the "I-Thou" relation as a possible site of the erotic. In his *Introduction to Philosophy*, Heidegger comments on his selection of the word *care, Sorge*, to name the essence of existence. Others find *Sorge* all too dire, says Heidegger; they wish that he would recognize that there is also *love* in life. Heidegger snaps back: "So, who wanted to deny it? . . . Yet it remains to be asked whether every great love, the only sort of love that tells us of love's essence, is not at bottom a struggle—not only and not in the first place a struggle to win the other, but a struggle on the beloved's behalf—and whether love does not wax precisely in inverse ratio to all sentimentality and contentment. But enough of this!" (27:327). Heidegger is clearly much better at *Zorn* than *Mitleid*. When he writes in the 1930s of the darkening of world and earth, neither sun nor moon appears, unless under the incessant yet utterly obscure rubric of "the truth of beyng." And nothing like compassion graces Heidegger's furious rejection of his contemporaries, the lot of them.

One last *Beilage* (again, in my view, from the early 1950s) is particularly noteworthy—number 14. It consists of a quotation from Hannah Arendt's *Rahel Varnhagen: Lebensgeschichte einer deutschen Jüdin aus der Romantik*. The editor cites the 1959 Piper Verlag edition, but it is possible that Arendt herself provided Heidegger with a copy earlier in the 1950s

---

argument, developed in the next few lines of my text, is refuted in the strongest possible terms by Friedrich Beißner in the second edition of his *Hölderlins Übersetzungen aus dem Griechischen* (Stuttgart: J. B. Metzler, [1933] 1961), 179n243. Which is not to deny Heidegger's interest in Michel's reading. (I am grateful to Alexander Bilda for his tracking down the Michel reference.)

or even much earlier than that. The quotation affirms that toward the end of a lifetime the importance of beginnings becomes clear. It is as though Arendt or Varnhagen herself is commenting on that line of Hölderlin's *Der Rhein*—one of Heidegger's favorite lines—which says that what one was in the beginning is what one remains, the beginning being what is "proper" and "indestructible" in a life, indeed, the very "core" of that life (95:265). We recall that this "core" has most to do with *birth*, the "other end" of Dasein, and with "the ray of light that / Comes to meet the newborn."

When earlier on I mentioned Heidegger's apparent disregard of the fates of his best students, who may themselves have been thinkers of being, readers may have been shocked to find no specific mention of Hannah Arendt. They would be right to feel aggrieved. Already by 1925 Arendt has told Heidegger of her fascination with Rahel Varnhagen, and that fascination appears to have become Heidegger's own (see HA:17). We know that in 1930, in Berlin, Arendt makes her first public presentation on her new research project concerning Varnhagen, a project Heidegger supports. Two years later, during the winter of 1932–33, alarmed by Heidegger's outspoken support of the National Socialists, Arendt writes to Heidegger, and he replies. It is their last exchange until February 1950. Her letter does not survive, but Heidegger's reply merits quoting in full:

Dear Hannah!

The rumors that are upsetting you are slanders that are perfect matches of other experiences I have had to endure over the last few years.

I cannot very well exclude Jews from invitations to my seminars, if only because I have not had *a single* seminar to invite anyone to during the last four semesters. That I supposedly do not greet Jews is such a malicious piece of gossip that in any case I will have to take note of it in the future.

To clarify how I behave toward Jews, simply the following facts:

I am on sabbatical this Winter Semester and so in the summer I announced well in advance that I wanted to be left alone and would not be accepting student papers and the like.

The person who in spite of this comes and urgently needs to complete his doctorate, and who is very well able to do so, is a Jew. The person who comes to see me every month to report on a large work in progress (neither a dissertation nor a habilitation project) is once again a Jew. The person who a few weeks ago sent me a substantial text for my urgent reading is a Jew.

The two fellows of the *Notgemeinschaft* whom I helped get accepted during the last three semesters are Jews. The person who, with my help, is getting a stipend to go to Rome is a Jew.[6]

Whoever wants to call that "raging anti-Semitism" is welcome to do so.

For the rest, I am now precisely as much an anti-Semite in university questions as I was ten years ago in Marburg, where, because of this anti-Semitism, I found myself supported even by Jacobsthal and Friedländer.[7]

All this has nothing to do with my personal relationships with Jews (e.g., Husserl, Misch, Cassirer, and others).[8]

And *a fortiori* it cannot touch my relationship with you.

The fact that for a long time now I have been generally quite withdrawn has as one of its causes my work's meeting with hopeless incomprehension, along with some less-than-pleasant personal experiences having to do with my teaching. To be sure, I have long since given up expecting any sort of gratitude or even mere respect from so-called "pupils."

For the rest, I am contentedly at work, although the work gets more and more difficult, and I greet you heartily. (Signed: M.) (HA:68–69)

---

6. Heidegger is referring to Karl Löwith.

7. The two scholars cited here were members of the "Graeca" reading-group at Marburg. Paul Jacobsthal (1880–1957), an archeologist, was forced to retire in 1935 and emigrated to England, receiving a post in Oxford at Christ Church College. Paul Friedländer (1882–1968), whom I mentioned earlier, and whose three-volume *Plato* was a mainstay for everyone studying the Dialogues during the 1960s and 1970s, was forced to retire in 1935. In 1938 he was arrested and sent to the concentration camp at Sachsenhausen. Miraculously, for reasons I do not know, he was released from the camp in 1939 and emigrated to the United States, where he taught at Johns Hopkins and UCLA.

8. Edmund Husserl is of course is well known, and Heidegger's relation to him and treatment of him is often discussed and debated. Georg Misch (1878–1965) was a fellow philosopher at Göttingen University; in 1939 he escaped to Great Britain. Ernst Cassirer (1874–1945), the distinguished neo-Kantian, whom Heidegger met several times during the 1920s, left Germany in 1933.

Antonia Grunenberg, whose book on Arendt and Heidegger is the crucial source, suggests that Heidegger is here implicitly reminding Arendt of his recent letter of recommendation in support of her to the *Notgemeinschaft der deutschen Wissenschaft*, a letter that Karl Jaspers had urged him to write.[9]

Critics will easily dismiss Heidegger's letter to Arendt as the familiar sort of schizophrenia in racists of all stripes: "Some of my best friends . . ." Yet the schizophrenia in the case of Heidegger would seem to run deep. Or at least the self-pitying Narcissism: once again it is Heidegger who is the victim of misunderstanding and ingratitude. He is the one who suffers slander and slights at the hands of others. I can do no more than repeat my astonishment and chagrin that in Heidegger's private jottings of the 1930s and early 1940s not a trace of concern for former students and colleagues, nor of lost loves, appears.

⁂

To repeat a point made earlier: among the aspects of the *Schwarze Hefte* that are most disquieting are those that mirror our own time and our own politics and practices. We hate to admit this proximity, but there it is. For example, when Heidegger berates his own times for "*die rücksichtslose Organisation einer* systemmatischen Verdümmung" (96:192), that is, "the relentless organization of a *systematic stupefaction*," I am forced to recall a piece I wrote during George W. Bush's second term, a piece I called "The School for Stupefaction." I do not recommend it to my readers. For by now we are so much smarter. . . . But my point is that many of Heidegger's lamentations are ones we are forced to share, we who are of a different nation, a different time, and a very different temperament, whereas we would like to set these *Notebooks* aside and recognize nothing of our own situation in them. That too is a mark of tragedy, is it not? The more one lashes out at others and the more self-righteously one condemns them, the more likely it is that the lash will recoil and strike home.

For the sake of our own time and our own nation, let me add a brief remark. Heidegger has some bad news and some good news for us: "By 2300, at the earliest, there may be history once again. By that time, Americanism, disgusted by its own inanity, will have exhausted itself" (96:225). So, we may relax; time is on our side.

---

9. See Grunenberg, in the French edition (cited in chapter 5), 182–83.

As to the vexing question concerning how the *Schwarze Hefte* relate to Heidegger's best *thinking*, which occurs elsewhere, my response is marked by hesitation. Move Heidegger's books to the "Nazi propaganda" section of the library? No, not even if there is precious little in these particular volumes that merits the word *thinking*. Shall we then claim that these notebooks have nothing to do with Heidegger's thought? No, that will not do. The headlines of the newspaper reviews of *Gesamtausgabe* volumes 94–96, reviews that had to be written before the volumes could possibly have been read, are not entirely sensationalist: "The blinded prophet," "The poisoned heritage," "An extreme case of silencing." Blinded not by the goddess, as in the case of Tiresias, but by the worst aspects of Heidegger's own "today." Blinded also by his own kerygmatic faith in *Seyn* and his chiliastic rhetoric on behalf of it. Poisoned by the worst of his own time, as we may be poisoned by the worst of our own—philosophy does not seem to be successfully prophylactic, neither then nor now. And the silences? Heidegger appears to have been deafened by the silence he felt compelled to keep, a silence we are unable to break for him, which therefore remains unforgiving.

That said, neither the roundhouse slam against "ontology," as in Adorno's *Negative Dialektik*, nor Emmanuel Levinas's efforts to subordinate ontology to an ethics convince me. There is too much of genuine philosophical—and thoughtful—achievement in Heidegger's *Sein und Zeit* to justify the roundhouse, and the *should* of ethics continues to bump its head against the recalcitrant *is*. I hope that the first part of the present book has shown that much is still to be gained by a critical reading of Heidegger's *Being and Time*. Likewise, the extraordinary essays of the early 1950s, along with the revolutionary essays on language and poetics from that same decade, will continue to be read. Is it then simply a problem of the 1930s? Should one excise that decade? But that would be to abandon Heidegger's extraordinary reading of "Anaximander's Saying" and to miss his most trenchant critique of modernity, "The Time When All the World Becomes an Image," *Die Zeit des Weltbildes*, the essay that is so important for Derrida's first seminar on Heidegger. It would be to overlook Heidegger's thought-provoking and enormously influential essay, "The Origin of the Work of Art," which has meant as much to practicing artists as to philosophers of art and beauty. And even if one resists Heidegger's readings of Hölderlin every step of the way, must one not *take* those steps *with* Heidegger, must one not continue to *read*? It is clearly a matter of reading as much as one can as best one can and worrying ceaselessly about the blindness that accompanies insight.

True, we do not have to wait until the 1930s for Heidegger's blindness. Are we not struck by the apparently uncritical devotion that Heidegger expresses in section 74 of *Being and Time* for "heritage," *das Erbe?* Why is there no call for a *Destruktion* precisely of the "heritage" that so fatally—and so natally—introduces a commitment to one's generation, one's community, one's people, one's nation, and one's militant destiny? To be sure, at the end of section 74, Heidegger poses a whole series of questions that ought to have invited a more detailed *Destruktion*, so that even this section of Heidegger's magnum opus can and must be *read*. Yet soon after the publication of *Being and Time*, in the 1928–29 *Introduction to Philosophy*, we find the troubling insistence that the philosopher's "duty," which has been "planted" in his Dasein, is "to assume something like a leadership role [*so etwas wie eine Führerschaft*] in the given totality of our historical being with one another" (27:7). Not so much in public life, Heidegger hastens to add; it is not as though one must become "the director" or "the supervisor." Even so, one must become a "model," *Vorbild*, precisely as one who understands in a more original way the ultimate possibilities of existence. This has nothing to do with delusions of moral superiority, Heidegger insists. In fact, the reverse is the case: "The responsibility that precisely an unsupervised and altogether nonpublic leadership must assume is the constant and intensified opportunity for the moral failure of the individual [*eine ständige und verschärfte Gelegenheit zum moralischen Versagen des Einzelnen*]" (ibid.). The claim is disconcerting for both its arrogance and its prophetic force.

There is something about *Seynsdenken* in general that is particularly worrisome. The more Heidegger counts on beyng, and the more his rhetoric rises on an afflatus of "event" and "decision" and "another commencement," the less *Seyn* seems to mean. Is *Seyn* then indeed a vapor and a fallacy? Or worse, a phantasm, a *fata morgana*, a will o' the wisp, an effect of *Zerstreuung*, a placebo for troubled times, another chapter of German ideology? As for the avatar of beyng, namely, "the last god," the more assured one is that this last one is fundamentally different from the earlier incarnations, and the more convinced one is that Heidegger has liberated himself from the ontotheological tradition, the more one needs to go back and read Nietzsche's *Antichrist* and *Beyond Good and Evil*. And, above all, *Thus Spoke Zarathustra*, "*Von den drei Verwandlungen*" ("On the Three Metamorphoses"), from which Heidegger's entire apocalyptics seems to take its inspiration:

Aber in der einsamsten Wüste geschieht die zweite Verwandlung: zum Löwen wird hier der Geist, Freiheit will er sich erbeuten und Herr sein in seiner eigenen Wüste.

Seinen letzten Herrn sucht er sich hier: feind will er ihm
werden und seinem letzten Gotte, um Sieg will er mit dem
grossen Drachen ringen. (KSA 4:30)

But in the loneliest wasteland the second metamorphosis occurs:
here spirit becomes a lion who seeks freedom as his prey; he
would be lord in his own wasteland.
     Here he is seeking his last lord: he would be an enemy
to the last lord and to his last god; he seeks victory; he would
wrestle with the great dragon.

All well and good. Wrestle away with the dragon! Yet where in Heidegger do we find the *third* metamorphosis? Heidegger himself, responding
to Nietzsche, insists that he does not wish to lionize the will. Perhaps we
were not so far off when we went in search of Bébé Dasein?
     If it is the chiliastic piety of Heidegger's *Seynsdenken* that causes us
worry—and any claim to a reign of a thousand years should give us pause—
we must try to release Heidegger's thinking even of *Gelassenheit* from the
piety that appears to buffer or suffocate it. Like Heidegger himself in his
final years, we will want to try to develop a language of response, an *Ent-
sprechen*, a language not so keen to proclaim, a tongue better able to listen.
Why not, since by this time we philosophers have become past masters of
the impatient and the puffed up. All we can hope for is that in our own
wasteland Heidegger does not become the dragon with whom we wrestle.
Life will have been too short for that. So why not a third transformation?
Why not *transition* in general, since *Übergang* was the favorite word of both
Hölderlin and Nietzsche?
     The editor of these three volumes, Peter Trawny, in his Afterword to
all three, tries to convince us of the singularity and exceptional value of the
Schwarze Hefte. This is what an editor is supposed to do and is bound to
do. Occasionally, a book reviewer will enthusiastically agree. In one instance,
a reviewer exclaims that the *Schwarze Hefte* enable readers at long last to
get to the "central core" of Heidegger's thought.[10]
     My own judgment differs from those of both editor and reviewer.
These jottings by Heidegger are by and large not thought provoking; the

---

10. Thomas Meyer, in the *Süddeutsche Zeitung* for Tuesday, March 25, 2014, "Die
Literatur," 70:14.

"notebooks" are not "Denk*tagebücher*." There are, in these twelve hundred
book pages, very few passages that are worth reading, at least if one is
interested in Heidegger's *thinking*. There is virtually nothing here that Heidegger does not write with greater care, rigor, and insight in other places,
principally in the books and essays that he himself published. And there
is much here that one wishes Heidegger had never written. For one whose
pride was in thinking, the *Black Notebooks* of the 1930s and early 1940s
represent a tragic collapse. What would augment the tragedy would be our
taking the *Schwarze Hefte* to represent the "core" of Heidegger's thinking.
The greatness of Heidegger's thinking rests secure in dozens of his books
and essays, and a chastened readership will continue to find that thinking
not merely *provoking* but *thought* provoking. To that extent it still behooves
us to magnify what is great in Heidegger's thinking, even if what is great
will not be found in these *Überlegungen*.

⁊⯮

For what reason, then, and for whom were they written? This question
nags at us, and no answer seems to satisfy. Perhaps the qualities that are
missing from them—the capacity for self-criticism or for self-awareness of
any kind, that is, an awareness that would avoid the self-stylization and
the ego-inflation mentioned earlier—are missing precisely because these are
not journals or diaries at all. Perhaps the absence of expressions of care
and concern and the presence of many passages that seem hard-hearted
and even ruthless have to do with the happenstance that these notes are
philosophical throwaways? They are not notes to self, in any case. They are
more like broadsides aimed at everydayness—broadsides that are themselves
ensconced in everydayness. For the most part, they read as though it was
always Heidegger's intention to publish them, an intention that is, however,
both perplexing and even alarming. Michel Tournier would call them *un
journal extime*, as opposed to *intime*, but he would also surely concede that
the *Schwarze Hefte* lack the wit, the profundity, and the agility of the pen
that such a *journal extime* demands.

The omnipresence of Nietzsche in the *Notebooks* makes me think that
Heidegger is trying to emulate the master; the fact that he denies that he is
writing "aphorisms" only confirms the suspicion. And it is true, in a way:
he is *not* writing aphorisms—his pen is too heavy-footed, his thinking too
humorless and compulsive, his foreign languages (in spite of his Scholastic
Latin and Classical Greek) and his culture generally too underdeveloped to
be able to write in any of Nietzsche's many styles. The situation improves in

the 1950s, when Heidegger develops a style of his own. Signs of an independent style doubtless appear already in his best writing and thinking of the 1930s, in "On the Essence of Truth," "The Origin of the Artwork," and "The Time When All the World Becomes an Image," but that style does not mature until "Building Dwelling Thinking," "Poetically Man Dwells . . . ," and "The Thing." As for the *Black Notebooks* of the 1930s, one is compelled to recall a remark Heidegger is reported to have made in his later years, "*Nietzsche hat mich kaputt gemacht!*" The remark makes most sense if we think of Heidegger seeking to emulate Nietzsche's trenchant styles of writing—and failing. If Nietzsche's thoughts come on doves' feet, Heidegger, at least in the *Notebooks*, fits out his doves with hobnailed boots.

It is surely naïve, however, to think that even a *journal intime* is written truly for oneself alone: there is something about writing that longs for a reader, and even the writer of intimate notebooks is in the unfortunate position of having to hope for a response. Yet the absence of Heidegger's best qualities, namely, his ability to focus and to reflect self-critically, and the presence of his worst, to wit, his aggressive polemics against everything in the world except his own *idée fixe*, is what the *Schwarze Hefte* so far offer us. It will be interesting to see if this changes with the *Notebooks* of the 1950s. But that will be for a new generation of readers to determine. For the moment, as one recalls the power of *Being and Time* and the reticence and responsiveness of *Underway to Language*, the *Black Notebooks* can only strike us as tragically, catastrophically flawed. They are self-inflicted wounds to the Heidegger corpus.[11]

---

11. It may be that the self-wounding is not at an end. At the final proof stage of the present book (March 9, 2015), I learn that *Gesamtausgabe* volume 97 has just been published. I have not seen it and have no first-hand information about it, other than that it contains the *Black Notebooks* from the years 1942 to 1948. The years immediately after the War, with the full disclosure of the Shoah, or Extermination, are terribly important for the issues raised in my own book. All I can do at the moment is pledge that I will read volume 97 as soon as I can. The "Conclusion" to the present book, which now follows, may have to be revised; yet I ask readers to bear with me a few pages longer and consider it.

Conclusion

In the Preface I described this book as a symptom of "galloping schizophrenia." The description might be accurate, unfortunately, but no one should be quick to accept it, least of all me, if only because schizophrenia does not gallop. Like psychoanalysis, it limps. Is there any way to help the book along so late in the day, any way to resolve the discord between its two parts, which reflect the ecstasy of a thought-provoking text, *Being and Time*, and the tragic catastrophe of the *Black Notebooks*? It cannot be a question of some dialectical resolution by means of which the two parts of the book would be viewed simply as two "facets" or "aspects" of Heidegger's thinking; no shiny bright third "determinate object" could possibly emerge from such an abrasive dialectic. However, I would like to trace my own reaction over the past forty years to the expanding revelations concerning Heidegger's involvement in National Socialism, and to reflect a moment longer, with the reader's indulgence, on that parlous decade of the 1930s in Heidegger's life and thought. At the same time, I will try to remember some of the principal difficulties in the analyses of ecstatic temporality—a future that is "closed," a having-been that can be trapped in a self-occluding "oblivion," and a "readiness" and "resoluteness" that fail to temporalize.

I no longer have the text of the original edition of Heidegger's *Basic Writings*, which I prepared for Harper & Row during the years 1974–76. But I do recall writing about Heidegger's involvement in National Socialism in the second part of my General Introduction to the volume. I had researched that involvement principally on the basis of Guido Schneeberger's anthology of political writings by Heidegger and the debate carried out during the 1950s and '60s in the pages of *Les temps modernes*, but also in the light of Heidegger's own statements in his defense. It became necessary to emend and expand my remarks when the second edition of the *Basic Writings* was being planned in 1991–92; there was a great deal more material to take into account, thanks to the research of Bernd Martin and Hugo Ott, which poked significant holes into Heidegger's defense. Simultaneously, a second (paperback) edition of Heidegger's *Nietzsche* volumes demanded of me a more comprehensive and more critical account. Referring to articles and books by Ott and Martin, but also to reflections by Jacques Derrida and Dominique Janicaud, my introduction to the paperback edition of Heidegger's *Nietzsche* had this to say:

> Their research [i.e., that of Ott and Martin] indicates that Heidegger's engagement in the university politics of National Socialism was far more intense, and his statements on his own behalf after the War far more unreliable and self-serving, than anyone has suspected. His role as Party member and rector of the University of Freiburg in 1933–1934 was not merely that of a reluctant fellow-traveler caught up in a fleeting episode of political enthusiasm. Heidegger was not a dupe, not a victim of his own political naiveté. The problem is not that Heidegger lacked a political theory and a political praxis but that at least for a time he had them. He devoted his rectorship to devising and carrying out plans for the full synchronization or con-solidation (*Gleichschaltung*) of the German university with the Third Reich. In this regard he worked closely with the National Socialist culture ministries in Karlsruhe and Berlin, that is to say, at both the state and national levels. His active support and leadership of the "reformed" (that is, Party-dominated) student government, his proselytizing on behalf of Hitler and National Socialism in those crucial early years, and, above all, his plan to cripple the university senate and to arrogate to himself as rector full administrative power, to serve as the *Führer-Rektor* of the university and as the spiritual-intellectual guide of the Party as a whole, are the most damning consequences of that involvement. Even more sinister are his denunciations of university students and colleagues who were recalcitrant to the "Movement," or who could be made to seem so. Finally, Heidegger's efforts in his own defense after the War are, to say the least, less than candid. Both his statement to the denazification committee in 1945 and the *Spiegel* interview of 1966 distort the record on several important matters, including Heidegger's nomination to and resignation from the rectorship.

In spite of all the talk today, not much more is known about these matters, so that I believe I can safely reaffirm these remarks from 1991. Yet the passage that followed them, as severe as it seemed to me back then, needs to be revised—and in the direction of something even more damning:

Yet what Heidegger *said* after the War pales in comparison with what he left *unsaid.* Whether for reasons of shame or feelings of helplessness and hopelessness; whether in proud refusal of public apology or in avoidance of the almost universal sycophancy of those days, the endless number of ex-Nazis who claimed to have seen, heard, said, done, and been nothing nowhere at no time whatsoever; or whether simply because of an incapacity to face the brutal facts, facts beyond wickedness and imagination—whatever the reasons, Heidegger never uttered a public word on the extermination of the Jews in the death camps of the Third Reich. While always ready to commiserate with the German soldiers and refugees in eastern Europe, and while always prepared to bemoan the plight of a divided Postwar Germany, Heidegger consigned the horrors of the Holocaust to total silence. A silence intensified by his acknowledgment of the sufferings of his countrymen and his fatherland, a silence framed and set off by what he did lament. A silence, in short, that betrays and belittles the matter of his *thinking*—which he claimed to be his sole concern.

For certain issues in his thinking cry for an end to the silence. His meditations on the technological reduction of human beings to mere stockpiles, on the upsurgence of evil and malignancy in the wake of the departed gods, and on the limitations of contemporary ethical and political thinking remain fundamentally incomplete if they fail to confront the Extermination. The death camps cry for painstaking thinking and writing, though not overhasty speech. And Heidegger's silence is more deafening than all the noise of his rectorship.

I would have to emphasize now more than I did then the things Heidegger *did* say and *did* write than these terrible silences of his. The reader has doubtless had enough of the bitter taste with which the *Black Notebooks* leave us. But let me be more specific about Heidegger's statements after the War. In the first lecture course that he was permitted to teach after the War, the 1951–52 *What Is Called Thinking?* Heidegger says nothing about the Holocaust or about the systematic persecution of Jews, the Roma peoples, homosexuals, and the political left throughout the 1930s and up to the very end of the War. Yet he says this to his Freiburg students:

[Spoken prior to the lecture on June 20, 1952:]

Ladies and Gentlemen!

Today the exhibition "Prisoners of War Speak" has opened in Freiburg.
     I request that you go to it in order to hear its soundless voice and I ask that this voice never abandon your inner ear.
     Thinking is remembering. Yet remembering is something other than a fleeting presentification of things past.
     Remembering ponders what matters to us. We are not yet in the appropriate space to think about freedom, or even to talk about it, as long as we close our eyes to this annihilation of freedom *as well.* (WhD? 159)

Now, there is nothing wrong about remembering the suffering of the German prisoners of war. Some of the most horrific and terrifying stories I have heard involve infantry soldiers who, after their release or escape from prison camps, walked back to their home villages—the trek from the East often taking four or five years. So many of my own German contemporaries, the friends I have made in Germany from the 1960s onward, have related to me their own "family stories." Most of these stories go back to World War I, which none of my friends experienced firsthand but which they remember with astonishing intensity now, precisely one hundred years after its onset. They think intensely about the havoc it wreaked on their grandparents, followed then by the chaos of the Weimar years and the horrors of the Third Reich, the havoc now enveloping the lives of their parents—and their own lives as children. Nothing in these accounts is self-serving or complacent, nor are the friends who tell them blind to the suffering and the death of others. They see the larger picture, and they shudder. It is the nightmare from which they will never awake.
     If we think now of Heidegger, must we not ask: If "remembering ponders what matters to us," is it not important to expand a bit the scope of what matters to "us"? Is that not what university teaching is all about, especially when teaching—which, in Heidegger's own words, involves *let-*

ting one's students *learn*—must pose the question, "What is it that *calls on us* to think?" Do not these calls emanate precisely from the "weak voices" that Walter Benjamin could not help but hear, voices of the defeated and the defunct? And if the danger in our growing wasteland is what Heidegger himself calls "the high-velocity expulsion of memory," should one not strive to be increasingly aware of one's own forgetfulness, one's own limits and limitations? Should not the labor to expand one's awareness of catastrophe be the essential labor? Should not a meditation on being, however one may spell it, expand one's capacity to remember? Should it not disperse the narrow and the parochial? Or is the ecstasis of self-occluding oblivion complete, so complete that it devastates all our chances to reflect on the past and alter our future?

Earlier on in the lecture course Heidegger asks, "What did World War II properly decide, to say nothing of its frightful effects for our fatherland, especially its having been torn down the middle?" (WhD? 65). The War decided nothing, says Heidegger, repeating what he was already saying (by way of anticipation) in the 1930s. He is thinking of the political categories that consistently fail to live up to the challenges of the times, especially the challenge of global technology. And yet. Did not the War decide something for millions upon millions of human beings, especially for those who did not survive it, but also for those who did? Surely Heidegger's vaunted decision-ism decided much less than the War itself did. If Heidegger's decisionism stems from his confidence in a resolute openedness that runs ahead, *die vorlaufende Entschlossenheit*, perhaps we should take some comfort from the happenstance that the "readiness" for resolve never seems to temporalize. If the circularity of anxiety, readiness, and resoluteness seems vicious, per-haps the attunement of anxiety may interrupt a decisionism that is hardly innocent.

To say the least, there is something about Heidegger's silence even after the War that reflects an astonishing mindlessness. Philippe Lacoue-Labarthe, especially toward the end of his own life, was rightly obsessed with this mindlessness; his colleagues and friends—Derrida, Janicaud, Lyotard, Nancy, and others—were also haunted by this terrifying oblivion in Hei-degger. The militancy of Heidegger's nationalism, which seems to be respon-sible for much if not all of the oblivion, is truly disconcerting. Heidegger invariably appeals to Nietzsche and Hölderlin whenever Germany is under discussion—but Nietzsche prided himself on being "a good European," and Hölderlin, who loved Revolutionary France and the French, felt that "Germany" was bounded by the fields of his childhood town of Nürtingen. No reader of Heidegger can or should be able to make his or her peace with Heidegger's (or their own) nationalism, militancy, and decisionism. Yet would not militant nationalism and decisionism be at least slowed down if one were to think more critically about *all* the things we are born into: a contingent place and time, a sex and gender that are configured in astonishingly narrow and constricting ways, a generation that is too soon old and too late smart, along with a community that seems a pretty mixed bag of the good and the bad? Perhaps a continued meditation on the closure of our finite future, the forgetfulness that nestles comfortably in our having-been, and the mindlessness of our everyday present would at least put a damper on the militancy?

We encroach precisely on Heidegger's *thought* when we worry about his call for "decision." That call, which marks and mars the *Black Notebooks*, but not them alone, is related to the "historic destinalism" about which Dominique Janicaud wrote many years ago—Heidegger's conviction that Germany was destined to play a privileged role in rescuing Greek antiquity for the future of the Western world. And to the extent that such "destinalism" inheres in Heidegger's thinking of the "sending of being" and of the "history of beyng" in general, an enormous shadow is cast over that thinking. It is not a passing shadow.

The mindless and hard-hearted remarks on "world Jewry" that we have confronted in the *Black Notebooks*, along with the endlessly repeated polemics against all and sundry, make that shadow more ominous than ever. It becomes almost impossible to take Heidegger seriously when he talks about resisting polemic and magnifying what is great in past efforts at thinking. And yet in that selfsame lecture course of 1951–52 that I have been citing, Heidegger says that "tactfulness" and "good taste" alone demand that we abjure polemic. We heard the following words back in the Interlude of the present book: "Every kind of polemic fails from the start to attain the stance of thinking. The role of an opponent is not the role of thinking. For a thinking is indeed thinking only when it pursues what speaks *for* a thing" (WhD? 49). It is *almost* impossible to take him seriously. And yet here is where I *do* take Heidegger seriously, both in the astonishing achievement that is his *Sein und Zeit* and in much of the later work—including the work of the 1930s. The greatness of the *work* calls for (critical) magnification.

One brief word more, then, about that decade. I have already mentioned several times the essay that Derrida discusses in his 1964–65 seminar, which I prefer to translate as "The Time When All the World Becomes an Image," *Die Zeit des Weltbildes*. Many of Heidegger's complaints about his times appear in that essay, yet it is not the work of a crank. It is one of Heidegger's most penetrating essays. I recently suggested to the publishers of

Heidegger's *Basic Writings* that we add this essay to the volume; my suggestion was not accepted, but the request reflects my admiration of the piece. The perplexing and even disconcerting fact is that Heidegger did an extraordinary amount of serious work precisely at the time he was jotting polemics, lamentations, and pieties into his *Black Notebooks*. Another example of work from the 1930s, one I have not mentioned so far: in 1936 Heidegger offered a course on Kant, today published as *The Question of the Thing*. A brief selection from this book appears in *Basic Writings* as the sixth reading, "Modern Science, Metaphysics, and Mathematics." Here Heidegger analyzes in a truly brilliant way the shift away from the Aristotelian and Medieval conceptions of "world" and "thing" and their transformation by Galileo and Descartes for all of modernity to come. In my view, this is Heidegger at his best, and our study of the history of science—I think, for example, of Thomas Kuhn's lengthy study of Copernicus—confirms Heidegger's essential points. There is nothing cranky about Heidegger's observations on the history of physics and cosmology. It would be a terrible thing were this kind of serious work to lose its standing because of the *Notebooks*.

Even more terrible would be the loss of *Being and Time* to serious students of philosophy in our own time. No doubt, our reading of that work has to be critical. As I tried to show in the first part of this volume, not everything about that book's analyses "works." Yet Heidegger's effort there is really quite extraordinary, and to rise to its level is not so easy. Ironically, some of the most problematic passages in the book (for example, section 74, on "heritage," "choosing one's hero," "community," "generation," "nation," and "struggle") respond to one of its most creative and self-critical moments, namely, the moment when "the other end" of human existence—not death but birth—enters the discussion. One wishes for Heidegger's work the sort of birth, or rebirth, that Hannah Arendt invoked: new possibilities for change and for a greater, if more critical, openness in the public sphere.

If Heidegger himself damaged his thinking—massively, even tragically, catastrophically—it is up to his readers, chastened and chagrined by these failures, to magnify what is thought provoking in it even as they decry its failings. Perhaps that is not schizophrenia but a regimen for health.

Index

Made in the USA
Middletown, DE
14 February 2022